A story that neede

ST LEONARD'S ROAD

To David, Brenda and Sharon, three special cousins. I hope you enjoy this book. It's not always an easy read for reasons you will appreciate.

Lots of love,

Joe

JOE CONNOLLY

First published in Great Britain in 2025

Design, typesetting and publishing by UK Book Publishing.

www.ukbookpublishing.com

ISBN: 978-1-917329-75-0

For my grandchildren Lucy, Joe, Rose and Sam

Annie McAvennie Billy McAvennie Alfie Weymond Billy Grover the coalman Nora, nanny Powell's friend Miss Bell Miss Reed Elsie Sweet Ada Sweet Winnie Weller Miss Nottle Pastor Thomas Mildred Shkolnik Josie Breslaw Mrs Voshvell Mrs Byford Miss Woods Miss Williams Mr Thake Mr Clark Geroge Mills Mr Howell Mr Enervor Doctor Stern Ray Levitt Percy Palaver Grumpily Grimp Mrs Beard Lilly Beard (Lily Levy) Mr Levy Christine Levy David Levy Doll Herring Albert Herring the little Herrings Old Mill Little Marie Big Marie Hughie Honey Patsy Honey Old Mother Jones Albert Jones Rosie Jones Mrs Counter Wally Smith Nell Smith Benny Smith Joey Smith Joycie Smith (Joycie Bannister) George Purton Emma Purton Granny Sims Jack Chambers Georgie Purton Eileen Purton Johnny Purton Stan Dray Laura Fry Emmie Brown Dolly Brown Tiddles Brown Ernie Miles Joan Miles Sheila Miles Mr Miles Mrs Miles Joanie Miles Dougie Miles Kitty Sharp (Kitty Jackson) Frank Jackson Masie Jackson Frankie Jackson Alf Allen Ethel Allen Doll Butler George Butler Maureen Butler Babsie Butler Georgie Butler Frankie Butler Aunt Mary (Mary King) George King Mrs Woodyard (Sookie Woodyard) Mr Woodyard Albert Woodyard Pauline Woodyard Brenda Woodyard Spanner Woodyard Wendy Woodyard George Mitchell Eileen Mitchell Alf Strecker Mrs Strecker Julie Strecker Danny Strecker Terri (Theresa) Strecker Tony Strecker Mr Wardell (Punch) Nell Wardell Nellie Wardell Violet Wardell Margaret Wardell Kathleen Wardell Patsy Wardell Carol Wardell Terry Blancke Mr Farnham Mrs Farnham Jeanie Kilduff Bennie Kilduff Linda Kilduff Cyril the paper boy Vi the other 'paper boy' Charlie Bromley (Old Brum) Jeanie Bromley Mr Mead Mrs Mead the two Mead brothers Mr Masser Mrs Masser Artie Masser Bessie Masser Valerie Masser Mrs Stock Mr Stock Sarah Stock (Cos) Arthur Cos Mary Cos Pamela Cos Charlie Johnson Flo Woodford Mr Woodford Eileen Woodford Joanie Woodford Joanie's husband Mrs Cable Mr Cable Ernie Cable Kenny Cable Evelyn Cable Evelyn's boyfriend Fan Watton Mr Watton Johnny Watton Mrs Besant Nellie McAvennie Rosie McAvennie Joycie McAvennie Mrs McAvennie Mr McAvennie Joe Paddles Girl P Betty Clery Albert Robinson ('Old Rob', 'Sheekie') Aileen Robinson Mr Mudge Ann 'the Singing Nun' Denis Barnes Canon Wright Father Haines Father Ellis Jim O'Mahony Sister Pat Ernie Williams Elizabeth Connolly William Connolly Uncle Will (William Connolly) Kitty Meacher Aunt Nan (Mary Ann) Bradford (Connolly) Aunt Nell Nell Burleson (Connolly) Steve Burleson Uncle Tom (Thomas Connolly) Aunt Aggie Rita Connolly Tommy Connolly Uncle Jack (John) Connolly Helen Connolly Dorothy Connolly John Connolly Aunt Kit (Kathleen) Snasdale (Connolly) Joe Snasdale Tom Brown Uncle Pats (Partrick Connolly) Aunt Nellie Whitnell (Ginger Nell) Patrick (Patsy) Connolly Janice Connolly (Aunt Mabel) Mabel Kilgor (Connolly) Johnny Kilgor Maureen Kilgor Christine Kilgor Pat (Patricia) Kilgor Uncle Peter (Peter Connolly) Rose Connolly John Connolly Roger Connolly Brian Connolly Uncle Danny (Daniel Connolly) Sally (Sarah Connolly) David Connolly Brenda Connolly Sharon Connolly Ronnie Kitts Ann Field Colin Hogarth Jackie Painter Ann Radley Terry Martin John Rodway Elaine Nurse White Mrs Skeets Pamela Lyons Raymond Holmes Keith Williams Mrs Barnett Mr Barnett Dougie Barnett Ernie Barnett Thelma Barnett David Barnett John 'Jock' Burnett Nessie Burnett 'Dinya' 'Mummy's Boy'

'Dikko' 'Blakie' 'Hauntsie' Tom Clark Mavis Potter Betty Smith Jean des Touches Terry Lawlor Dave Bryan Jim Godfrey Huw Croxford Bill Fuller Colin Fuller Gladys Middleton Victor Middleton Pete the pianist Mr Price Nell Vint Fred Vint Joe Gaylor Flo Gaylor Christine Smith Arthur Edwards Ann Edwards John Edwards Paul Edwards Ann Marie Edwards Maura Ryan (Maura Slater) Joe Slater

CONTENTS

FOREWORD I

THE DEBRIS 1

NANNY POWELL 9

HOPPING 21

THE FIVE WAYS 29

OUR HOUSE 43

ROSE, HENRY AND CHARLIE 57

EDUCATION 79

A COUNTERFACTUAL 1951 89

THREE ENCOUNTERS WITH HISTORY 97

A WEE WITH CLEMENT ATTLEE 101

A WALK DOWN THE ROAD 109

A WALK ON THE OTHER SIDE 149

FAITH OF OUR FATHERS 171

THE CONNOLLYS 181

THE FACTS OF LIFE 227

IN SPITE OF ALL THE DANGER 235

LOUSY BUT LOYAL 255

SIR LUCY LAWRENCE 261

GOING ON HOLIDAY? 285

THE GASSIE 293

THE PEOPLE WHO CAME 303

OLD ROB 315

AUNT GLADYS 321

JEAN DES TOUCHES 327

THE EDWARDS 341

THINGS CHANGED 347

THE IRONS 363

AFTERWORD 389

PLAYLIST 391

ACKNOWLEDGEMENTS 393

BIOGRAPHY 395

FOREWORD

This is the book I always wanted to write, but what was to have been a simple account of growing up in post-war Poplar, took on a life of its own and has become something more profound. It is not just any other East End memoir; it is the story of a community that survived the Second World War only to be destroyed by a crude and insensitive slum clearance programme. It was bulldozers, not bombs, that ripped Poplar apart. In explaining what happened, I have tried to rebuild that community from the people themselves: person by person, house by house, until it becomes something solid, credible, almost tangible. Wherever I could, I have told the story in the words of the people themselves by using their sayings and phrases and expressing them in their own language of cockney.

The years that followed the Second World War were harsh and difficult ones. The country was bankrupt, its infrastructure was in ruins, food was rationed, millions of people were without homes and many of the houses that survived the bombing were no more than slums. America abruptly ended its 'Lend-Lease' financial support in 1945 and 1947 saw the worst winter in living memory. Despite all that, the early years of my life were ones of vision and optimism. Many of the changes put in place then, especially those in health and education, ensured that my generation had a far better quality of life than our parents ever did.

Other things emerged during the writing too: how architecture affects our lives for good and ill, how my primary school set me up for life, my experience of religion, and how the National Health Service probably saved my life. I have written about my family too: my mum, dad and sister, my extended family on my mother's side and the outrageous and sometimes unpleasant antics of the Connollys. As the story concludes I describe the changes that took place in St Leonard's Road towards the end of our time there: an increase in crime, the obsession with building high-rise flats, and the futility of our attempts to be rehoused in Poplar.

Throughout the book I have been as honest as my memory would allow: everything that takes place really happened to the best of my knowledge. Inevitably, names have been changed to protect the privacy of individuals (many now dead) and their families. In doing that, I have tried to strike a balance between protecting people's interests and telling the truth, and I have endeavoured to be fair. Factual accuracy is important too and I have checked a wide range of sources to verify the claims I have made (about numbers of road deaths, for example, or infant mortality rates.)

Whenever I could, I have obtained copyright permissions for the use of photographs and text from other sources. This has not always been possible because extensive searches have not always been successful. If there is objection to the unacknowledged inclusion of photographs or text, I will ensure that the item is removed from subsequent editions.

The book is strongly critical of what I have called 'the architectural establishment.' These were the architects and planners in the social housing programme who didn't ask us what kind of homes we wanted to live in or where we wanted to live, because they had already decided that for us.

That idealistic arrogance, combined with civic ineptitude, put millions of British people through the awful experience of slum clearance and destroyed hundreds of communities across the country. The destruction of communities in post-war Britain is one of the great social injustices of modern times but it has never been addressed. Maybe this is because it was done to working people who did not have a voice of their own.

KEY PLAYERS

Joe (Joseph) Connolly, my father. Nell (Ellen) Connolly, my mother. Doreen Connolly (later Clery) my sister, Rose Powell (Nanny Powell, my maternal grandmother), Rose Powell (later Oliver, Aunt Rose my mother's sister), Charles Oliver, (Uncle Charlie, Aunt Rose's husband), Henry Powell (Uncle Henry, my mother's brother) Roderick (Rod) Clery, our next-door neighbour who later married Doreen.

ST LEONARD'S ROAD

THE DEBRIS

Freed by German bombs from their entombment, the seeds of Oxford Ragwort that had lain dormant for the best part of eighty years had taken in sunshine and rain and were now abundant. It was four years since the war had ended and their flowers were everywhere; flecks of yellow confidently showing themselves between burrs, rye grass, wall barley, and sturdy aromatic plants that we knew only as 'weeds.' And other flowers too: daisies, buttercups, clover, white-flowering vines of bindweed and beautiful deadly nightshade that could kill with its seductive berries. I stood in the middle of all this; my feet apart, eyes squinting under the brightness of the sun, an inch of white underpant showing below each trouser leg like businessmen's cuffs. I was four years old.

"Don't pick them, you'll wee the bed," said one of the big girls as I reached for the ragwort. "They're Wee the Beds, don't touch 'em." I pulled my hand back sharply. "Why don'tcha go and pick somefink else?" said the big girl. We always played with big girls. The war had kept our fathers away for six years so ours was a street of big sisters and little brothers. There were big boys too but they never bothered with us. The big girls were always there, though. They had to be. They were expected to look after us; but they didn't seem to mind. Maybe they saw it as their destiny; a rehearsal for when they would be mothers themselves.

That morning, the girls had made a house and I was sent to pick flowers for it. Girls liked making houses. They'd collect bricks from across the debris and lay them out in lines to make bedrooms, sculleries and the rest. The walls were never built up though; girls liked to play houses not build them. When I was older and played with the big boys, we made houses too but we called them 'camps' and they had real walls and roofs that we covered in turf to withstand the impact of enemy attacks. "Go and pick some diff'rent ones," the big girl said, so I left the house and went to see what I could find. There were plenty to choose from: orange marigolds, yellow buttercups and purple flowers like daises on long stalks. I came back clutching a bunch of wilting stems and went to offer them.

The big girl who'd saved me from a wet bed was Annie McAvennie. Annie was Billy McAvennie's sister and Billy was one of the little brothers like me. I entered the house to give Annie the flowers thinking she would be pleased but she wasn't. "You can't do that," she said with a hint of annoyance in her voice. "You've come in through the wall, you can't come in through the wall." I didn't understand. "Go out and come in through the door," said Annie. "You can't come in through the wall." So, I stepped over the wall, walked round to the front door and went back in.

Our 'debris' was vast or so it seemed and there were 'debris' everywhere. Two of the corners of our block had been bombed and a bomb had taken out three of the houses in-between. Most of the ones that once backed onto ours had been bombed too, leaving the swathe of uneven land that was our debris. Beyond that, many of the houses in Woodin Street had gone too and the land from there to the railway was one enormous bomb site. South of that was a third site with brick air raid shelters and an emergency water reservoir still in place.

The bombing must have been fierce to have caused such destruction. Poplar was a particular target because of its docks and with the river to show pilots the way, it was easy to find. On moonlit nights the Thames shone like a twisting silver ribbon and people prayed for cloud. At The Imperial War Museum in London, there is a picture of a Heinkel bomber over the great 'U' of the Thames between Greenwich and the Isle of Dogs. It was taken in 1940 and below the bomber the streets of Poplar are easy to make out: East India Dock Road, West Ferry Road, Chrisp Street and, somewhere to the north, St Leonard's Road, our home. A chill went through me the first time I saw it, as I realised that my family were sheltering somewhere below.

My mum was terrified of the bombing. If she couldn't get to the shelter in time, she would sit in the coal cupboard under the stairs holding my sister Doreen and trembling until the raids were over. When the bombing grew fierce, she would put her fingers in her ears and Doreen, little more than a toddler, would comfort her. Such was her fear that Doreen once led her along the street to Nanny Powell's with shrapnel raining down on them. Much of the bombing that caused the destruction around our home may have occurred on just one night because my mum often told me that she looked out of the shelter during one raid and everything around her was in flames. Maybe it was proximity to the railway that made our streets a particular target.

My mum lived in fear throughout the war and experienced terrifying dangers. It didn't get any better as the war went on; there was no let-up. When the bombing raids grew less frequent, the rocket raids began. First came the V1's: pilotless jets that whined across the sky until their fuel was spent and they dropped to earth to detonate their powerful explosives. People were terrified when the engine went silent because they knew that the destructive load was now dropping down on them at speed from above. Then came the V2's, faster and more destructive than the V1s. Death from V2s came without warning. Because of their speed, their explosions occurred before the rocket was heard; with V2s, death came with a macabre kind of bonus.

In the spring of 1945, my mum was pregnant with me and in March a rocket exploded about a mile away as she was cleaning the windows. She wasn't very tall so she stood on the window ledge to reach the highest panes. The blast from the explosion was so powerful that it shattered the window and flung her to the ground; a terrifying incident in anyone's life but for her it was only one of many.

Shortly after the war began, she and Doreen were evacuated with Nanny Powell to the relative safety of Hertfordshire. It proved to be a miserable experience. The family they were sent to resented their presence and treated them badly. They never called my mum by her name but referred to her as 'evacuee' instead. They didn't allow her and Nanny Powell into the rooms except for meals and the food they were given was meagre. For much of the time, they had to sit in the garden or on the stairs. It was the woman of the house who showed the most resentment. Her husband was ashamed of her ways, but it was only the son who acted towards them with any humanity. Once, when his mother wasn't looking, he slipped my mum a fried egg, carefully balancing it on the blade of his knife because he didn't want to be caught offering her his plate. When I think of my mother on those stairs, denied the respect of a name, afraid for her family in London, fearing for her husband at sea, a single parent with a dependant toddler and little money, I wish that I could go back in time and confront those people for their pitiless lack of humanity.

Eventually Nanny Powell had had enough. "We're better off facing the bombs than being here with these," she said. So, they returned to Poplar and that's how they came to be sheltering from a Heinkel bomber in St Leonard's Road instead of sitting on the stairs of an unwelcoming home in Hertfordshire.

* * *

My parents married on the second of August 1936 and moved into two small rooms in Aberfeldy Street. When larger ones became available in Chadbourne Street, they grabbed the chance and moved to number seven and there, on the twenty fourth of March 1938, Doreen was born. By the time the war began they had moved again, this time to a flat in Uamvar Street, just along St Leonard's Road. Then the war caught up with them because their house was bombed and they lost everything they had. With nowhere to go, they moved in with my grandmother, Nanny Powell. Nanny Powell's house at 217 St Leonard's Road was already home to four adults when my parents came to live there. There wasn't much living space and only two bedrooms so there must have been tensions at times. But my nan was a woman with special qualities and she managed to keep the home together despite overcrowding and the uncertainties of war. It helped that my dad looked on her as a mother and she showed him the affection of a mother to a son.

Between 1936 when he got married and 1940 when his house was bombed, my dad moved home five times. He was filling in forms, giving details, writing his address, updating information over and over again. Eventually the frequent moves caused him one enormous problem when, in October 1941, the police came to arrest him. My mum was in the bedroom with Doreen when they arrived. She heard a heavy knock on the door and noise coming up from downstairs but things happened so quickly that, before she knew what was going on, the police had put him in handcuffs and taken him away.

He was accused of avoiding conscription. He hadn't done that of course; it was just that his call-up papers went to previous addresses and he had never received them. He asked if he could say goodbye to his wife and daughter, but was refused and bundled into a car and taken away. The family never saw him for a long time after that and it was a while before they even knew where he was. He went on to serve with the Royal Navy until he was 'demobbed' on the 18th of February, 1946. He had given four years and four months to his country and earned medals for his service in Gibraltar, North Africa and the Atlantic Ocean.

Accommodation was scarce before the war but it was even harder to find once the bombing started. When Nanny Powell learned that her neighbour two doors down was moving away to live in Dagenham, she asked the landlord if my mum could take over the tenancy and he agreed. The house was bare when my she and Doreen moved in; the bombing had taken everything they owned, but she was fortunate to find a place at all and especially one just two doors down from her family.

The house was 213 St Leonard's Road and it is where I was born on the 20th of August, 1945.

What had the world put in place for me then? What was my inheritance? At the very heart of my new life was a loving mother, an absent father poised to return to show the love that he had in abundance, and a seven-year-old sister who would always look out for me and show me care. Not bad. And then there was the next layer, the extended family of my nan, Aunt Rose, Uncle Henry and Great Uncle Harry. Then another layer; a community of people who had come through it together, looked out for one another, knew what the East End was about, understood why mutual support was essential, were generally civil and sometimes funny. And then England, Britain, a country that was united, a country of people who had decided that the future was to be about fairness and equality, good health, better housing and higher standards of education; how lucky I was to be born into all that.

But there was another side. The house where I was born was virtually a slum years before it was demolished for slum clearance twenty-four years later. We had little money. Poplar was a patchwork of old terraced blocks and bomb sites. The air was dirty with grime from factories. There were shortages. The country was broke, much of the infrastructure was ruined. And during the early years of my life things got worse.

NANNY POWELL

Save for the addition of several layers of wallpaper and a few coats of paint, the back room in Nanny Powell's hadn't changed much since it was built in the 1860s. That went for the rest of the house too. Most of it was as it had always been: the brown-bannistered staircase with its brown oil-clothed stairs, the pokey scullery with its yellow ochre sink and the bedrooms with iron bedsteads weighed down by flock mattresses and bedclothes of wool, linen and feather. It was a Victorian worker's dwelling and Nanny Powell and my Great Uncle Harry were Victorians. The way they spoke, the things they ate, their manners and attitudes were all of the times they had grown up in. I spent hours in Nanny Powell's when I was small and, because I did, I feel I have experienced something of Victorian working-class life.

There was one window in the little living room that Nanny Powell called the kitchen. It looked out onto the back yard. The wall of the house next door rose to the left shutting out the light, so the kitchen was dark. Opposite the door, on the far wall, was an alcove with a Welsh dresser. Below it was a cupboard where things were kept but never brought out. Next to the dresser was the chimney breast and, in the hearth, a cast iron stove with an oven and fire. Kettles were kept on it for hot water and the stove was lit even in the summer. Two flat-irons sat face down on the hob to catch the stove's heat for ironing; as one cooled the other was ready to take its place.

To the right of the chimney breast was another alcove and in it a free-standing cupboard. On top of it was a radio with a face that lit up when it was switched on and a tuning dial that could take listeners on a journey to interesting places at home and abroad: Hilversum, Hamburg, Luxembourg, London, Home, Welsh and more. Next to the radio was an exotic blue and white teapot. Its shape was sinuous and complex and its glazed surface was decorated with scenes of elephants processing through Imperial India.

A table stood against the wall behind the kitchen door; a fine table of good size. It was made of pine and, although the legs had retained their dark-brown varnish, the top had been scrubbed white over the years leaving a broad knotted surface that spoke of honesty and authenticity. Hiding under it was a joy for me, especially when it was draped with a tablecloth. I'd play tricks on Uncle Henry by pulling the bottom of his trouser leg or squeak like a mouse to frighten Aunt Rose. Boots and shoes were kept under the table. It made sense to keep them there; out of sight but always available.

Old Harry would sit to the left of the stove in a fine old Windsor chair. The wood of the arms was varnished dark brown but resting hands had worn it away to a pale honey over the years. Harry was Henry Mason, my nan's brother. He was born about 1868 and was several years older than her. Although Harry was in my life for less than three years, I remember him clearly; a short figure in cheese cutter cap, collarless shirt and black 'weskut.' He had an old face lined by time with droopy eyes and the thick bushy moustache of a man of his times. His placid nature was tempered by an ability to cut in with guileful remarks that could deflate egos and make people laugh.

Everyone liked him. Harry called me 'Iggly Snow Shoes'; it was a name unique to him and to me. No one else called me that. Because of Harry, the span of spoken language in my life reaches far back into the nineteenth century.

Old Harry was almost blind when I knew him, his failing eyesight was probably due to cataracts. For much of the time he would sit in the big Windsor chair smoking a clay pipe. The pipes were brittle and often broke but Harry always had another to hand when a stem snapped. I would watch him closely as he made long tapers to light them with; carefully folding strips of newspaper into thin batons that he could light from the fire. They were such simple, lovely objects and so skilfully made. Nanny Powell preferred snuff to tobacco and Harry sometimes took a pinch of snuff too.

Harry would also cut squares of newspaper which he kept in the hearth for spitting into. When they needed to, both Nanny Powell and he would spit into the paper, screw it up and throw it into the fire. I was never put off by that; I just thought it was an hygienic way of getting rid of something nasty, which of course it was. To Harry and my nan's generation, spitting had a different significance to ours. In their day it was common and necessary for working people to spit because the filthy air of industrial Britain had such a damaging effect on their lungs.

Old Harry died in 1948 and it was the first time that my life was touched by death. I wasn't quite three and, although I cannot recall how or why he died, I do remember the day of his funeral and the big black Daimler cars coming down the street to take the mourners to the cemetery. A few weeks later, the same black cars returned but this time it was to take Aunt Rose to her wedding. When I saw her getting into a funeral car, I feared the worst and ran towards her shouting "Don't go, Aunt Rosie, don't go!"

I still have a copy of Old Harry's memorial card. When I was a boy, it would turn up from time to time and whenever I read it, it would make me sad:

Hold Thou Thy cross before my closing eyes
Shine through the gloom and point me to the skies
Heaven's morning breaks, and earth's vain shadows flee
In life, in death o Lord, abide with me.

* * *

Nanny Powell smelt of dry things; of dried leaves, of herbs, of hops, and pepper. Her smell was pleasant and reassuring and, burying my face in her apron, I would breathe it in and feel wanted and safe. She was thin and tall, although her tallness was more a case of being a little taller than the people around her. Her face was long and thin and she had slender lips, a full nose and high cheek bones. Her fine grey hair was worn in a bun. Her eyes were pale-green or, possibly, a shade of greyish-blue. Her voice was clear and cockney. Except on special occasions, she wore a pinafore. She never dressed up much but when she did, she looked good.

Nanny Powell's life was a hard one. She never had money and faced challenges that many would find too hard to bear. As a teenager she lived in fear of Jack the Ripper as he went on his murderous rampages a few miles up the road in Whitechapel, but she never spoke of it. Neither did she go on about taking in an orphaned child, or giving birth, or coping with babies during the uncertainties of the First World War. She never spoke of the General Strike, though she had some troubling stories to tell, or of being widowed during the Great Depression, or of suffering the death of her adopted son, or of living through the firestorms of the Blitz. Instead, she was a steadfast presence: someone people turned to; someone who knew what to do. Her house was a haven for me; a place to run to when life grew stormy and somewhere to linger when times were good.

I spent hours with my nan. She would look after me when my mum was shopping or doing housework and I saw her every day. She was seventy when I was four but we played together like children. As a little one I would climb the stairs to her landing, sit at the top and bump my way down stair by stair until I reached the bottom. Then I would climb back up and do it again. Once she asked if she could do it too. "Yes, nan." I replied in disbelief and delight. So, she climbed the stairs and came bumping down on her bum one by one, leaving me helpless with little boy laughter. Laughter was my reward for being her grandson and her reward for making her grandson laugh.

When I was a little older, I learned how to slide down the banisters. I would mount them at the top, then, facing the landing, speed my way down, gripping the rail to slow me as I got nearer the bottom. As when I bumped down the stairs, Nanny Powell asked if she could have a go too. Lifting her leg over at the top, she let go of the rail and came swiftly down. It left me rocking with laughter. Then she suggested we come down together so we did, with me in front and her behind. It was such a funny thing to do and it must have been difficult for her, but any discomfort she felt was never shown, because nothing would be allowed to deny me my right to laughter.

Nanny Powell called me 'Dick Barton' after the 'special agent' hero of the radio series. We all loved 'Dick Barton' and never missed an episode. Dick was an ex-commando who got into some terrible scrapes. The story lines had death machines, swarms of killer rats, threats of drowning and a good supply of nasty villains. It should have been frightening listening for a little boy, but I loved the 'Dick Barton' programmes. In 1951 the BBC decided that Dick had to go and his place was taken by 'The Archers,' an early soap series about farming and country life. It was meant to promote modern agricultural techniques. Nanny Powell and I listened to it together from the start; it was our special thing. She would sit in her chair below the radio and I would sit on the other side of the fireplace in Old Harry's chair. I never listen to The Archers anymore, but it gave comfort to me when I was young and things weren't going well, because it brought me closer to Nanny Powell.

* * *

Sometimes on summer mornings, I would sit with my nan in her front room shelling peas. It was cool in there; a nice place to be on a hot day. She would pop open the pods, slide her thumb along the inside and let the peas fall into her apron. I was always given a few to shell, but more went into me than into the apron. In the winter when she made pies, she would give me a little pastry and stewed meat to make a pie of my own.

Nanny Powell cooked traditional food; London food that she'd eaten all her life. Much of it was fish. As London was on a tidal river, it was easy to bring fish up the Thames from the estuary or the open sea. Meat was scarce during the war and when I was small it was still on ration. "There's liver up the butcher's," someone would shout and my mum would stop what she was doing and run up the road to Hedges as fast as she could. My nan cooked fish most nights: bloaters, sprats, plaice, cod, rock salmon, mackerel, kippers, sardines, conga eel and smoked haddock. She would oven-poach mussels in milk and cooked smoked haddock the same way. Fish roe got a similar treatment. Some roes were smooth, others had a crumbly texture and both were delicious. On Sunday mornings Uncle Henry often took me on his bike to buy live shrimps from the fishmonger in Poplar High Street. He made a little wooden seat so I could sit on the crossbar and I loved riding there on it. When we got home, he'd cook the shrimps in boiling water and bring some in to us for our tea.

I'd often be in my nan's when Uncle Henry came home from work. Henry worked as a welder in an Ilford firm that made barges and he got home just before six. When I saw him coming round the corner by the church, I'd call my nan and she would get his tea ready. Henry spent ages washing his hands when he came in from work but, eventually, the two of them would sit down to eat at the old pine table. Often, I would be given a 'bit of gravy tater.' Gravy tater was a dollop of potato served in a small enamel bowl with thick brown gravy and, sometimes, a few vegetables or some meat. I always said "yes" to gravy tater and after I'd eaten it, I would go home and have my tea.

Henry and my nan would finish their meal with 'afters' and a cup of tea. Posh people called afters 'dessert' and even posher people called them 'pudding'. Pudding was a good word for Nanny Powell's afters because she made lots of delicious puddings: spotted dick, jam roly-poly, and treacle pudding, all steamed for hours in a saucepan. Her rice puddings looked good before and after they were cooked. The milky rice was topped with egg custard and finished with grated nutmeg. When the pudding came out of the oven and the surface had caramelised, it looked even better. Once it cooled, she would cut me a portion and sprinkle it with sugar, turning her back on Henry as she did, pretending to hide what she was doing from him. Sugar was rationed and she would contrive a little dispute with him to make me feel we'd got one over on him.

"What's that you're putting on 'is rice pudden? It ain't sugar, is it?"

"No. Salt."

"Salt on rice pudden? Never 'eard of it. You sure it ain't sugar?"

"No! Salt!"

For my sixtieth birthday my son and daughter took me to Langan's Brasserie for a birthday dinner. Langan's is a special place and the menu that night offered an interesting combination of complex cuisine and plainer food. I had a smoked haddock dish to start with. It came with a perfectly poached egg and I followed that with a plate of calf's liver. I chose a crumbly treacle flan to finish with a small jug of cream. It was a perfect meal. As Alice and Joe waited for the bill, something dawned on me. "Smoked haddock, liver and treacle tart," I said. "I chose a meal my nan would have cooked me."

* * *

Sometimes Nanny Powell sang as she worked. The song I remember most is *I'll Be Your Sweetheart* a 1940s number written in the style of a music hall ballad. Its verses are unremarkable but the refrain that links them is beautiful; a simple message carried by the most perfect of tunes. It is gentle but insistent; whatever happens I will be with you and I will love you:

I'll be your sweetheart if you will be mine
All my life I'll be your Valentine
Bluebells I've gathered, keep them and be true
When I'm a man, my plan will be to marry you.

Nanny Powell had the singing voice of a Victorian, so when she sang 'gathered' it sounded like 'gath*urrred*.'

When my youngest granddaughter Rose was a baby, she suffered dreadfully from acid reflux, a painful and unpleasant condition. It was difficult to calm her when she felt such pain, but I had the knack. I would take her head on my right shoulder, cup it in my hand and hold it against my face. Then I would rock to and fro and sing old-fashioned songs to her until I felt her little body relax. It usually worked and baby Rose often fell asleep to gentle old songs like *Underneath the Arches, The Umbrella Man* and her great-great grandma's favourite *I'll Be Your Sweetheart*. I think that this goes to show how those fortunate enough to experience familial love can pass it on through the generations. Through me, Nanny Powell was helping baby Rose to find comfort.

Nanny Powell died in July 1954, a few days after her seventy-seventh birthday. She had suffered a stroke and was taken to Poplar Hospital. Her sudden illness threw the family into shock. Her death was unexpected despite her age. As a nine-year-old, I witnessed the business of adults trying to deal with a crisis. I listened to their reports from hospital visits. "She's in a coma," said Henry and I asked what a coma was. Days went by and there was no sign of progress. One evening I was standing under the lamppost by Nell Smith's door when Uncle Henry came along from the hospital. I asked him how Nanny Powell was. "She tried to say something to us but we couldn't understand her," he said. "Some kids at school are hard to understand and I'm used to them, so let me have a go," I said. Nanny Powell wasn't in hospital for long and with every day the lack of improvement began to sink in. I loved her and I didn't want her to die. "Henry's took it bad," people said when it was all over. The nicotine stains on his fingers were testament to that.

People came and went: neighbours, tradesmen, relatives and people I've never seen before, all of them well-meaning and kind. And the clichés flowed. "She's in a better place now." "She didn't suffer thank gawd." "She wouldn't 'av wanted to 'av bin a burden." "She's up in 'eaven lookin' down." Arrangements were made. Francis and Chris Walters would do the funeral. The Walters family was well known in Poplar. Two of the daughters were successful comediennes whose comedy characters, Gert and Daisy, were very popular, and their brother Jack was famous for playing the television policeman, George Dixon. Francis and Chris Walters always did the funerals in St Leonard's Road.

Nanny Powell had nothing much to leave. She had no money, so there was no will to be dealt with and Uncle Henry and Aunt Rose took care of the official requirements that come with a death. The neighbours organised a collection to buy a wreath. "We're genna get 'er a nice Gates of 'eaven," said Mrs Jones. The neighbours' wreath was always a Gates of Heaven; an upright arch of white flowers with two doors, one ajar as if about to open to let the loved one in. "We're 'avin mum 'ome," Aunt Rose told Mrs. Purton when she asked about the funeral.

Curtains were drawn along the length of the street when the hearse came to bring Nanny Powell home. Flowers arrived and a constant trickle of people came to pay their respects. The front room was darkened when I went in to see her. It was unexpectedly different; a familiar place transformed. It smelt different too; the fragrance of lilies, the perfume of other flowers and the rich sweetness of coffin varnish, melded into one aroma that came to mean the smell of death. The coffin was oddly appealing with its light varnished wood and polished brass handles. Nanny Powell was laid with her head facing the window. The coffin lid was pulled back to reveal her face and she looked so nice; like Nanny Powell but younger and peaceful with her face unlined. She was shrouded in white linen trimmed with lace. The Victorian lady was getting a Victorian funeral.

Wreaths were ordered. On the day of the funeral, more flowers and wreaths arrived; so many that they filled the airie outside. Johnny Grover the coalman, Alfie Weymond from the green grocer's stall in Chrisp Street and Hedges the butcher all sent wreathes. These were traders whose families had known Nanny Powell for years and they held her in such high regard. When the hearse arrived, the wreaths were placed on the roof of the funeral cars. As was the custom, the Gates of Heaven was put at the front; a sign of respect both to and from the neighbours.

I wasn't allowed to go to the funeral. Sarah Stock looked after me while it took place. "Go to the street door Joey, your Nan's going now," she said. I looked out from Sarah's front door and saw the hearse creep slowly away led by an undertaker, his measured gait expressing dignity and respect with every step. It seemed many hours before the mourners came back but it probably was no more than two. Then my mum called for me and I crossed the road to Nanny Powell's house, but it wasn't Nanny Powell's house anymore.

* * *

Death isn't static. It doesn't stop with the sudden ending of a life but continues on like a car on ice; skidding, sliding, carrying on. The one you have lost will never speak to you again, or breathe the air you breathe or blink their eyes, or stare again, but they continue on because the very essence of what they were is there in your mind unaltered by physical death. And because of that, the feelings you had for them do not go away but continue on too and you cannot rid yourself of them. To the completeness of a person, the physical presence is just the frame for the bigger picture. When I was devastated by grief my head was filled with one recurring thought: I have all this love for her and nowhere for it to go.

HOPPING

For working-class East Enders, hop picking was their holiday: a chance to get away from the grime and polluted air of home and into the lovely countryside of Kent. 'Hoppin' started in the first week of September and continued for the best part of a month. The war never stopped it; harvesting hops for beer was essential war work or, if it wasn't, it certainly should have been. Although the hop fields were mostly untouched by the war, my mum told me of an encounter she had with a German pilot when she was 'hopping' in 1941. As he was taken at gun point from the wreckage of his plane, he saw her holding Doreen and made to speak. I can imagine the tension this must have caused and how apprehensive my mum would have been, but common humanity prevailed, and he was allowed to say something. "Your little girl is very lovely," he said "I have a little girl like her too," and from his pocket, he took a picture of his daughter and held it up for her to see. For a moment the two of them were brought together; no longer enemies, but parents. A man who was obliged to kill Doreen and my mum was a father too, with all the feelings that go with parenthood; feelings that he and my mother shared. How does it come to this?

Nanny Powell always went hopping; the Powells had been 'goin down 'oppin' for years; I have pictures of them picking hops in the 1930s. Most of the grans I knew went hopping too. When hopping day came, they would sit outside on their trunks waiting for the lorry to arrive. I was two when I went for the first time. I remember the lorry coming that day and the excitement that went with it: the driver letting down the tailgate, men heaving Nanny Powell's trunk into the back, the greetings and laughter. I remember being lifted into the lorry and seated next to my mum on Nanny Powell's old green hopping trunk. Then moving off, the lorry lurching and groaning and me looking out over its open back as Poplar slipped away: Dewberry Street, Brunswick Road and then through the Blackwall Tunnel. On into Kent and the ladies started singing:

'When you go down hoppin, hoppin down in Kent,
See Old Mother Riley spending all the rent
With a tra la la, a tra la la....'

The journey to Hunton was about sixty miles but it took a long time. The lorry crawled up hills and managed only about forty miles an hour on the flat. Kent was hilly and Wrotham Hill was very steep. When the over-burdened old lorries tackled it, the women got out while the men gave a push up the hill. Our route passed through Maidstone and Yalding along ever-narrowing roads through lovely woodland until my nan and her friends recognised the familiar. "The Bull's still there Rose," her friend Nora said as the lorry made its way through the village. "Good job an' all," said Nanny Powell. "We'll 'av one in there tonight if we're lucky."

We lived in tin huts well away from the hop fields. They were attached to one another in lines and each one was about the size of a beach hut. The walls and roofs were made of corrugated iron and a long wooden bench ran the width of the inside to make a platform for our bed. We slept together on mattresses stuffed with straw. They were prickly but they smelt delicious and I slept happily and secure on our platform surrounded by my family.

By the hut door was a table for cooking and a stove that smelt of methylated spirit. The smell of meths started the morning of every day and reminded me that we were away from home and in the country. Outside, fires were kept burning for hot water and warmth. Hubble the farmer gave us plenty of faggots to burn, so the fires never went out. It was the smells of hopping that I loved most: the smell of wet grass in the morning, the smell of woodsmoke at night, beer on the breath of grown-ups when they came back from the pub, the mattress straw, the cooking stove and the smell of the hops themselves. The aroma of hops is something I relish. Crush the flower of Lavender and it releases its perfume, sweet and perfect. Crush a hop flower and it is just as good, but its perfume isn't sweet, it is dry and savoury; it makes you hungry.

The sound of the morning was the squawking of crows; there were dozens of them, high in the trees or circling around in the air. It was always cold, or so it seemed, and getting dressed was uncomfortable in the chill of the unheated hut. The walk to the hop fields was another challenge. To reach them we had to cross a field of heavy yellow clay, wet from rain and furrowed from ploughing. Then, on through long wet grass that soaked our feet and ankles until we reached the hopping bins.

Hops grew on bines; sinuous stems that twisted upwards along strings attached to wooden posts. Because they rose so high, they had to be pulled to the ground for us to access their flowers. Picking was a simple process: the flowers were tugged from the bines and thrown into long canvas bins. But it was hard work and back-breaking too. It meant standing all day and picking had to be fast if we were to earn enough money to make it worthwhile. At the end of the day, the foreman would call: "Pull no more bines," and we had to stop. Then the pickings were weighed and the weight was recorded.

Nanny Powell was a good hop picker; she could pull hops at speed without damaging them or leaving any flower on the stem. Sometimes I helped with the picking too and at the end of the day, my fingers would be stained ochre-green. When picking was over, the hops were sent to the brewery in Faversham where our day's work would be turned into beer. In the evenings Nanny Powell and her friends would turn their day's work into beer too at *The Bull* in Hunton. *The Bull* was the hoppers' pub. It wasn't big, just two bars not much larger than living rooms. The ceiling was low and the walls were stained yellow with nicotine. It came alive at night when the hoppers were there, chatting noisily or singing, each with a glass of black beer to help the evening along.

There was more to hopping than just picking hops. It was a change of scene, a chance to spend time away in a place without slums or bomb sites; a place where the air was clean. Kent was a lovely part of England. The brewing industry and the fertile Kentish soil had produced a unique landscape of hop fields, fruit orchards and huge swathes of wheat. In rural Kent it was as if the war had never happened. Old buildings stood intact unscarred by bombs and shrapnel. There were ancient villages of red-brick houses with red-tiled roofs that continued down onto their upper-storey facades. There were half-timbered houses too, their wood petrified into something resembling stone, and, everywhere, the fat old oast houses standing like jolly nuns, their round red walls and conical roofs topped off with white louvered vents.

There must have been other children for me to play with, but I was too young to go with them, so I never went far. I was told there were dangers too: ditches to fall into from which you would never come out, bulls that would trample you to death and foxes that would bite you and eat you up. The hedgerows were full of poisonous berries and, in the big field across from the huts, there were gypsies who would kidnap you and never bring you back. It was troublesome stuff to fill a little boy's head with and most of it was nonsense. No one died in a ditch or was eaten by foxes or poisoned or abducted, and Nanny Powell said that gypsies were all right anyway (though I never risked putting that to the test by going too near them.)

One day a farm girl gave me a ride on a horse. His name was Dobbin and he was so tall that I wondered how I would ever get up onto his back. Dobbin was the most unoriginal name a horse could have, but it suited him. He was gentle and I had no fear of him. I was used to seeing big horses like Dobbin harnessed to huge brewers' drays. I often saw them outside pubs with their heads in nosebags, waiting patiently while the draymen loaded barrels of beer into pub cellars before going inside for an hour or so to help empty them again. For sport, we would run under the horses' bellies, rushing through as quickly as we could before one of them stamped a foot or sprayed us with an enormous wee.

There were three steps set against the wall of one of the houses in the street at Hunton; a block for mounting horses that must have stood there for centuries. I climbed it and, with a little help, was lifted onto Dobbin's back where I sat with the farm girl behind me. How different the world looked from up there. I could see along the street, over hedges and down onto Dobbin's enormous neck with its lovely mane of wispy black hair shifting lightly as he nodded and plodded his way along.

Not long ago, I went back to Hunton with some friends. I was looking for the places I had known as a child. I walked around the village trying to recognise at least one landmark or location, but it was no good, I could find nothing. I was about to give up when suddenly it all changed; like a tablet screen realigning from horizontal to vertical, the picture altered and I knew where I was. The configuration of road, the incline, the trees, made sense to me now and I knew I was approaching the path to Hubble's farm. I carried on, hoping to get into the field where our huts had been but the entrance was blocked. I knew it was the right place though; the slope of the ground told me that.

We walked back into the village, turned into the road we'd come from and there, a little way down on the left, was *The Bull*: the low roof, the front garden where the hoppers drank when the weather was fine and the doorway set back from the road. *The Bull* at Hunton, a place where I had witnessed the singing, the knees-ups, the drinking and laughter of Poplar people a lifetime ago; no longer a pub, now someone's home. Back in the village I found the stone steps I had climbed to mount Dobbin. I climbed them again; they were smaller than I remembered. What I hadn't noticed all those years ago, was how perfectly located those steps were in a small street of ancient buildings that hadn't changed in centuries.

When my mum died in September 2001, I wanted to mark the days she had spent picking hops; days that meant so much to her. Standing by the grave at her funeral, I took two sprigs of hops and handed one to Doreen. We threw them down onto the coffin below. Hops have always been a part of my life. They are a reminder of my mum, my nan and the people I come from. Their flowers and perfume are beautiful.

THE FIVE WAYS

My father was a Catholic but my mother was not. When he was twenty-two, he was engaged to a Catholic girl, but then he met my mum, broke off the engagement and proposed to her instead. Some of the Connollys bitterly resented him marrying a Protestant and made life difficult for them both. His sisters Nan and Kit would call after my mum when they saw her in the street. They taunted her and accused her of taking their brother away from his family. She never forgot that and, over the years, his family were the cause of more arguments between my parents than anything else.

Doreen and I were not brought up as Catholics. We were both baptised in the Church of England, but when the time came for her to start school, my dad wanted Doreen to be educated as a Catholic. Maybe this was to pacify the Connollys or perhaps he thought it was the right thing for a Catholic father to do. My mum took a different view. Catholic schools had a reputation for harshness. I remember hearing people say that in Catholic schools "Nuns are strict" and "They are spiteful; they hit you over the knuckles with a ruler." As things turned out, Doreen's first day at the *Holy Child* school never happened. My dad took her there, but my mum told her to come away if she didn't like it and that's what she did. She went to the *Hay Currie* school instead, and when the time came for me to go to school, the question of a Catholic education never arose.

Doreen and I were baptised Anglicans but we never went to church. Instead, we were sent to Sunday school at The Five Ways Mission, a little meeting hall opposite the war memorial in St Leonard's Road. The Five Ways got its name from its location, being at the convergence of five roads that met there. It was part of London City Mission, a Christian organisation established in the early 1800s to *...bring them to an acquaintance with Jesus Christ as Saviour,* 'them' being the poor children of London; children like Doreen and me. The London City Misson wasn't a denomination. It wasn't like Methodism or the Church of England; it didn't have liturgies or rites. Instead, it had plenty of singing and Bible stories and lots and lots of Jesus. Its purpose was to bring children into the fold and keep them there.

The mission hall was about the size of a large shop. It had two doors facing onto St Leonards Road: one was the entrance and the other was always kept locked. It was like a chapel inside with wooden chairs in rows facing a raised platform that was not quite a stage and not quite an altar. Above it hung a large coloured picture showing Jesus in a white robe, his arms open in a gesture of embrace. Surrounding him were children of different races. A caption read: *'Suffer the little children to come unto me.'* It was a picture I liked and a sentiment I appreciated.

Half-way down the hall on the right was an organ. It was brown and dark with pedals to push, stops to pull and keys to press. When played by someone who knew what they were doing, it made a good sound. At intervals along the ceiling, white-shaded lamps on long cables cast a dull yellow light from above. Below them, radiators ran the length of the room pumping out heat on cold afternoons in winter. The mission walls were wood-panelled and painted: the upper half white, the lower half green. Over the years, sunlight, traffic fumes and pollution from factories had turned the white paint ivory.

Sunday school started at two and ended at four. I began going when I was four and for a few years, Doreen came with me. To me it was a duty and a chore; something I was made to do and grew increasingly resentful of. One week was much the same as another: we were told stories, taught scriptures, said prayers and sang songs. The songs we sang were called 'choruses' and singing them was one of the things about being there that I liked. Some had actions to illustrate the words. *Away Far Beyond Jordan*, had a line that went: *'We'll meet in that land, oh won't it be grand,'* and when we sang it, we crossed our arms and shook hands with the children on either side. Sometimes, as an act of subversion, the handshaking would become very animated and over vigorous.

Our Sunday school teachers were like characters from an Ealing comedy. There were four of them. Miss Bell was in charge and she was assisted by Miss Read, and the Miss Sweets: sisters Elsie and Ada. Occasionally the four were joined by Winnie Weller, a neighbour of the Sweets from Mills Grove. Miss Reed was about seventy, Miss Bell probably in her late forties and the Sweets in their sixties. Somewhere in the background lurked the shadowy presence of Miss Nottle but mostly it was just a team of four.

Miss Bell was taller than the others; an upright figure who wore floral dresses, a bottle green coat and sensible shoes. She used 'flannel graphs' to tell her stories and they brought colour to my generally colourless world. To do them, she would stand in front of a cloth-covered board and illustrate her story by sticking felt pictures onto it. When she told the story of Zacchaeus the tax collector, she would begin by pressing a cloth tree onto the board. Then, when little Zacchaeus arrived, she would stick him onto one of its branches. When Jesus turned up, she'd flatten him in place under the tree and we would sing:

Now Zacchaeus was a very little man,
And a very little man was he,
He climbed right up to the top of a tree
So the Saviour he could see.
And when the Saviour passed that way
He looked into that tree
And said "Now Zacchaeus you come down,
For I'm coming to your house for tea."

As we sang, we did actions to go with the story. We would hold a flat hand level with our waists to emphasise Zacchaeus' lack of height and shield our eyes from an imaginary sun as the Saviour looked up into the tree. 'Tea' was represented by holding one forefinger across the other to form the letter T.

For scripture lessons, the chairs were arranged in circles and we sat in small groups. These Bible classes were the most mind-numbing thing of all. To sit still listening to readings from the Old Testament, spoken in Jacobean English, followed by a protracted explanation of the text, was more than tedious for a boy who would much rather be playing on the bomb site with his mates. In time I learned that the best thing to do during scripture, was to engage in an entertaining distraction whilst appearing to pay attention. On sunny days I would fascinate myself by staring at the rays of sun that came streaming in through the windows, imagining them to be searchlights and enjoying the sharp contrasts of the shadows they made. Most of all, I enjoyed gazing at the minute specks of dust that were caught by the rays; millions of them, all moving haphazardly and defying gravity. When Miss Reed took the class, the rays of sunshine also caught the tiny specks of spittle that she projected from her mouth and I would dodge about trying to avoid them. "Sit still Joe," she would say. But 'sit' and 'still' were unfortunate words because they produced even bigger sprays of spittle and I had to dodge about more.

Elsie and Ada Sweet were an unlikely pair of sisters or, unalike perhaps describes them better. They were both short and both held a deep love for Jesus but in most other respects they were different. Ada was less engaging than Elsie. She lacked Elsie's warmth, was more serious and harder to like. She wore dark clothes; coats in black or brown and a black 'Robin Hood' hat with a feather on the side. Horn-rimmed glasses gave her angular face a harsh look. She smiled less frequently than Elsie and I suspect she was the more practical of the two. But for all her plainness and lack of charm, Ada, like Elsie, was a good person. Elsie had a soft, open nature. She was quick to praise and ready with a smile. She wore scarves and dresses of pale chiffon and smelled of lavender water. Her cheeks glowed unnaturally red with rouge and her lips were ever-scarlet. I can hear her voice quite clearly even now, rich and fruity, praising me and never forgetting to mention Jesus.

Elsie and Ada lived in Mills Grove, a quiet street tucked away between the busier St Leonard's and Brunswick roads. I went to their house a few times when Sunday school was relocated there whilst The Five Ways was being repaired. It was a neat, old-fashioned place and unlikely to have changed much since the Sweets grew up there in the latter years of the nineteenth century. Strings of glass beads, hanging by the front door, jangled as you passed through them into the passage. In the front room, pictures of flowers and pastoral landscapes hung on the wall above heavy brown furniture. On a stand in front of the window, a potted aspidistra partially obscured the view into the street.

Elsie and Ada lived busy lives and were confident in their surroundings. They were 'out there.' In summer they would go for long evening walks and when they passed our door they would stop for a chat and praise me to my mum and dad for the way I recited the scriptures. I can still picture them coming down the street towards us; Elsie a soft form in pastel colours; Ada a sharper, darker figure; Elsie on Ada's right arm and both walking in step with one another. And when I think of them, my heart melts and I wonder what became of them when the cruel sledgehammer of demolition came crashing down on our community.

* * *

I was popular with my Sunday school teachers because, even at a young age, I could remember psalms and verses from the Old Testament and recite them. As a reward I was given a book called *Stories of the Bible*. I treasured it for its illustrations and in particular for their colour. Inside was an elaborate sticker inscribed with the words: *'To Joseph Connolly for Saying the Scriptures Well.'* It is dated 1949. One evening I had to recite a poem before 'invited guests.' It was a ploy to encourage people to put money into the collection plate:

You guess what I've got in my pocket,
It isn't a knife or a ball,
Nor chocolate nor sweets nor an apple,
No, it's something quite round and quite small.
Oh no I am not going to spend it,
It's for the collection you see.
Look, it's a bright shiny penny
That my mother has given to me.

At the words "Look, it's a bright shiny penny," I had to put a hand in my pocket, take out a penny and hold it up. We rehearsed several times with Miss Bell constantly correcting me. "It isn't you *GAS* what I've got in my pocket, it's you *GUESS*." I remember a lovely family moment when my mum and dad sorted out the penny for me; my mum finding the best one she could from her purse and my dad shining it with metal polish to a bright gold before checking my pockets for holes and sending me on my way.

Sometimes we went on outings with The Five Ways. The Sweets took us to Barking Park once; just a bus ride away but a treat nonetheless. A better trip was to Hampton Court where we went on a river boat. It was there or Barking Park where Eileen Purton got splashed and her knickers were soaked. Without hesitation, Ada reached into her bag and took out a clean pair for Eileen to have. Ada was indeed the practical one.

Winnie Weller was an occasional addition to The Five Ways team. She was short and dumpy with a face that could always show a smile. Maybe it was because of her happy demeanour that she was known as Winnie and not Miss Weller. Winnie was a friend of the Sweets and part of a broader coterie of unmarried Poplar ladies who were known as 'churchgoers.' The group included Miss Nottle, but Miss Nottle wasn't the usual type of lady churchgoer because she had a dark secret.

When my dad was away at sea my mum sent him parcels; little luxuries and comforts to help see him through. Often the parcels didn't get to him and when that happened, she received an official note saying 'Ship lost at sea.' It was a dispiriting experience especially for my dad who watched as other sailors helped themselves from parcels of biscuits, cigarettes, chocolate, toothpaste and soap. Miss Nottle may have felt a little sad too as she was the postmistress who had to dispatch the brown paper parcels with their precious contents. But everyone accepted these losses; we were at war afterall, and 'worse things happen at sea.'

The post office was next door to The Five Ways so maybe Miss Nottle got to know Miss Bell and the others because of that. I remember her serving at the counter there before the post office was relocated to better premises further along St Leonard's Road. Miss Nottle was ideal for the role of postmistress; she was knowledgeable, practical and efficient. The post office ran well under her management and it was always busy. I liked going in there. It smelt of officialdom: of rubber stamps, ink pads, wrapping paper and wood. And even at a young age, I felt it connected me to a broader, outward-facing society beyond the constraints of working-class Poplar.

When the old post office building became empty it was converted into a shop. Several years later, new owners moved in and it was taken apart for refurbishment. That was when Miss Nottle's dark secret was revealed for, when workmen entered the cellar, they found it full of parcels destined for the armed forces. Miss Nottle had hoarded them; kept them for herself. A dreadful wrong in so many ways: theft, depriving men who were risking their lives of a few comforts, stealing from poorer people who spent what little they had on supporting their loved ones and using her position for her own advantage when the country was at war. Miss Nottle was found out and sent to prison. One special parcel did get through. In it was a small piece of coal, wrapped in tissue paper and wound in string. It was sent from my mum to my dad with a message that said *This is in case the ship runs out of coal so that you can come home safe.* He treasured it and brought it home. I still have it.

* * *

When Miss Bell left The Five Ways, Pastor Thomas arrived. Pastor Thomas was the first male preacher I remember. He was as Welsh a non-conformist minister as one could be. A short, slight man in his forties in a grey double-breasted suit and always with a bible under his arm. He had a fine Welsh accent and never relied on volume to preach the gospels; he was no 'hwyl' preacher. Pastor Thomas had several children and their number prompted ribald comments about his potency from some of our mothers.

There were always occasions when parents came to The Five Ways: carol services, harvest festivals and prize-givings, but these were one-offs. Pastor Thomas wanted to make family involvement a more regular part of his ministry so, soon after he arrived, he organised an outing to Chalkwell, a seaside town near Southend. This suited his plan because most of the mothers came with their children. On the morning we left, we had a group picture taken and Pastor Thomas played a lively hymn on his accordion before we got onto the coach. Unfortunately for him, he was unaware of the ways of coach outings in Poplar. Meeting by a coach, having a group photograph taken and singing a song before going on a trip had all of the hallmarks of a pub beano and to some extent that's what it became.

It was a sunny day and Johnny Watton, Billy McAvennie, Johnny Purton I spent the morning playing together on the beach. At midday I sat with the others to eat my sandwiches and, a little after that, our mums asked Pastor Thomas if he would mind keeping an eye on us while they went for a walk. He was happy to agree and, with his blessing, they set off.

The route the walkers took led directly from the beach to a pub and apparently that is where it ended. Nothing happened to us while they were gone, but by the time we left for home I was red with sunburn. Johnny Purton and I were both suffering. We were fair-skinned and blonde. Billy Mac and Johnny Watton were darker and not affected much, but I suffered badly and when we got home my dad was annoyed with my mum for neglecting me. I would have burnt anyway because we didn't know how to prevent sunburn. We applied olive oil because we thought it offered protection when in fact it did the opposite. Calamine lotion eased my pain for a while but over the coming weeks I lost layers of skin.

In later life, the sunburn I had when I was young has caused me problems and I have had treatments and operations to remove lesions and prevent cancerous skin damage. When the country was locked down during the COVID *pandemic* in 2020, I spent some time writing poems for my grandchildren. Some were just for fun but others were intended to help and guide them in their lives. This is what I wrote about being exposed to the Sun:

Precautions

Never take the Sun for granted.
Don't be hoodwinked by its charm.
For every ray, the seed it planted,
Later on, may do you harm.

Enjoy the beach's summer glory,
Build a castle, dig a hole.
Have a picnic, read a story.
Keep beneath a parasol!

Fall asleep within its cover,
Drift into your summer dream.
Have a swim, then have another.
Put on tons and tons of cream!

Love the Sun for all it brings you:
Light and warmth and food and life.
Know too that the Sun can harm you,
Make you ill and bring you strife.

Always cover up in summer.
Wear a T-shirt in the sea.
Shade your eyes and put a hat on.
Then you won't end up like me.

* * *

I often tried to get out of going to Sunday school but it was difficult. My mum and dad insisted I went even if I feigned a headache or complained of a sore throat. If I wasn't well, Doreen could always bring me home. Sometimes when she went earlier than me, I made the weekly trudge up to The Five Ways on my own and one Sunday I contrived a plan to avoid going. I decided to fall over, hurt myself (but not too seriously) and run home in tears. If it worked, I would be let off and wouldn't have to go back. Unfortunately, my parents had taught me that lying was wrong and The Five Ways had taught me that God could see everything I did, so I couldn't pretend that I had fallen, I had to fall. I ran along the 'airies' as far as Doll Herring's house and threw myself forward, hitting the ground with enough impact to produce a few grazes. I limped home in tears. The plan worked but I couldn't try it again.

When I was ten, I left The Five Ways and went to church instead. It wasn't through choice, though; if I'd have had my way, I would have spent Sunday mornings reading comics. St Michael's and All Angels was a high-Anglican church: incense was burned, 'Hail Marys' were said and there was even a confession box. The building was of an unusual Victorian design; a kind of modern Gothic. A pointed clocktower, tiled in grey slate, rose above its eastern end and at night when its clockfaces were lit, it reminded me of a huge witch with yellow eyes.

Going to St Michael's had some advantages, the main one being that, as it was bigger than The Five Ways and there were more people in the congregation, it was easier to sit quietly and hide. But the disadvantages were significant, particularly the tedious over-long sermons. It was a passive experience too; there were no flannel graphs or recitations, no interaction with the priest or getting your name mentioned from the front, and the mass was predictable and dull, but I enjoyed the hymn singing and the thumping church organ and I enjoyed the feast days and festivals when the priests wore different vestments. It was good to get a palm on Palm Sunday or a posy of flowers on 'Mothers' Day' too, but all that aside, going to church, like attending The Five Ways, was a chore to be endured.

OUR HOUSE

I think that I must have a good memory because the people who shared the events of my life have told me so. I have a strong visual memory; I see the past in pictures. In my mind's eye now, I can see a river to my left and, over it, a railway bridge. A black steam train crosses the bridge from right to left. I point to the train, toddle towards it and towards the river. Adults rush in and my dad picks me up. Much is made of what has just happened. What I am recalling is my earliest memory; I was taking my first steps by the river Lee at Rye House in 1946. I was eleven months old. The pictured memories of my early life come in tones of light and dark. The times I spent on the debris are always light, but the houses I knew were dark: the winter streets, my first school, the doctor's surgery, the Sunday school, all of them were dark. My home was cold and the winters of my early years were fierce, yet I never think of it as dark or cold.

My dad did all he could to keep us warm but with not much money, there were limits to what he could afford. Coal was expensive and we used it sparingly but, because he worked at the gas works, he could buy coke at a cheaper price. So, we burnt lots of coke. He brought it home on his bike: a sack for us, or for my nan, or for a neighbour. It was to keep the kitchen warm because that was our living room and the only room that we could afford to heat. On bitterly cold nights he'd bank up the fire with coke until it burned pink with the intensity of its heat and we would sit around the hearth listening to the radio until the coke turned to ash. Then, with mottled legs and glowing faces, we would go upstairs to brave the cold of the bedrooms.

Our beds were made up with sheets and blankets and covered over with a thick eiderdown. In the deep months of winter, ice formed on the inside of the bedroom windows and as we exhaled, our breath would be visible in the coldness of the room. My dad always came to check that I was warm enough and when he came to tuck me in, he would take the great navy overcoat that he had worn on the North Atlantic and drop it heavily onto my bed. Then he would kiss my forehead and say, "Goodnight, God bless and spare yer."

One of his less successful ideas for keeping us warm was to attach a spring to the door so that it would close behind us after we came through. He hated seeing a door left open because the draughts were strong and the air was cold. "Shut that flamin' door!" he'd say if one of us went out without closing it properly. As was often the case with my dad's home improvements, the door spring wasn't such a great success in practice. The problem was that the spring he attached was the most powerful one he could find; it was an industrial spring and quite unsuitable for a family home. It took some strength to pull the door open and a good degree of nimbleness to pass through before it swung swiftly to a close. The result was a number of minor injuries including grazed heels, bumped heads and the occasional bruise.

Another of his ideas was to paint the kitchen, stairs and passage all one colour. Unfortunately, the colour he chose was Battleship Grey. It was an authentic shade of Battleship Grey because it actually came from a battleship or, at least, from a

Royal Navy store somewhere. He had managed to get hold of it for next-to-nothing so I can only conclude that it 'fell off the back of a battleship.' "Looks clean, doesn't it?" he said when the job was done. No one wanted to disagree; he'd worked so hard but in fact it looked dreadful; truly a colour for its times. In the misery and gloom of post-war Britain, we were surrounded by grey.

The grey walls went in time and the paint was papered over. Whenever papering was finished, we would assemble with my dad to appraise the result. "Looks clean, doesn't it?" he would ask, just as he did with his battleship grey. Wallpaper was always brighter than battleship grey so we could agree with him every time. "Makes the room look bigger too, doesn't it?" he would add. He wallpapered the kitchen several times and always said that. Were his assertion to have been true, the illusion created by the accumulation of years of papering would have given our little house the look of a suburban villa.

Without doubt, my dad's most outstanding addition to our home was the garden. It was his garden. He created it, tended it and made it beautiful. He loved plants and knew how to grow them. He raised flowers from seed, pricked them out, potted them and planted them. He knew so many varieties and brought them to flower in sequence over a long season. It was only a small plot, but it was filled with colour from May to October. There were flowerbeds along each side and at either end, and a small patch of grass in the middle. The Chrysanthemums that flowered in the autumn had blooms the size of small dinner plates. My dad grew things for us to eat too: runner beans, Cos lettuce, peas and tomatoes. He taught me so much about flowers and plants but never in a formal way; he'd just talk about them and show me what to do.

So proud was he of his garden that he decided to enhance it with fantail pigeons. His plan was to let them flutter among the flowers and bring a sophisticated, almost Italianate look to his small estate. My mum, Doreen and I thought it was not a good idea but he went ahead anyway and stocked what had once been the chicken shed with a number of the white fantails. His vision was doomed from the start. When the birds were in the shed their scratching and cooing was incessant. When the shed door was opened, sometimes they wouldn't come out. A cat caught one once and the result was a mass of white feathers and one bird less. By the second week, the fantails had gained in confidence and started to spread their wings. One afternoon they flew out of the shed en masse and disappeared over the roof. We ran to the front door, saw them circling and feared they might fly away altogether. Eventually they settled on the upstairs window sills of the houses opposite. This became their routine whenever they were released. Their cooing and pooing began to annoy the neighbours and they complained. Jack Chambers in 209 was annoyed too, because they would settle above his pigeon sheds and his birds took a fancy to them. Instead of flying into their shed after a race, they would flirt with their pretty cousins instead. The end came when one of the fantails got stuck down Mrs Mead's chimney. She could hear it fluttering just above the hearth. My dad managed to retrieve it but the fantails had to go.

For the first nine years of my life, food was rationed. We never went hungry but things were scarce. My mum did so well during that time. With so little meat, she improvised and created tasty meals to make it go further. She used tinned corned beef with onions to make delicious pies. She mixed beef mince with bread, fresh sage, eggs and onions to make rissoles that tasted good. Nothing was wasted; leftover meat from a Sunday roast would become a pie for Monday night's tea. Dripping from roast meat was poured into a basin to harden and later we would spread it on thick slices of bread for supper.

As well as the food he grew, my dad also raised chickens. We got plenty of fresh eggs and he killed a bird for us to eat from time-to-time. He joined a pig club and we got pork in quantities that we never could have had from the butcher. Pig clubs were common when food was scarce. Working people got together to buy pigs and would take it in turns to tend them. When they were grown, they would be slaughtered and butchered and the meat shared out. The pigs were fed on leftovers from school meals and factory canteens. Our pigs were kept in an old kennels in Fairfield Road, Bow. My dad would take me to feed them and clean out the pens. Sometimes Johnny Purton came too. I loved going there and I loved the pigs, though the big sows could be intimidating. The meat we got from them was the best pork I ever ate; particularly the fat which was rich and succulent. When rationing ended, food became more plentiful and the nation, myself included, became chubbier.

* * *

Doreen had lovely hands; long, elegant hands. She could span an octave on the piano with each one. Doreen's hands were always cold. "Good for making pastry," she used to say. "Cold 'ands warm 'art," Aunt Rose would often add. When she was very young, Nanny Powell taught her how to sew. She taught her knitting too. Even as a little girl there was a neatness to her stitching and her talent for needlework set her apart from other girls. As she gained in confidence she learned how to embroider and I liked to watch her as she patiently secured the colourful embroidery silks onto linen until, gradually, patterns and flowers emerged.

She passed her needlework exams comfortably. In the sixth form she made a housecoat in powder blue. When her school was inspected, it got a special mention in the inspection report: *One girl in the sixth form has made a housecoat of which she is rightly proud,* it said. Her work was, and still is, painstakingly precise. Cloth is cut cleanly and there are no fraying threads. Stitches repeat along a line; each almost identical to the one that went before. Hems are pinned and carefully tacked until she is satisfied that they are good enough for sewing. Linings are made to fit perfectly.

When she was fifteen, my dad bought her a sewing machine. It was a shiny black Singer, tough, durable and attractively decorated with elaborate gold patterns. It sat in a well-crafted case of light walnut and she still uses it today. She took to it right away and soon it was earning her money. Eileen Mitchell, a neighbour, sewed handbag linings for a bag factory in Walthamstow and gave Doreen some to make. The unmade linings came a gross at a time. She got only a few pennies for each one, but the money soon mounted up, so the incentive was there to always do more.

I hated the handbag making. We had such a small living room and Doreen took it over; the noise was unrelenting and there was no chance of watching television. The machine was set up on the table with un-made liners of beige nylon stacked beside it. When the pedal was pushed, it started up noisily like a revving car. As each lining was finished, the thread was pulled and cut and the liner dropped onto a pile on the floor. Cast-off threads got everywhere. "How many more?" I would ask. "Only another six," Doreen would say, but six would take ages.

Doreen could turn her hand to anything. She was an excellent cook and her pies and cakes were like illustrations from a cookery book. I have never seen a better pastry cook or needlewoman. She says her achievements are down to the hours she spent with Nanny Powell who, according to Doreen, was a patient and gifted teacher. Unfortunately for me, her money-making schemes also included hair perming. 'Doing perms' was even worse than making linings because of the disgusting smell that went with it. Each perm took about two hours. They began with a hair wash at the scullery sink and rinsing with hot water. After it was washed, the hair was patted dry, combed into strands, wetted with perming lotion and bound tightly around curlers. Then the perm was left to set. The perming lotion had an awful smell like powerful ammonia and it lingered for hours.

* * *

Doreen's use of the kitchen as a hairdresser's and dressmaker's shop was noisy, smelly and untidy, but as it was our living room, we had to endure it. The front room was bigger but we never considered living in that. It was only used at Christmas and sometimes when people came. No one in the street used their front rooms for living in, they were just kept for best. We used ours for several days over Christmas and going in there made Christmas special. A fire was lit and fruit laid out in bowls with nuts and boxes of dates. It always smelt so good; the rich aromas of fruit and fire smoke merged together to make a special smell that always meant Christmas. When the holiday was over, the grate was cleaned, the room was tidied and the door kept locked.

I wasn't allowed into the front room very often but I liked being in there. It was a calm, quiet place with big comfortable chairs and a small round table of 'contemporary' design. There was one window that looked onto the street and my mum spent lots of her time cleaning it or changing the curtains. On a stand in front of the window was a large plaster ornament in pale metallic pink. It was the figure of a lady leading two greyhounds and the desirable form of her body was perfectly explained by the drapes of her clothes. She wore a wide-brimmed hat and had the look of a lady in a Gainsborough portrait.

In the corner by the window stood a glass cabinet containing some of my parents' wedding presents: two lovely Art Deco plates in cream earthenware edged in pale blue and two colourful water jugs. The cabinet also contained my mum's wedding headdress and the decoration from the top of the wedding cake. There was a piano in the front room too; a fine modern upright in black wood. My mum and dad bought it for Doreen and she learned how to play. She practised diligently and could soon sight-read from a manuscript. One of her earliest pieces was *Lavender's Blue*. She would play it with gusto and I would sit beside her singing out the words.

* * *

The front room stayed much the same until it was time for Doreen to have a room of her own. Until then, she and I had shared the front bedroom upstairs. With only two bedrooms when we needed three, the front room was the only option, so she moved in and I was given the back bedroom upstairs. It was small and sparsely furnished with a window that faced the debris. My dad decorated it for me in monochrome wallpaper that had a repeating pattern of a tiger at rest in a jungle. "It's contemprie," he said. Contemporary was a word of its time; a contemporary look was a good thing to have in those days. It expressed modernity and taste, though neither applied to us.

One summer's evening I was in bed suffering from measles, when my mum rushed in, lifted the bedclothes and threw in several boxes of tea. "Don't say nothing," she said and hurried downstairs. I lay there wondering why she did it and who it was that I should say nothing to. She came back later and took the boxes away. Panic over. The tea was stolen, 'knocked off.' There were often stolen things to be had when I was a boy. Most of them came from neighbours in the street or the men at the gasworks. That evening, firemen had come knocking on doors to raise money for charity. My mum saw a blue uniform, assumed it was the police and panicked.

I liked my room but it was cold and small. The window was loose-fitting, the panes of glass were cracked and there was no heating until my dad put in a paraffin stove on winter nights. When the stove worked it was fine and I would lie awake watching its patterned-glow on the ceiling. But most of the time it smoked so badly that my school uniform reeked of fumes and the next day I would be embarrassed if any of my schoolmates came too near.

I had my bedroom until I came home from college and for a while after that. It was never ideal, just a place to sleep, but it was my own and it gave me privacy. It had a bed, a dressing table, a cupboard a 'tallboy' and nothing else. I found it hard to do my homework there because there was no surface to work on. I wrote essays with my books on my knees and drew maths diagrams with graph paper resting on the dressing table; and because it was above the kitchen, there was always noise from the television downstairs. Sometimes when the homework was particularly hard, I felt such a sense of helplessness.

I read dozens of books in my bedroom: all of the Biggles and Jennings stories, most of Just William and classics like Treasure Island and Tom Sawyer. When I was older, I read French novels by Zola, Balzac and Gide and books by Steinbeck and Orwell that spoke of idealism and social conscience. I took a copy of Great Expectations to bed with me one evening and read until I heard the dawn chorus; I had been reading all night. When I was older, I got a radio and it was in that little room that I heard Sergeant Pepper's Lonely Hearts Club Band for the first time.

* * *

As Doreen got older, she started making her own clothes from dressmaking patterns. The patterns came in packets with pictures of sophisticated women on them, all adopting poses that brought a flamboyant 'swish' to their jackets and skirts. Inside were tissue paper sheets marked out for cutting sections of a garment. Doreen would lay them over the dress material, pin them in place and cut around them carefully. My mum was so proud of her dressmaking and brought armfuls of dresses down to show visitors when they came. I would feel embarrassed as the pile grew bigger but nothing was going to stop her from showing them what her clever daughter could do.

Doreen was canny with money and always earned enough for the extras she needed. She worked for quite a while as a Saturday girl at Woolworths in Chrisp Street and, after that, she got a job in Breslaws, a ladies' clothing shop in St Leonard's Road. The Breslaws were a Jewish family. Poplar was a dockland borough with Irish connections so, unlike Bethnal Green or Whitechapel, it didn't have much of a Jewish community. The only Jewish people I knew were shopkeepers and Doreen's friend Mildred Shkolnik, so Jewish people were something of a mystery to me.

The Breslaws were fond of Doreen and she got on well with their two daughters. One Saturday when they saw a lady about to enter the shop, the girls hurried out the back to hide. "It's Mrs Voshvell," said Josie. "You serve her Doreen… please." Doreen was thrust forward and found herself face-to-face across the counter from the dreaded Mrs V. "Good morning, Mrs Voshvell, how can I help you?" she asked. "I vant knickers, my size no-bigger-no-smaller." Doreen went to the drawers behind the counter and took out several pairs. "These are the pure linen ones, Mrs Voshvell, and these are cotton." As she spoke, suppressed giggles were coming from the back of the shop. After some indecision, Mrs Voshvell made her choice and bought two pairs of cotton bloomers. "Thank you,

Mrs Voshvell, goodbye," said Doreen. When she'd left, the Breslaw girls came back into the shop almost collapsing with laughter. "What's wrong?" Doreen asked. "Mrs Voshvell's not her name, we don't know her name," said Josie. "We call her Mrs Voshvell because when she buys something she always says 'Does it vosh vell?'"

* * *

I hated it when my parents argued. Their rows would threaten like a storm, erupt and then subside. Doreen was better at coping with them than I was. She carried on through them unfazed, but I would put my fingers in my ears and pray for them to end. Most of their disputes were about my dad's family. My mum resisted their influence and she had good reason to. When we were invited to Connolly events she would refuse to go if certain members of the family were there, and this would lead to a row. On the whole, I sided with my dad because I often thought that my mum was being unreasonable. When Aunt Nan's husband Joe Bradford died, he went to the funeral on his own because my mum did not want to be in the company of Nan and some of the other Connollys. She didn't want my dad to go either and I thought that was unfair.

Rows were a regular but not frequent part of our lives in St Leonard's Road and family life was good. Sometimes my parents would play together like children; he would grab her and tickle her or she would pull faces at him in mock defiance. From time-to-time Doreen and I would set about my dad as he sat in his chair too. "Let's play our old tricks on him," one of us would say and we would fall on him and tickle him from all sides. We laughed a lot; often at the antics of my mum. She loved to laugh and I am so fortunate that she gave the gift of laughter to me. She had the ability to make others laugh too and for someone often perceived as shy, she could be flamboyant and carefree at times.

My dad had none of her expressive ways and couldn't make others laugh, but he enjoyed her antics and egged her on when she got going. When they came home from the pub on Saturday nights with Aunt Rose and the others, my mum would sing a funny song or do a dance to make them all laugh. One of her songs was *The Spaniard Who Blighted My Life*, a fiery number from 1911, written by the music hall singer, Billy Merson. She would perform it with gusto and stamp her foot down hard every time she sang *'he shall die.'*

... When I catch Alfonso Spigoni the Toreador, tralala
With one mighty swipe I will dislocate his bally jaw, tralala
When I catch that bull fighter the blighter I'll kill
He shall die, he shall die, he shall die tie tie tie tie tie tie tie
He shall die, he shall die
For I'll raise a bunion on his Spanish onion when I catch him bending tonight!

Sometimes she would fetch two carving knives from the kitchen drawer, cross them on the floor and do her version of a Scottish sword dance. She danced with tremendous energy and her steps and gestures looked quite authentic to me. She still performed her dances well into her sixties.

* * *

In September 1956 Doreen began a two-year teacher training course at St Gabriel's college in Camberwell. It must have been an expensive time for my parents because she needed things for college when I needed things for my new school. Before she started at St Gabriel's, I went with my dad and her to Green Street in Upton Park to buy a holdall for her things. He chose a large one in navy blue canvas with tan leather straps. When we got it home, Doreen found that the zip was faulty and wouldn't close properly. The next Saturday my dad went back to change it and took me with him. He showed the stallholder the problem and she took the bag from him. She held it up, tried the zip but couldn't get it to work. She scanned the bag from end to end, looked inside and held it close to her face. "There's a stain on it," she said, pointing to a small blotch the size of a blob of rain. "I can't take it back with that on it." "Take it back and give me another one." "I ain't taking it back, it's stained." "That's not a stain." "Yes it is!" "We didn't stain it, give me another one." "No, it's stained." "Give me my money back then." "No!" A crowd had gathered by now and I felt dreadful. "I'm not going 'til you give me another one," said my dad. "Anyone else want serving?" asked the stallholder looking around dismissively. But the crowd was more interested in how the drama would play out and no one came forward to buy. My dad got his way and Doreen went off to Camberwell two weeks later with a new holdall. Now, for the first time in my life, I was living in a household of three.

ROSE, HENRY AND CHARLIE

AUNT ROSE

Aunt Rose was short, stout, sometimes generous, sometimes mean, often loving, occasionally envious, gullible, combative, vain, unconsciously funny and wonderful. She was three years older than my mum but clipped a couple off so that Charlie, her husband, would think she was younger than she was. Rose is there in my earliest memories; standing before the mirror in Nanny Powell's scullery, applying Amami Wave Set and Conditioner to her hair, or powdering her face before going out for the evening. She met Uncle Charlie in *The Germans*, a pub in St Leonard's Road where he worked as a barman. She was well into her thirties by then and still hadn't found someone to settle down with. In those days women married young. Rose and Charlie got married in 1948 and moved in with Charlie's dad at 84 St Leonard's Road. Mr Oliver was a nice old man, an ex-soldier who had married a French lady, so Charlie had a French mum. When Nanny Powell died, Rose and Charlie moved into her house to share it with Uncle Henry. They never had a home to themselves in all their married life until Henry died in 1991 and then they had just a few months together before Rose died too.

One of Aunt Rose's most endearing characteristics was that she often mispronounced her words. Many of her best examples have passed into legend and are often repeated at gatherings of family and friends. In 1968 she and other council tenants went on a rent strike and refused to pay a steep increase imposed by the Greater London Council. The strike dragged on for months. Eventually the strikers were given support from a young lawyer and Rose was jubilant. "I think we're genna win Joey," she said "We've got a young banister behind us now." She told Doreen once that one of Charlie's nephews was so clever that she would get along well with him: "You'd like him, Dor. He's very educated, you can reverse with him on anythink."

Once Doreen pulled up outside Rose's flats just as she was leaving and they had the following exchange:
"Hello Aunt Rose, do you want a lift?"
"That'd be good Dor."
"Where do you want to go?"
"Take me to MI5."
"MI5, Aunt Rose?!"
"Yes, I'm in a bit of a rush."
"You sure you want to go *there*?"
"Yes! a'course I'm sure.
"Why are you going there?"
"I wanna have a good look round."
"What, the spy place?"
"What bleed'un spy place? I wanna go to MI5!"
"Do you mean M-F-I Aunt Rose?"
"Yes."

MFI was a furniture store.

Sometimes Aunt Rose's mispronunciations could be interpreted in more controversial ways. In the mid-1960s, when she was trying to get rehoused, she wrote to Ian Mikardo, the local MP, to ask for his support. Mikardo was never much of a constituency man; he had bigger fish to fry as a leader of the Labour left. He sent her a stock reply that appeared to offer hope and it seemed to Rose that at last someone had taken up her cause. Unfortunately, she never got Mikardo's name right and always called him 'Mikarios.' Archbishop Mikarios was the President of Cyprus at the time. Rose would tell people "I wrote to ole Mikarios and 'es genna take it up for me." This caused surprise and not a little envy, particularly amongst the women Rose worked with who thought she was gaining unfair advantage from an international statesman and a foreigner at that. Mikardo's promise of support never came to anything and a disillusioned Rose then told everyone: "Old Mikarios is no bleed'un good and he ain't getting my vote any more either." It is possible that Rose's withdrawal of her support for the president of Cyprus raised eyebrows again at work, because now it seemed that she had voting rights in two countries. We laughed at what Aunt Rose said but we never laughed at her. Her wonderful mix-ups just made us fonder of her. Others were not so kind and I think that some of the women she worked with sometimes made fun of her.

Rose and my mum were so unalike. Mum was a worrier and Rose was a warrior. They were both short, but Rose was chubby and Nell was thin. Rose had no children and went out to work, while mum had a family and worked full-time as a housewife. Rose showed me affection, she was fond of me, but my mum gave me the love of a mother. Mum avoided confrontation but Rose met it head-on. When she was at school, my mum was bullied by a girl called Beatie Ballard.

When Rose heard about it, she caught Beatie and gave her a thump. There is an irony in that because one of Rose's proudest boasts was that on Empire Day, she was always chosen to be an angel of peace.

In the late 1950s, the American company Proctor and Gamble promoted their Fairy Snow washing powder by sending a man from door to door dressed as a snow man. If the householder could produce a packet of their detergent, he would give them a five pound note. When my mum answered the door to the Fairy Snow Man, she was terrified by the enormous white presence on her doorstep and ran back inside. "What's wrong?" asked Rose. "There's a man at the door all in white," said Nell. "He's frightened the life out of me." "Let me see 'im," said Rose and she hurried to the door where the snowman was still waiting for my mum to return. "Clear off you dirty old sod, coming round decent people's houses all dressed up," said Rose. "Go on! Clear off!" The Fairy Snow Man hurried away. Rose and Nell didn't know about the promotional stunt and thought they had been visited by a madman.

The two sisters were good together though the relationship cooled at times. They only really fell out once and for about three weeks they never spoke. I was like an emissary passing between two camps. Eventually I used to make fun of the situation to expose the ridiculous position I was in. They had both been at fault and not speaking made no sense at all. The thaw came and they stayed close for the rest of their lives.

Rose was always fond of me. Just as Uncle Henry favoured Doreen, so she favoured me. I was a rascal to her at times when I was a boy and played the sort of tricks on her that boys like to play. I bound my head in white crepe paper once and smudged the front with tomato ketchup to make it look like blood. Then I went into Rose and adopted an unassuming manner as if nothing had happened. "Oh my gawd, what you done?" cried Rose. "Nuthink, Aunt Rose," I said. "That ain't nuthink, look at yer 'ed!" "Oh that, I just bumped it."

Years later when Rose was addicted to the television soap opera *Peyton Place*, I was a student at Bath Academy of Art. The show was broadcast in the West Country several months before it went out in London, so I was able to give her 'plot spoilers' for her to tell the women at work. It worked to her advantage for a while until I started making up plot lines that became increasingly outrageous. "Grandpa Harrington murders Rodney," or "Norman Harrington is really a woman," and so it went on. Because of my pranks, Rose called me 'Candy Camra' after the *Candid Camera* TV programme that filmed pranks from a hidden camera. 'Candy Camra' is, of course, an 'Aunt Roseism' in itself.

I wrote the following in Paris when I was in my mid-twenties. I had just ended my engagement to my fiancée Christine. She and I had stayed in Paris several times together and now, after four years, I was on my own. The evening that I wrote this, I was feeling abandoned by my French friends; they had gone out together and I was left in their flat feeling miserable. In my sadness I reached into my roots for reassurance and turned to Aunt Rose. This is my letter to her. An appreciation. I am telling her the things that, through her uncomplicated East End life, she had already told me.

'Johnny turned to his Aunty Fackeral. "Aunty Fackeral," he said, "beware of pretty houses, use them wisely. Beware of bankers and

bad art. Take cover when you find an option and only come out when it is safely considered. Make sure that your comforts are taken for granted or they will be granted and not taken. Guard your instinct, for instinct is your precious inheritance and can so easily be lost. Keep your generosity for that is the manifestation of your love. Mind your language and keep it as you found it from your birth, it is your culture and they will take it from you if they can."

"Aunty Fackeral beware of good taste and property. Use things when you want them and leave them dirty if you are too tired to make them clean; use them or they will make use of you. Do not worry about fashion, it will pass and it has not the means to defeat you; but watch it closely in the hands of others."

"Aunty Fackeral, these things conspire to take away your love. Guard your love above all else for nothing can match its value; there are no substitutes. Not everyone has such love and there are people who destroy the things they cannot have."

"Aunty Fackeral, you are not offended by the things that I have said? Was I wrong to say them? But it was you..."'

I came in from work one evening in July 1991. Pam came close and held me. "Aunt Rose has died," she said. I wept.

UNCLE HENRY

Uncle Henry was stuck in his ways and could be stubborn but he had a good sense of humour, was unflinchingly loyal and always supported us. He and my mum were close. They shared a sense of fun and sometimes I caught a glimpse of what they were like as children. "Do you remember when we used to play *Ugly and Pretty*?" Henry would ask, and the two of them would begin the game of funny faces they played when they were young. When "Ugly" was called, tongues poked out, mouths were turned down, ears were pulled forward and chins jutted into gurning contortions. "Pretty" involved a rapid transformation. Eyes opened wide, eyelashes fluttered, heads moved graciously from side to side and top lips were tucked tightly into bottom ones.

Henry knew how to make my mum laugh. She would tell him some outrageous tale, often with tragic elements, and he would react with feigned incredulity. She would keep going and he would keep giving until my mum was helpless with laughter. I loved those encounters and Henry's responses were all the better for being expressed in his strong cockney accent. "Gawd stone me 'ooray!" was one of his stock responses to Nell's ever-increasing tales of woe.

Henry was the youngest of the siblings and the most talented. He was a capable craftsman and well-regarded at work for his skills as a welder. He was good at mending shoes and did repairs for all the family. He loved music and had a good ear for picking out a tune on the piano. His style was rambling and free. He played with energy, attacking the keys and thumping his feet on the pedals as he hit out a tune. He was confident too and would skate over his mistakes and continue on as if it didn't matter. Unsurprisingly, he was in demand as a party pianist. He was popular too. People liked 'Enno' and not just because he could play. Like all of the adults in my life, he loved the songs of his youth. Al Jolson was his idol and *Mammy* was Jolson's song:

I'd walk a million miles
For one of your smiles,
My... Maaaammy!

Waiting for the Robert E Lee was Henry's favourite and, although Jolson's music is not to my taste and I find the blackening of his face gratingly bad, I must admit that his 1947 recording of *Robert E Lee* is tight, expressive and highly original.

Henry carried on playing his songs and added to his repertoire. He bought sheet music but only for the lyrics; dots and lines on a page meant nothing to him. He played by ear and practised every Sunday morning for at least two hours and he loved to sing. In 1964 his music and his stubbornness came together in a strange impasse when he won a prize in an Irish lottery. The first prize was a small car but Henry came second and had a choice of alternatives: a new radiogram or half a Friesian cow (the words 'only in Ireland' come to mind.) Wisely, he chose the radiogram and six weeks later, a large cardboard box with the 'gram inside arrived.

Aunt Rose asked the delivery men to put the radiogram in the kitchen for when Henry came home and I made sure I was there when he did. But there wasn't much of a response from him when he saw it. He just gave the box a look, muttered a few approving remarks and went off to wash his hands in the scullery. "Ain't yer genna open it, 'En?" asked Aunt Rose when he came back. "I'll do it later on," he said and went upstairs to his room. There followed several months of prevarication. "Yer can't keep it in 'ere, 'enry, there's no room," said Rose. The box was still in the kitchen and taking up too much space. "Open it up so we can see what it's like," reasoned Charlie, but

Henry stuck stubbornly to his wish to "do it later." Eventually the cardboard package was moved into the front room where it sat unopened for three or four months. When Henry finally opened it, the radiogram turned out to be a very nice piece indeed with a sleek varnished cabinet, modern record deck, hidden storage space and a two-band radio. Things changed after that. Henry started buying records. I was now in my teens and we were on course for a generational clash.

Max Bygraves was a comedian who became a versatile all-round entertainer. He was a huge star in the 1960s and regularly topped the bill at the London Palladium. We all liked Max; he was a cockney like us, one of the few people in public life that spoke like we did. He was from Bermondsey; not the East End exactly, but much the same. He was a warm, down-to-earth family man except that, after he died, we learned that he frequently cheated on his wife, disowned the women he had made pregnant and never supported their babies. As a boy I had liked Max's jolly songs about toothbrushes falling in love or tulips from Amsterdam, but by the time the Beatles had arrived I was sick of them. My increasing passion for the Beatles, Bob Dylan and the Rolling Stones was matched by Henry's increasing passion for Max Bygraves.

Henry could afford to buy as many of Max's records as he liked and most of them were 'long players' – *Singalongamax* (several volumes) *Singalongaparty Song, SingalongaMaxmas, Singalongamovies*, the list went on and on. With his new radiogram, Henry could stack up to twelve albums to play automatically and he often did. Family gatherings became an awful endurance for me, particularly at Christmas when my friends weren't around and I had nowhere to go. Max would play on automatic for the entire evening. I can imagine what Henry would have felt if I had made him listen to hours and hours of *Blonde on Blonde* or *Revolver* or *Out of Our Heads.*

None of my family could accept the outrageousness of the Rolling Stones. Whenever she saw the Stones on television Aunt Rose would say "Good gawd a'mighty, look at the beauties!" But Henry, now in middle age, took the music of my generation personally, seeing it almost as a threat to what he believed to be good and right. Charlie and my mum and dad were more open-minded. I heard my mum singing *All My Loving* once when she was ironing; "I like some of the Beedles," she said. Charlie occasionally bought records that had made it into the charts. His choices were often updated versions of old songs like *What Do You Want to Make Those Eyes at Me For?* by Emile Ford and the Checkmates, but they were records that I liked too and that made a nice point of convergence for us both.

Eventually I reached a nice point of convergence with Henry too, when I discovered the recordings of George Formby. I was at art school by then and one of the third-year students had taken to playing George at high volume from his bedroom window. The promotion of his idol worked, and the 'gormless lad' from Blackpool became something of a cult figure at Bath Academy. One Saturday, Henry and I sat listening to George together, laughing at the cleverness of his songs and the upbeat joy of his performance. It is to George's credit that he offended prudes and pleased millions in his time and still offends prudes today though perhaps of a different sort.

* * *

It must have been difficult for Rose and Charlie to share their home with Henry but it was Henry's home first. He had the tenancy and despite his single mindedness and funny ways they got along well enough most of the time. When they moved from St Leonard's Road to a maisonette in Bow, Henry had a better room for himself; a personal, special place. It was a home within a home; not much, but enough. He spent hours there making things for Doreen's school: toys, stools and other things, and got delight from seeing the children use them. He made a wooden sledge for Alice and Joe when they were small and we had hours of fun with it. I have passed it on to my grandchildren and it is still perfect.

Henry loved London and when he retired, he would buy a Red Rover travel ticket and spend a day discovering parts of the capital that he hadn't seen before. Our paths crossed one day when I was at work. I got off the train at Holborn and there he was on the platform. It was so nice to see him. "Where you going, 'en?" I asked. "I thought 'I'd go 'an 'av a look at Covent Garden," he said. We swapped platforms and went our different ways. "'Enrie knows 'is London," Rose would say. In middle age he took up with Millie, a lady friend, and they spent days and days going around London together. "I think I'll get 'em a little bus conductor's uniform each," said Uncle Charlie.

Henry's other pleasure was strolling. On Saturday nights he would set off scrubbed and tidy for a walk around Poplar, dropping in at pubs along the way. When he came home, he would tell us where he'd been and his reports were often detailed and tedious. "I went up Violet Road, 'ad one in *The Bun House*, then up Devons Road over to North Street and went in *The Sabbarton*. Young Micky Clark was in there with his mates, so I had a couple with them and…" "I went up St Leonard's Road and run into Billy Jennings in *The Hearts of Oak*. Cor, 'e ain't arf altered." His entire route was covered in his reports and they included individuals and numbers; "There was a tidy few in The Germans," or "It was very quiet in The Prince." I'd try to cut him short by asking where he ended up, but, having answered, he would always return to the precise spot from where he had left off. "Anyway, it was all quiet in The Prince but I stayed 'til the last knockins."

When I was a teenager, Henry would give me ties. He had far too many of them and was always buying more. He'd come in with a selection and from about a dozen, I might take two or three. Clothes were more formal then; some men wore ties to football. "'Enrie's got some lovely books for you upstairs, all about the war," Aunt Rose would tell me from time to time. "E's genna give 'em to yer, he said." Henry never denied he had the books and once or twice he mentioned them to me. "Lovely books," Rose would often say, "You oughta see 'em Joey, they're worth a lot of money." I never did get them from him and he never showed me them, but when I was in my twenties, he gave me one of his rings. It is a fine buckle design in gold. I take it out and look at it sometimes but I have never worn it because Henry had big fingers and the ring just falls off mine.

Uncle Henry died in early 1991 from a heart attack. There were no ambulances because of a strike by drivers and there was a long wait before help arrived. When it came, he was taken to hospital in a military ambulance with soldiers carrying him on a stretcher. To my mind there is something eternally sad about that. His funeral was well-attended and as he was taken away for burial, *Maybe It's Because I'm a Londoner* was played.

When Doreen and I went to clear his room, I was struck by how little of value he possessed and yet how much his room contained. Clothes mainly, packets of shirts, lots of jackets and trousers, cufflinks and rings, expanding armbands to keep shirt sleeves in place and shoes aligned and polished. We found a few unopened wage packets and a savings account book and shared the money between Aunt Rose and my mum. Most touchingly, we also found the few tools he had used to made such perfectly-crafted things. On the tallboy by the window were photographs of Doreen and me. Mine was still in the metal frame he put it in when he was given it in 1953.

After Doreen left, I stayed on to finish clearing the room. Standing on Rose's kitchen steps I reached far into the cupboard shelf. There at the back was the set of books, some still in the brown paper they came in when Henry had first got them: *The War Illustrated. Hammerton, Amalgamated Press.* It was a bound collection of magazines that were published throughout the War. These and the ring are my inheritance from Henry, but he gave me so much more.

UNCLE CHARLIE

Uncle Charlie had a goodlooking face and he was broad but, at five feet five inches in height, he wasn't very tall. I remember him with fondness; caught with a smile on his face, in mid-sentence and about to make me laugh. He was funny and witty too. The art of Charlie's humour was to take the ordinary, alter it just enough to make it absurd and re-present it as a funnier version of itself. He did it with people by processing their characteristics and acting them out in a slightly altered form. Vic, the estranged husband of a family friend, would creep into the lounge when his wife had company and surreptitiously take an apple from the bowl in the hope that no one would see him. It was a simple enough thing to do but when Charlie did his parody, he added a slight shuffle to the step and made a few 'tut tut' sounds as the apple went to mouth; nothing much in that, except that it was very funny when Charlie did it. Charlie's parodies were never cruel because he had a basic sympathy for people, but we were always left laughing *at* his victims and not *with* them. My mum had a sense of fun too and he knew know to make her laugh. Sometimes she would be doubled-up with laughter as he delivered his lines with a smile and an upward glance of his eyes.

There was something vulnerable about Charlie too. I think he may have used his wit and humour to conceal a more uncertain side. His mother died when he was young and perhaps her death took away his confidence. She was French and that would have set him apart from other children at school. Maybe he was picked on for being the son of a foreigner; people were suspicious of foreigners when he was a boy. He was semi-literate too; he struggled with reading and could barely write a line. Being short would not have helped either. It isn't wise to speculate, but perhaps all of these factors came together to undermine his confidence.

Of all the adults in my family, Charlie was the least educated but he was clever in ways that the others were not. He could figure things out in a practical way and he was artistic. When he moved to Bow with Rose and Henry, he painted the patio slabs in different colours, each one carefully chosen to contrast the ones around them. The effect was original and interesting, like something by Paul Klee or Piet Mondrian. None of the others could match Charlie for humour either, although Henry could be very funny at times.

Charlie had a placid nature; I never heard him raise his voice. It was Aunt Rose who 'wore the trousers,' but theirs was a true partnership and they thought so much of one another. I don't think Rose ever quite got over the fact that she had managed to find Charlie and I think that Charlie needed someone strong like her to protect him, so the marriage worked well for them both.

Uncle Charlie served in the Army during World War Two. Rose often said that he had been at Dunkirk when the British Expeditionary Force retreated from France in 1940. "It was so terrible he never wants to talk about it," she'd say. All Charlie ever told me about being in the army was that he learned how to drive a lorry when he was a soldier and still had an army driving licence. He had a smattering of French too. His favourite phrase was: "Voolie voo promonay avec mwa madamwarsel?" It was a standard Tommy line. My dad doubted that Charlie had been at Dunkirk, the details were too sparse, but the photograph of him in army uniform on top of the piano was proof that he had been a soldier.

When Charlie died and we cleared the house, I found his military record and it was very revealing. It showed that he had indeed been in France at the time of the Dunkirk retreat and that he had joined the army not long before. The record goes on to show that shortly after that, the army dismissed him. He was honourably dismissed but no reason was given. The few short sentences on his record are sympathetic. The last one says "This man should never have been admitted to the British army." Charlie had a short war and we may speculate that he wasn't mentally strong enough to be a soldier. He probably was at Dunkirk and the events he experienced there may have terrified him. He suffered some form of post-traumatic shock as a result and could not continue as a soldier. But the phrase 'should never have been considered' is tantalising. Did it mean that the flaws in his mental make-up were there even before he joined?

Charlie was different to Uncle Henry. He didn't resent my music, for example, but engaged with it genuinely and without condescension. We shared some tastes in clothes too; if Charlie bought a shirt he thought I'd like, he'd bring it down to show me. It was the same with shoes. Henry was kind to me in so many ways; he was my blood relative and he was a good uncle, but Charlie had a more natural way of engaging with me.

When Aunt Rose died in 1991, Charlie found himself on his own for the first time in his life. His last years were sad, lonely ones. Doreen worked locally and would visit him regularly but I lived further away; my job was in Suffolk and I had a family too, so my visits were not frequent. I often rang him, but when I did, I dreaded hearing the sadness in his voice at the other end of the line. Our conversations taxed me as they always began with the challenge of trying to lift his spirits, but I would persist and I usually managed to leave him on a cheerful note. I often asked him to stay with us and Doreen did too. We invited him to Christmas every year but he became wary of leaving his home unattended. Many of the older tenants in his flats had gone and some bad people had moved in. There were burglaries and the occupants of a flat four floors up had taken to throwing burning objects down into the gardens below.

In his last years, Charlie was befriended by a young woman a few doors along. She lived on her own too and I think that keeping an eye on him gave her some company. Her name was Rosina. She was intelligent and kind and we were indebted to her for the way she supported him in those last years. Charlie didn't have much of a family. His brother and sister had died. He had two nephews who saw him occasionally but they had never been close and they never gave him much support.

In his grief and loneliness, Charlie turned to drink to ease his pain. I don't blame him for that but it took its toll in due course. Doreen saw him just before he died. She was passing between appointments one lunchtime and decided to look in on him. As she pulled up outside his flats, he was getting into a taxi. He looked yellow and dreadful. "They're sending me to the 'ospital," he said. He was examined by doctors in outpatients and admitted that afternoon. When Doreen saw him that evening, he was sitting in a chair beside his bed alone and without pyjama bottoms. She was appalled by the lack of care he had been shown and berated the ward sister for allowing him to be so neglected. I was in Ipswich that day and I rang the hospital from my office. I asked the nurse on his ward to tell him that I was asking after him and would come to see him the next day. I wanted to reassure him that he was not on his own; Doreen and I were there. But I never got the chance to see him because, before I got to the London Hospital, he had died.

Uncle Charlie died penniless. He had nothing. His home was clean and tidy but there was not much food in the fridge. Doreen and I cleared the house. There were clothes he had kept of Aunt Rose's and some suits and shirts of his own. In a bottom drawer I found a large family bible; its inside page was half-filled with the names and dates of members of the Oliver family. The fact of its existence, the formality of its content and the carefully-written entries were so unlike anything I would have associated with Uncle Charlie. On the tallboy in his bedroom was a picture of Aunt Rose and beside it in a vase, a solitary plastic flower; it was a red Rose.

ROSE, HENRY AND CHARLIE

It was always 'Rose, Henry and Charlie' never any other order of their names. Was that because of their ages, or did it just work out that way over time? Whatever the reason, the three of them lived together for thirty-seven years and, given that Rose and Charlie were a couple and Henry was so set in his ways, I think they coped well. Henry had been used to being waited on by his mother; he didn't help around the house and he was stubborn. He'd take his time coming to the table when the dinner was ready or hog the sink when it was being prepared. He had his own way of doing things and was hard to budge when he put his mind to something. That tested Charlie at times. "Yer Uncle 'enry's terrible higerant," he would say. "'E comes in from work, goes straight to the sink, washes 'is hands and don't say allo or nothing." "'Enry's set in his ways," Aunt Rose would add. But despite his sometimes selfish behaviour, he was a good brother to her and my mum and the frictions of everyday life that Rose and Charlie experienced with him were compensated for in other ways. The three of them often socialised together and had friends in common. They had some holidays together too and they wouldn't have done that if they didn't get on well.

Rose and Charlie had no particular friends of their own, they tended to be part of a group, but occasionally my mum's cousin Ivy would visit with her husband Jim, and when she did, they would go out together as a foursome. Ivy was cold and rather unpleasant and I didn't like her very much. I got the impression that she didn't like me either and didn't like children in general. Ivy was 'a cut above.' She dressed well and spoke a more cultivated form of cockney that was hardly cockney at all. She had been a very good swimmer when she was young and had won awards for racing. Jim was always in her shadow and didn't say much. He had a big nose like a bulbous strawberry and I had to look away quickly at times in case he caught me staring at it.

I think Henry felt excluded when Ivy and Jim came. It was the same when Charlie's brother Sid and his wife Charlotte came too. Charlotte was cunning and unpleasant like Ivy. She had a slyness to her eyes that left me feeling uncomfortable and she lacked warmth. Sid had a big nose too like Jim but, unlike him, Sid was cocky and verbose. The presence of Ivy and Charlotte brought the worst out in Rose. She cosied up to them and sang their praises to my mum in a way that implied that she was excluded. Henry was never exclusive like that and had little to do with them.

Rose, Henry and Charlie could be a funny trio, particularly when they'd had a few drinks. Drink brought Rose into song and most of the songs she sang were chosen because they had roses in the lyric: *You're the One Rose; Just a Rose in a Garden of Weeds; Saint Theresa of the Roses,* she knew quite a few. She had a robust singing voice, low in register and with an old-fashioned style of delivery. She wasn't unpleasant in drink, neither were Henry or Charlie, they were just 'happy drunks.'

Late one Saturday night I was in our front room with two or my school friends when there was a tapping on the window. I pulled back the curtain and it was Charlie. He was obviously the worse for wear. "Yer Uncle 'enry's drunk," he said with a grin, his finger pointing to his left. Henry appeared, his face red and equally as sozzled as Charlie. "Yer Uncle Charlie's drunk," he said, his finger pointing the other way. They remained there, two faces side-by-side until a pair of hands parted them and the sozzled face or Aunt Rose thrust itself between the two. "They're both drunk," she said with a grin and then they disappeared. "Who were they?" asked one of my friends. "Oh...er…em…," I replied.

* * *

One hot night when I couldn't sleep, I stayed downstairs listening to records. It was getting on for one o'clock when I finally went up to bed. As I passed the landing window, I saw torchlights flashing on the far side of the debris. Someone was on the railway. I watched for a while and as my eyes adjusted to the darkness, I could see several men moving around, obviously up to no good. My mum and dad were still awake and I went into their room and told them what was going on. My dad got up to see for himself. "Go and tell Henry and Charlie and I'll phone the police," he said.

Then everything happened at once. My dad dressed and rushed off to the phone box and I ran to 217 and knocked on the door. Before anyone came to answer I saw Henry at the front room window. Like me, he was too uncomfortable to sleep and was sitting downstairs to keep cool. "What's up?" he asked through the window. "There's someone over the back," I replied. "Dad's gone to phone the police."

Then the upstairs window opened and Charlie looked out. "What's 'appening?" he asked. I looked up and saw him leaning out of the window. "There's men over the back. Dad's gone for the police," I said. "Stay there and I'll open the door," he replied and was down the stairs in a flash. "I'll go out and 'av a look; you go up and wake up Henry." I told him that Henry was downstairs in the front room but by then Charlie had already gone. Everything was happening at speed. The opening and closing of doors and windows, people running around, a drama taking place out of sight, it was like a scene from Michael Frayn's *Noises Off.* I went back to the front room window but Henry was gone.

Charlie went back to his room to fetch the pickaxe handle he kept under the bed, then came rushing down heading for the backyard. To his shock and horror, the backdoor was wide open; the crooks had obviously been inside. He ran into the yard just as the last of them was climbing the fence. "Got you, you bastard!" he shouted and started flailing at the man's legs with the pickaxe handle. "Wo! Wo! Wo!" yelled the culprit, kicking back to protect himself. "Leave off! Leave off!" Charlie paused the action and put down the handle. The 'escaping intruder' was Henry.

The police arrived in no time. Non-uniformed officers. They came into our house, went upstairs and asked a few questions. We showed them the landing window and they had a look for themselves. The gang were still there doing whatever they were doing and the police went off to deal with them. We watched for a while to see what was going on but it was too dark to see much. Eventually the police came back. "It's nothing to worry about," one of them said. "It's just a gang of workmen on the line." I'm sure that when I told Henry and Charlie that there were intruders "over the back," I said "over the back *on the railway.*" I'm sure I said that. I must have done…surely…

EDUCATION

My grandad, James Powell, must have been a clever boy because, according to my mum, he "passed the scholarship and went to George Green's." George Green was a selective school, a kind of grammar school of its day. "... but his mum and dad couldn't afford to keep him there and they had to take him away." So, Grandad Powell never got the education that could have changed his life because his parents didn't have enough money. When he died in 1927, the 'clever boy' was working as a cartman for a removal firm.

Unlike her dad, my mum struggled with her learning. She was a nervous, shy little girl and illness punctuated her schooling with periods of absence. She was frightened of her teachers and of one in particular: Madam Morgan. Being scared of Madam Morgan, she kept her head down and tried not to be noticed. My mum thought herself a dunce. "I'm no good at reckoning up," she'd say or "I ain't no good at spelling." But her writing was reasonably satisfactory and her reading was good. She read to me a lot when I was a boy and when she did, she read with fluency, emphasis and expression. In later life she was never without a book and got through Mills and Boon and Ruby M. Ayres novels by the dozen.

My dad was more capable than her in every respect. His handwriting was better, his spelling less prone to mistakes and he was good at calculating sums in his head. He read well too. Like my mum, he enjoyed reading and always had a book on the go. Gangster novels by Mickey Spillane and Hank Janson were his favourites, and books about the Second World War like *The Cruel Sea* and *The Guns of Navarone.* I think he too may have been a bright boy like Grandad Powell but, as with Grandad Powell, school never helped him to a better life.

Both of my parents left school at fourteen. They had experienced nine years of didactic teaching reinforced by threats and physical punishment; my mum facing the fearsome Madam Morgan and my dad kept in his place by cane-wielding priests, nuns and teachers. In September 1950 I began my education and, although I didn't know it then, like Grandad Powell, I too was a clever boy. Unlike him, however, I was fortunate because school led me out of the challenges of working-class life and gave me prospects for something better.

My education began at Alton Street Primary two weeks after my fifth birthday. Alton Street was the other side of Sprattsies Steps and a good walk away from where we lived. It was an old, sombre building, built in the previous century by the School Board of London to a design still seen in parts of the capital today. We went in convoy on that first day: a little group of boys and girls, mums and grans from St Leonard's Road and the streets around, over the bridge into Fawe Street, across the Barchester Street ruins, along Brabazon Street and into Alton Street where the school rose ominously above the little cul-de-sac in which it stood. Then, through a metal gate, across the playground, through a door and along to the classroom where our mums were kept outside as we were ushered in. The moment of letting go was as I imagined it would be: the ache in the pit of my stomach, the brink of tears, the words of protest, the reassurance, the distraction, the turning around to find my mother gone and then…it all began.

The classroom at Alton Street was built for children of another time. It was dark, with high ceilings and windows that didn't begin until half way up the wall. In its day it must have been functional; large enough to take classes of sixty or more. Putting windows high up was a way of preventing children from looking out onto the world outside, although the world outside at Alton Street amounted to no more than a playground enclosed by walls. Teachers were strict in Victorian times and children were controlled. They were taught facts and learned by rote. Questioning was discouraged and opinions were not sought. It was a model that raised standards of literacy and helped children become numerate, but it stifled creativity and nurtured social compliance. That was the learning experience for children when Alton Street opened and nothing much had changed by the time my parents were at school; but things were different when I started and my schooling was much better than that.

I was an unsure five-year-old; shy and nervous of strangers. Doreen inherited her father's confidence but I had the shyness and anxiety of my mother. Being anxious did not go well with starting school but the nervousness of the first morning faded surprisingly quickly and I soon settled in. The soft landing was due to my teacher, Mrs Byford, and from the day I started primary school until the day I left for secondary, I was fortunate to have had teachers who cared about children and knew how to bring out the best in them.

Mrs Byford was a tall, bespectacled women in her late forties and a good teacher. She could hold us all attentive in her grasp or set us free to do things for ourselves. She could make us laugh or quieten us down. I can never remember her being angry; she seemed to me to be always unflappable. Most of all, she knew how to teach. Soon I was a confident reader and books began to gain a significance in my life. I learned how to add, subtract, divide and multiply. I mixed paint and rolled plasticine. I sang songs and recited poems. Mrs Byford was active in the room; she didn't spend much time at her desk. She put up displays and kept the walls interesting. She organised the class into groups and not rows. We sat at tables and shared things. She may have been working in a Victorian classroom but there any connection to the School Board of London ceased.

At Christmas we put on a play for the older children. We were to be a Christmas tree and some of us were decorations. I played a candle. It was my first performing role and playing a candle would be a challenge for any actor. Holding a candle stick with a little white candle, I sang these lines:

I'm a candle gay,
Hanging on the tree,
See the little children
Dance around me.

It went fine on the day but there were problems at rehearsal because when I sang the second line, it always came out as: "I'm a candle gay 'angin on the tree." Mrs Byford would patiently correct me. "It's *HHH*an*GING* on the tree Joe, not 'angin." Eventually it came right and I got through with the help of a highly exaggerated 'aitch.' Twelve years later I was sitting in the music room at Bath Academy of Art being interviewed for a place there by Joe Hope, the Deputy

Principal. Joe had an easy way with him that enabled me to overcome the working-class awkwardness I so often felt in the presence of middle-class people. He put me at my ease and the interview went well. We talked about artists, painting techniques and exhibitions I'd seen. Then he wanted to know more about my personal qualities. "You say you are a school prefect so how do you manage the younger boys?" he asked. "Well, I have to supervise a fifth form class at lunchtime and that usually goes well," I said. "Usually? Are they difficult at times, then?" asked Joe. "No, I find they be'ave well," I replied. *Be'AVE* I felt the dropped aitch crashing down on me heavily from above. *Be'AVE* I had thrown away my chance of getting into art school with one dropped aitch. But Joe Hope was a good man and he continued as if I had pronounced the word perfectly. In 1963, others of his class would not have been so generous.

In my second term at Alton Street, the class had a setback. I came into the room one morning and saw Mrs Byford standing by her desk with another woman. When we were settled, she explained. "This is Miss Todd and Miss Todd is going to be your teacher for a few weeks. She has lots of exciting things she wants to do with you and I am sure you will enjoy your time with her." I looked at Miss Todd. She had a young, attractive face but it wore a cold expression.

For a while nothing much changed when Miss Todd took over but soon the mood altered. Small acts of autonomy like leaving our places to get a pencil or checking an answer with someone else, were challenged. We were corrected, we were controlled and gradually, we changed from happy confident learners to children who always sought permission and never speculated an answer. It didn't take long for us to realise that Miss Todd was strict and we didn't like her. One day she slapped Ann Field on the forearm and after that, our fear of her grew. Eventually her time with us came to an end and her teaching practice was over. No doubt she qualified as a teacher, but her methods sat more comfortably with those of the School Board of London than the more enlightened practices of the London County Council.

I made good progress in that dark classroom with my bright and thoughtful teacher and making progress was like being on a walk: taking in new things, feeling the pinch sometimes and enjoying the achievement of arriving somewhere new. Early in the summer term, Mrs Byford gave us some big news. Alton Street was going to close and we were going to get a new school on the Lansbury estate. It had just been built and it was called *Susan Lawrence*.

In our last days at Alton Street, we helped Mrs Byford clear the classroom. With her characteristic sense of fun, she turned a chore into a game by taking the tape from the displays and sticking it on the ends of our noses. The last day was orderly and unforgettable. We packed our things into the little metal boxes we kept on our desks and waited to be called. At ten o'clock we were lined up in the playground for the walk through the streets to our new school. Clutching our metal boxes, we made our way through a derelict landscape of rundown houses, bomb sites and blackened buildings until, quite suddenly, things changed and we entered the clean lines and newness of the Lansbury estate. The walk we made that day was a symbol of where our country had been and where it wanted to go; a whole school of children in one long line, walking away from poverty, war and dereliction into a brighter, better future.

* * *

I was fortunate to have been born when I was. Winston Churchill, Britain's greatest wartime leader, had led our country to victory over the obscenity of Hitler's Nazi regime. Because of Churchill, I was born into freedom; without him, things would have been very different. But despite leading the country to victory, the general election at the end of the Second World War saw him defeated. He was replaced by Clement Attlee, and Britain's greatest wartime leader was succeeded by its greatest peacetime prime minister. It was Churchill who gave me my freedom but it was Attlee who gave me my future.

Labour won the election by a landslide. The country was looking to the future and there was a great desire for change. But Britain was broke in 1945 and much of its infrastructure had been destroyed; building the future that the homecoming troops expected would be difficult because the country was on its knees. Hundreds of thousands of people were homeless and industries, geared to wartime production, had to be reconfigured or rebuilt. The railways, already clapped-out and losing money in the 1930s, were in urgent need of investment. The nation's health was poor; we were a country of bad teeth, poor eyesight and lung infections. A man could expect to live to sixty-five if he was lucky and a woman for just a few years longer. Abroad, Britain struggled under the burden of a crumbling empire and the Soviet Union threatened the freedoms of countries in what Churchill had called a descending *Iron Curtain*.

Attlee inherited a huge agenda and no money. But like Margaret Thatcher in 1979 and Tony Blair some years later, he was fortunate to have some highly talented ministers, many of whom had served in Churchill's wartime government. Attlee's government achieved so much in the first five years after the war: an enormous fighting force was demobilised, over one million homes were built, a welfare state was established with a National Health Service at its heart, key industries were nationalised, the education system improved, new towns established, 'green belt' land allocated around towns and cities and India was given independence.

Poplar became a focus for post-war regeneration. About 10,000 houses had been lost to bombing during the war and many of those still standing were war-damaged slums. The Lansbury Estate was conceived as a way of achieving regeneration within the traditions of the communities it replaced.

The philosophy of the design was that new development should comprise neighbourhoods, and that within the neighbourhood should be all that a community required – flats, houses, churches, schools, an old people's home, a pedestrianised shopping area and covered market. There should be pubs and open spaces, linked by footways. Traditional materials were used in the construction, such as London stock bricks and Welsh slate to counter the modern architecture.

(Wikipedia citing)

The Lansbury Estate was a success. It is one of the few examples I can recall where the idealism of architects was at one with the aspirations of the people. My school, Susan Lawrence, was at the heart of it all and it embodied the principles of Lansbury. It was surrounded by houses and low-rise flats, close to Chrisp Street market and a short walk away from Poplar Baths. Nearby was Lansbury Lodge, a care home for the elderly. It was modern and new like the rest of the estate. It wasn't hidden away but given a prominent position on the corner of Grundy Street so children could wave to their grandparents on their way into school.

Seeing my new school changed things for me and altered my perceptions of what a building could be. I had never been inside a building like it. Not Alton Street, or The Five Ways mission or any of the shops and houses I knew were like this. I was struck by the light and openness of it with its spacious entrance hall entirely glazed on one side and a wall of patterned yellow tiles running from floor to ceiling on the other. So much of it was new to me and different: the light elegant staircase up to the junior hall, the bridges from the upstairs corridor to the classrooms, the assembly halls with their polished floors and wide flat stages, the quiet coolness of the library and the novelty of Venetian blinds in every classroom. I never tired of the building. It was a joy to be in. A picture in the archive of the Royal Institute of British Architects shows the staircase up to the Juniors' hall, rising as if on air with nothing below it. To the left are the large windows of the foyer and through them, a view into the street showing a row of blackened slum houses. It is a remarkable photograph of Poplar caught at a moment in time; the problem and the solution captured in one frame.

Buildings have the power to change our perceptions of ourselves; they can raise us up or bring us down by association. When I was at secondary school in Blackheath, I was ashamed of my home. I kept it apart from my friends and didn't allow them there. But Susan Lawrence was different. It made me feel good about myself. I liked people to see it and to know about it. More than that, it lifted my horizons by showing me how things could be different; it gave me aspiration. That is the power of architecture. Buildings are more than just places to live or work in; they are symbols. They can build our self-esteem or diminish us in our own eyes and because of that, architecture is too important to be second-rate.

In 1951 the Government held a cultural event to celebrate the artistic, scientific and industrial achievements of the country. It was called the Festival of Britain and the Lansbury Estate featured as part of it. The festival site on the south bank of the Thames included two exciting architectural pieces: the Skylon, a thin elegant form over ninety metres high, and the Dome of Discovery, a large flying-saucer-like structure nearby. The festival captured the nation's attention and the Skylon and Dome of Discovery, together with the stylish Festival logo, became symbols of what Britain might be like in the second half of the twentieth century. My dad took us to the festival and seeing the Skylon and the Dome 'in the flesh' was like meeting someone famous in the street. And, although I would never have been able to articulate my response to them then, I knew that, like my new school, they were good to look at; they were good designs.

A COUNTERFACTUAL 1951

"JOE...weee, JOE...weee." It was my nan calling me to come in for my tea. "Yer nan wants ya," said Johnny Purton. Johnny, Billy McAvennie and I had been digging a hole in the path that led across the debris to the Chrisp Street steps. We were making a trap. When we finished digging, we were going to put sticks across the hole and cover them with turf to hide it. The trap was intended to catch baddies but for the plan to work, it required the baddies to be fooled by the untidy clods of turf we had piled across their path. If they were, and if they were foolish enough to tread on them, the police would find them injured in the hole and put them in prison.

I never wanted to go inside when I was playing but we were dutiful children and came when we were called. My nan was waiting in the gap that linked our street to the debris. "Yer mum wants yer for yer tea, come in and wash yer 'ands." "Oh Nan!" "Ten minutes more then." I ran back to Billy and Johnny to finish making the trap. The hole we dug was big enough to cover now and we started cutting the turfs. I had a perfect tool for cutting; a flat-headed metal spade with a T-shaped handle just right for my size. It could cut through roots of grass easily and it was strong enough to stand the strain of levering as I prised the roots from the ground. Billy and Johnny had already put the sticks across the hole and we were ready for the turfs. St Michael's clock chimed the quarter hour; a quarter past six. I was late. I tossed my turfs to Johnny and he put them in place, then we stood a while admiring our work. "If it's broke when we come in the mornin' then we'll know someone's fell down it," said Billy. "I 'ope they av," said Johnny." "I 'ope it's a baddie an'all," I said. Then I picked up my spade and ran.

I was late and I ran fast, banging my spade on the ground as I went. The path was bumpy and uneven. The surface was littered with rusty tins, stones and rubble. As I ran into the gap between the houses, I caught my foot on the spade and lost my balance. I fell forward and hit the ground with force, putting my hands out to lessen the impact. At once I felt a sharp pain in my right hand. I rolled over in shock. My knees were grazed and my hand was gushing blood. I stood up and started running again. Nanny Powell's door was open and I ran crying into the passage. "What's wrong, Joey? Let me see yer," she said, lifting my hand to examine the wound. We went into the kitchen. I was flicking my hand to rid myself of the pain and, as I did, specks of blood flew from me, splattering the walls with tiny spots of red. Uncle Henry came in. "What's 'appened?" he asked. "Go and get Nell," said my nan. When my mum arrived, she was shaken by what she saw; obviously my wound was more than superficial. I was still crying and my hand was hurting. My mum held me as Nanny Powell washed the wound over the sink. "Henry, run into Nell's and get the Germolene," said my nan. "It's by the bed on my side," said my mum, handing him a key.

Nanny Powell went upstairs to fetch some pieces of bed sheet that she kept for making bandages. Henry came back holding the tin of Germolene. Nanny Powell tore the sheet into strips and my mum dabbed the wound with cotton wool. The three of them were obviously concerned. "Germolene'll make it better," said my mum as she scooped a little from the tin and smoothed it gently across the wound. "It's stopped bleedin' now," said Nanny Powell in a consoling voice. But Henry was sceptical. "It looks bad to me," he said. "Should we take 'im up the 'ospital?" Henry had posed a difficult question and a look passed between them. "Is Joe on the panel at work?" he asked my mum. My father worked for the North Thames Gas Board at the gasworks in Bromley-by-Bow. "I think he's in the scheme," she replied. "You all in it?" asked Henry. "No, just 'im, you can't have your family in it," said my mum. The 'panel' scheme was an arrangement that companies had with their workers to cover medical costs. Without having that or private medical insurance, treatment had to be paid for, so working people treated themselves whenever they could, sometimes with terrible consequences. The bandage was securely in place and the dressing was dry but the wound was still hurting.

My dad was on the two-to-ten shift that day so I was in bed when he came home but still awake. "What you done?" he asked in a soft voice. "It narf hurt, dad," I said. "How d'ya feel?" "A bit sick." "You bin sick?" "No." "Do you wanna be sick?" "No, I'm all right." "I'll have a look at it in the morning, good night, God bless and spare ya," and he kissed me on the forehead. I didn't sleep much that night. My hand was throbbing and I felt hot. From time to time I wanted to be sick and I had a headache. In the morning my mum and dad came in to see me and my mum unwound the dressing on my hand. The wound looked red and sore. "How are you feeling?" she asked. "Not very well, Mum," I replied. "You can stay at home today," said my dad. "Do you want to go in our bed?" Going into mum and dad's bed was a treat when I was ill. Sometimes, if it was the winter, a fire would be lit in the grate but this was summer and the room was light. I lay there all day feeling ill. About one o'clock my mum brought me up a boiled egg and 'soldiers' but I had little appetite. By early evening I was hot and feverish but my hands and feet were cold. I tried some dinner but what little I manged soon came back up. My dad sat on the end of the bed and my mum looked worried. "He needs to see the doctor," said my dad, "I'll get old Stern."

Doctor Stern was my dad's panel doctor and the two of them had known each other a while. When Stern arrived, he didn't want to see my wound; not at first, anyway. Instead, he asked me questions. "Hello, young man, and what have you been up to?" "I fell over on the debris, Doctor," I replied, my voice thin and weak. "Can you tell me your name?" he enquired. "Joe Doctor." "And what school do you go to, Joe?" "Susan Lawrence Doctor." "And what's your teacher's name?" "Miss Woods, Doctor." Then the examination became a physical one. He felt my brow and held my hands and feet; they were still unusually cold. "I'm just going to unbutton your pyjamas, I want to look at your tummy," he said in a reassuring way. He undid the buttons, opened my pyjama jacket and looked carefully first at my chest and then at the rest of my torso. His face registered nothing but my parents were clearly shocked. "He's all red, look at him," said my mum with anguish in her voice. "I think I'd like him to go to the hospital," said the doctor, "is that all right?" The question wasn't one of seeking permission; if the doctor wanted me at the hospital, then that was that.

My dad didn't hesitate. "Whatever it takes Doctor, whatever it costs." "We can talk about all that later, Joe," said the doctor "but let's get him to the hospital first." "We'll pay for an ambulance," said my dad. "No need for that, I'll take him in my car." Doctor Stern's words panicked me. "I don't wanna go in 'ospital," I cried, "please don't take me to 'ospital." "The hospital can make you better Joe," said the doctor. "I wanna stay 'ere, please don't make me go to 'ospital," I sobbed. "Me and mum will be with you," said my dad "it's nothing to worry about.

At the hospital there were forms to fill in and questions to answer but I was seen quickly. A doctor examined me and another was called. Words were exchanged above my head: "liquids" "observation" "admission" "Penicillin." In time I was taken to a ward where I lay for a full day coming in and out of consciousness. A night of broken sleep followed and then, in the morning, I woke to find screens around my bed. I lay there for a second day. From time to time, doctors arrived to examine me and nurses came to do things. I was given injections and encouraged to drink. My pyjamas became wet with sweat and I was put into a clean nightgown. Out of consciousness and then back again, feeling ill, feeling hot. My mum and dad were there but I didn't see them. Then they were asked to leave. Doctors and nurses again, doing things to me, and me sliding back into unconsciousness...until...I died.

But of course, I didn't die. There were no panel doctors any more. Families like mine no longer had to agonise over the cost of medical treatment; it was there whenever we needed it with no bill to pay. This was 1951 and we had the National Health Service. The reality of what happened was different to the counterfactual I have described; maybe it was the difference between life and death. There was no hesitation that would have allowed the sepsis in my wound to spread and there was no charge for the antibiotic treatment I received to prevent it.

My mum and Uncle Henry hurried me along to Poplar Hospital that evening. On our way up St Leonard's Road, we passed Aunt Rose's house at 84. She and Charlie were just leaving to go to the pictures. I loved Aunt Rose and when she said that she would come to the hospital with us it was reassuring. So, we arrived at the out-patient department a little group of five. It didn't take long to be seen and it soon became clear that the wound was a particularly bad one; penetrating and dirty. The doctor cut a deep hole into the palm of my hand and opened it wide. Carefully, he felt around with tweezers and extracted a large piece of glass. "Here it is, have a look," he said, holding the glass aloft before dropping it into a small enamel tray. "We are going to give you stitches now but you can have a look first." I leaned forward and looked into the hole in my hand. It was impressively large. "Stitches," I thought, "I'll be able to tell my mates that I've had stitches." As a precaution against what he called 'blood poisoning' the doctor arranged for me to have a course of Penicillin injections. The injections were to be given into my buttocks. Like stitches, injections were a prestigious thing for a boy to have. Later I told my friends: "I 'ad stitches and they stuck a needle in me bum with pennercillian in."

The National Health Service is the greatest societal achievement of this or perhaps any country. It is based upon the assumption that medical treatment 'free at the point of need' shall be provided to all those who require it. Underpinning that simple idea are notions of humanity and equality that define a civilised society. Sometimes the NHS is attacked for mistakes and inefficiency and so it should be; it should not be above criticism and must always be held to account. But there are those who would abolish the NHS, privatise its services and follow the example of the United States. Some of its strongest critics suggest that to apply liberal notions of equality to health provision is a soft position to take. But defending the NHS is not an easy option, it is a difficult one because it requires us to defend the rights of people who may be undeserving in our eyes: the criminal, the neglectful, the ill-mannered, the aggressive and the disdainful rich abolitionists. No, defending the NHS is not an easy position to take, it is a hard one. The soft option is to get what you can for yourself and leave the rest to look after themselves.

When I am told that the NHS is failing and we should seek another model I ask myself who is telling me this and where do their true interests lie? A country that sold off its rights to provide clean water should be very careful before ceding its most precious possession to American insurance companies or Chinese banks.

THREE ENCOUNTERS WITH HISTORY

I never understood why Winston Churchill was so detested by the people of Poplar. Whenever his name came up it was always met with disdain and there was never any concession made to his leadership in the Second World War. As far as I can judge, at the heart of their contempt was his treatment of strikers in the General Strike of 1926. So often I was told that "Churchill sent the troops in." It is true that soldiers were sent to Poplar. Contingents of troops were drafted into the docks to unload ships and guard the premises, but it wasn't Churchill who deployed them; he was Chancellor so military deployment wasn't down to him. But when armoured cars and soldiers with loaded rifles and fixed bayonets were sent to East India Dock Road to guard lorries taking food from the docks to a depot in Hyde Park, Churchill was the toughest of advocates for their presence. He wanted machine gun posts to be set up along the route too, a move that Stanley Baldwin, the Prime Minister, rejected.

The stories I was told of the General Strike are awful. Strikers were attacked and beaten by police, food was scarce and people feared going out. My mum was twelve in May 1926 when the strike started and she told me this story of an encounter she had with a mounted policeman.

'Me and mum was coming back home down St. Leonard's Road when the police came after us. Mum took my hand and we run. I was

frightened. They were on horses and they had big sticks and they were waving them around. One of them come right up behind us shouting. All of a sudden, a woman opened her front door and said, "Get in quick." We ran in her passage but he kept following us and rode the horse right into the passage as far as he could. I was so frightened. In the end he backed it out.'

How distant we feel at times from those who take the decisions that alter our lives. How close do we ever get to the people who make history? When a string is pulled in government who is there to feel the impact it has on people's lives?

* * *

In 1931 Mahatma Ghandi came to London to attend the Round Table Conference on Indian independence. In keeping with his lifestyle, he decided not to stay in a West End hotel but chose a community centre in Poplar instead. Ghandi wanted to be associated with the poorest people of London and when Muriel Lester of the *Kingsley Hall* centre in Bromley-by-Bow heard he was coming, she invited him to stay there and he accepted. While he was there Ghandi made himself known in the community and he was popular. He visited houses and schools, used local shops and was seen around the streets.

One morning when she was seventeen, my mum was leaving for work when Old Uncle Harry noticed an odd-looking figure coming towards them from the direction of Bromley-by-Bow. As the figure drew near, my mum saw that it was a man in a loin cloth with a robe draped over his shoulders. To her astonishment it was Ghandi. He passed them as they stood on the airie of 217 and as he did, he smiled and wished them good morning. They wished him a good morning in return and followed him with their eyes as he made his way towards East India Dock Road. Of all my mum's stories it is the one I like best and I still find it amazing that she encountered this immense figure of world history just outside Nanny Powell's house.

I like to speculate on where Ghandi was going that day. Maybe he was on his way to another session of the *Round Table Conference* in Westminster but if he was, it would have taken hours for him to walk there. Perhaps he was heading to East India Dock Road to catch the 15 bus to Trafalgar Square; afterall he shunned the luxuries of the rich and likely travelled by bus as often as he could. It is also possible, however, that he was on his way to meet Charlie Chaplin who was in London at the time to promote his film *City Lights*. In his autobiography Chaplin writes: *"I met him* (Ghandi) *in a humble little house in the slum district off the East India Dock Road."* According to Chaplin the two discussed machinery and its impact on the lives of common people. Chaplin asked why Ghandi was opposed to machinery when it could do so much to improve his people's lives. *"I understand,"* said Ghandi *"but before India can achieve those aims, she must first rid herself of English rule. Machinery in the past has made us dependent on England, and the only way we can rid ourselves of that dependence is to boycott all goods made by machinery."* Five years later, Charlie Chaplin produced *Modern Times*, his critical masterpiece on the effects of mechanisation on people's lives.

* * *

In 1948 the United States Government initiated The Marshall Plan, an enormous package of financial and material aid to help seventeen countries get back on their feet after the Second World War. Part of the programme involved sending food parcels to schools in struggling communities and Hollywood film stars were sent to publicise the scheme. Alton Street was chosen for a visit by Charlie Chaplin's ex-wife, Paulette Goddard. She was glamorous, young and attractive. Doreen was one of the children chosen to join her for a carefully-staged publicity photograph. The picture is something of a classic. In it, Paulette is smiling radiantly and wearing a long, expensively-tailored satin evening coat with a tasselled bunny hat. She is leaning forward. A girl is receiving a large parcel of food from her and looking quite uncertain in case she might drop it. Doreen is in the picture looking bemused, and some of the other children are clearly un-interested. The photograph amuses me for the contrast it shows between Paulette's clothes and demeanour and those of the children. According to *The East London Advertiser*, she was wearing golden shoes.

A WEE WITH CLEMENT ATTLEE

One evening in March 1961 I was slouched in the armchair in Aunt Rose's kitchen reading the *Evening Standard* when my attention was drawn to a football competition in the sports pages. It was for schoolboys up to fifteen-years-old. From twenty-two players from London clubs, competitors had to select the best eleven. Was the best goalkeeper Jack Kelsey of Arsenal or Reg Matthews of Chelsea, for example, or Johnny Byrne of West Ham a better centre forward than Bobby Smith of Spurs? The prize was a very good one. The winners would be collected in a chauffeur-driven limousine and taken with a friend to Wembley Stadium to see England schoolboys play Wales. Not only that, but they would be hosted by Billy Wright and given lunch in the VIP restaurant behind the royal box. Billy Wright had been England's captain and played for his country a hundred and five times. He had recently retired and was in the news for marrying Joy Beverley, one of the Beverley Sisters, a singing trio who were popular at the time.

I was steeped in football. I knew all of the players on the list and had seen most of them play. My team fell into place quite easily, and after just a little haggling about which fullbacks to choose, I completed my list and sent it off. Not long after, a letter arrived telling me that I had won. I was naturally delighted but a little cautious too. Who would I tell and who would I take? I decided not to say much to the boys at school because to do so might seem like bragging, but one day in the gym I decided to tell Mr Ellis our PE teacher. Bill Ellis was a decent man and seemed genuinely pleased for me. He thought it was an achievement for me to have won the competition, so he announced it to the class. This was a good outcome for me because it preserved my modesty and gave my news with a minimum of fuss.

Deciding who to take was more problematic and I was faced with some tough decisions. Terry Lawlor was my closest friend at school and I was still mates with Johnny Watton at home. Then there were several boys who I got on well with, many of whom played football with me every day in Greenwich Park. In the end I settled for Ray Levitt. Ray and I were pretty good friends. He was in my class, we were in a five-a-side team together, and every Sunday we met up with a group of other boys to play football. Ray was easy-going and he had a good sense of humour. He loved football and was an avid Charlton Athletic supporter. He was self-deprecating and sometimes made himself appear to be more gullible than he really was.

Our five-a-side team was called *Eltham and Lee Athletic* and we played in a league at Sutcliffe Park in Sidcup. I was the goalkeeper, although I liked to play outfield too and often did. I was chosen to play in goal because I had quick reflexes and was prone to leaping about in a way that made even the most basic of saves appear spectacular. One evening, Johnny Watton came to watch me play and he gave me a few warm-up shots. His kick was so fierce that, although I managed to deflect the ball around the goal, the force bent my hand back and I had to play the game in quite a bit of pain. After another match, two scouts from Eltham Palace football club came up to me and asked if I would like to play for them. It was the pinnacle of my footballing achievements as the club was a good one, but I had to decline the offer because Eltham Palace were based even further away from home than my team was.

England schoolboy matches were huge affairs. The ones at Wembley attracted a crowd of 95,000 and the ground would have filled to its capacity of 100,000 but for a safety limit imposed because most of the spectators were schoolboys. When I was twelve, I went to the England versus Germany match with a school party from Roan. It was like no match I had ever been to or have been to since. The noise was loud and strangely odd; nearly 95,000 unbroken male voices at full pitch is a sound like nothing else.

On Saturday April the 29th 1961, a car arrived at midday to collect me. It was a huge black Austin Princess, sleek and gorgeous like a royal car with walnut dashboard, enormous comfortable seats and silver metal detail. The chauffeur was fully kitted out in cap and uniform and he treated me with the respect and deference he might have shown to the Lord Mayor of London. It was a strange, almost surreal experience to step down from the airie of our shabby house and have the door of a large limousine opened for me by a uniformed chauffeur, but I really enjoyed the moment. However, for all that, I felt awkward as I sat alone in the back, because there was an unspoken agenda going on. I was the client to be driven around as instructed and the driver had to do what he was asked. On the other hand, he was a man and I was a boy so we both knew where the power really lay. Sitting beside him in the front was a staff member from the *Evening Standard*. His job was to look after me and make sure that nothing went wrong.

Ray lived at the bottom of Vanbrugh Hill in Greenwich so we had to go through the Blackwall Tunnel to collect him and come back again to make our way on to Wembley. Neither of us could believe we were sitting in a chauffeur-driven car like royalty; it was such a funny thing for us to be doing. For much of the journey we communicated with a combination of hushed asides and grins. I starting giving stiff royal waves out of the window and we rocked with silent laughter. "Tell him you want him to stop at a sweet shop," whispered Ray, so I did. Then a little later he said, "Say you need to stop for the toilet now." "You tell him," I said, but Ray didn't chance it.

One thing I hadn't resolved on my way to Wembley was what I was going to ask Billy Wright when I got to speak to him. He was such a big star and over his long career he would have heard all the questions there were to ask, but I knew I had to say something. I had cut pictures from my football albums for him to autograph, but I had no idea what else I would ask of him. Then I remembered that he had given an interview a while back when he described what it was like to face '*The Hampden Roar.*' This was the intimidating greeting that opposing teams faced from 135,000 Scottish supporters whenever Scotland played at home. As England's captain, Billy would have got it full blast from the lusty Glasgow chorus bent on a tartan victory. So that became my question; I would ask him what it was really like.

When we got to Wembley the *Standard* man guided us through the fast-growing crowd up onto a terrace that overlooked Empire Way. Billy was there already, standing with the other competition winners and his stepson. There he was,

England's one-time hero, and I was now to be in his company. Billy was well-practised in situations like this and was chatty and easy-going. Despite that, I felt awkward and tongue-tied and kept to the back of the group. "Any more questions before we go inside?" Billy asked. So, I took my chance. "What was it like to face the Hampden Roar?" I asked. Quick as a flash Billy came back with a smart riposte. "The Hampden Roar? I haven't heard it since 1949!" The captain of England was never going to concede anything to the Scots.

We climbed the steps into the stadium and went inside. All the way up to the restaurant we passed through a throng of spectators jostling and pushing each other to get as close to Billy as they could. It was an eye-opener for me to see what fame really meant when someone famous gets close to the public. Billy took it in his stride and just kept ploughing on, smiling and acknowledging the adulation as he went.

The Empire Restaurant was of its time: functional art deco with lattice screens that gave a hint of Chinoiserie. Billy sat at the head of the table with Ray on his right and me next to him. The meal was of its time too, being both uninspiring and predictable: tomato soup with a bread roll followed by roast chicken leg, potatoes and peas. Almost certainly the dessert would have been ice cream or apple pie. We were given a glass of fruit juice and Billy had wine. Before we started to eat, a photographer from the *Standard* came to record the event for the paper. He was about to take his picture when Billy stopped him and covered his wine glass with his hands; years of experience had taught him that it would not be a good idea for the captain of England to be seen drinking alcohol with a group of schoolboys.

Apart from Billy's stepson, the other boys were younger than Ray and me and, as we were seated next to Billy, we got more of his attention. He was friendly without being condescending but despite that, I felt tense throughout the meal. Table manners were part of my problem. My dad had taught me plenty of table manners but his were mostly *don'ts*. Don't put your elbows on the table, don't speak with your mouth full, don't touch your food, don't eat off your knife. But these were our rules and there were other ones that posher people had that I never knew about. At this meal the problem for me was peas. At home I would load peas with my knife onto my upturned fork and shovel them into my mouth. But I was fairly sure that the *right* thing to do was to hold the fork face down and prong them, so I tried it that way. The result was that my portion of peas was reduced only slowly and a small mound remained stubbornly in place alongside the potatoes. My anxiety grew worse when the chicken proved difficult to cut and my knife made little impact on it. I resisted the urge to tear and hack and persisted with more forceful cutting motions. The chicken won and my knife went slipping off into the peas scattering them across the table in Billy's direction. There was enough of them to make a necklace, but I managed to collect them together and got them all back on my plate. Billy noticed and smiled sympathetically.

After the meal Ray and I thought it would be a good idea to go to the toilet before the game started. The Empire Restaurant toilets were in the same VIP area just along from the royal box. Like the restaurant, they were functional and not particularly luxurious. If this was how the other half lived it was not over-impressive. Ray, who had been standing on my left, finished before I did and when he went, it left a gap beside me. As I turned to wash my hands, I saw an old man a little further on standing straight-backed and intent on doing what everyone was there to do. It was just a subliminal impression but instantly I realised that it was not just any old man, it was Clement Attlee: Clement Attlee, Major Attlee, Earl Attlee, the hero of the Dardanelles, the outstanding young barrister, the conviction politician, Churchill's right-hand man throughout the Second World War, the leader of his party, the man who took a ruined country and stood it on its feet, the man who gave me my future. There he was, standing having a wee just like anyone else.

A WALK DOWN THE ROAD

PERCY PALAVER

St Leonard's Road starts at East India Dock Road and winds northwards for about a mile towards Limehouse Cut and Bromley-by-Bow. It was a lively place of houses and shops when I was a boy and it seemed like there was a pub on every corner. We lived at the northern end in a stretch of old houses between Cobden and Chadbourne Streets. On the corner of Cobden Street was a barber's shop owned by Percy Smith; 'Percy Palaver' we called him. Percy was a gentleman; old and polite, courteous and attentive. He was small and grey with a trimmed moustache that gave him an old-fashioned Edwardian look. Like Percy, the shop was small and old-fashioned too. I had my first haircuts there. My dad would take me and Percy would put a plank across the arms of the barber's chair for me to sit on. Percy called me 'Sunny Boy.' Maybe he couldn't remember names and called all little boys that, but I liked being called Sunny Boy.

I think Percy was the only barber in his shop and there was only one barber's chair. Facing it was a large mirror with display shelves on either side. On the wall beside it was a framed cartoon of an ice-cream seller pushing his 'trike' with its fridge box full of children. A caption read: 'Stop me and buy one.' Sometimes waggish older boys would point to the contraceptives on the shelves and swap the order of the first and fourth words. Sitting in the chair while Percy snipped away, I would look at the *Ona* and *Durex* packets and wonder what was in them. The advertisement said that they 'provide the maximum sensitivity and comfort for both husband and wife,' so presumably they were like slippers or gloves. When I was older and I knew what they were, I came to admire the discretion with which Percy handled the sale of them. "Anything else sir?" he would ask the younger men after their haircuts were paid for. Then with a nod and a quiet word the sale was completed.

THE BOMBED-OUT HOUSE

Next door to Percy's was a bombed-out house. Its walls were still standing and the joists of the upper floor were still in place but most of it was gutted. The front door and windows were boarded up but even as little ones we found our way in. Once, in search of wood for bonfire night, some older boys took me and Billy McAvennie inside. Albert Woodyard prised open the corrugated iron on the front door and we squeezed through. Inside the house was a wreck. Much of the roof and masonry had fallen through and was piled haphazardly across what were once the downstairs rooms. Any wood that had survived the bombing had long been scavenged from the ground floor but there was plenty to be had upstairs. Getting to it was difficult though because the only way to reach it was by climbing what was left of the staircase. We needed the wood, so we had to go and get it.

Albert Woodyard went up first. Albert was a tall gangly boy of about fourteen and one of the large family of Woodyards that lived along the road from us. He climbed up easily, his long skinny legs straddling the gaps in the staircase without much difficulty, but it was a bigger challenge for Billy and me. The first five stairs were still in place and there were more stairs higher up towards the landing, but between the lower and upper ones was a gap with nothing to hold on to. It was easy for the older boys but I couldn't see how I was going to do it. "Kenny'll give you a bunk up so I can reach yer," said Albert, "then I'll pull yer up." I climbed the lower stairs easily enough though some of them were broken and unsafe. I reached the gap and, looking up, I could see Albert's long dirty arm stretching down towards me. I hesitated but soon my thighs were held by Kenny below who shoved me upwards towards Albert. "Cum on," said Albert, waving his hand towards me in a beckoning motion, "give us yer 'and." I stretched my arm towards him and his grubby hand gripped mine. He tugged me up and for a while I thought I might fall, but I wasn't scared. Albert twisted himself round and edged his way upwards towards the landing taking me with him in a series of tugs until I landed on what was left of the upstairs floor.

Looking up I could see through the roof and into the sky. Around me I saw that there wasn't much left of the upstairs floor; just a few planked 'islands' linked by timber joists charred black from the bombing. There was plenty of wood to be had from them, but we would never be able to prise these heavy joists free. "Over there," said one of the big boys pointing to a pile of window frames and charred wood scattered across a stretch of what remained of the floor. "There's tons over there, cum on." Then, balancing on one of the joists, he made his way across; eyes forward and arms outstretched like a tightrope walker. "Cum on," he said again. We followed him across in turn and, still feeling no fear, crossed to the far wall with a series of carefully-taken steps. "Chuck the wood down through the floor," said Albert. I grabbed an armful and let it go. The thinner planks twisted in the air as they fell and the thicker pieces dropped heavily and landed with a bang. "Mind me 'ed, mind me' 'ed!" came a voice from below. We stacked the wood onto an old pram and wheeled it round to the debris. How dangerous this had been and how oblivious to the danger we were.

'GRUMPILY GRIMP'

Next to the bombed house lived a couple who no one really knew. I don't remember much about the man but, to my shame, I can recall the lady well. She had a pallid complexion and the creased, wrinkled skin of a smoker. She was middle-aged, slightly-built, and her thin hair was an unnatural shade of yellow. We never knew her name but we took against her and made life difficult for her. With no good reason, we decided that she was unpleasant and we called her Grumpily Grimp. Our unkindness to her was remorseless. We'd knock loudly on her door and run away or hide behind the little crenelated wall nearby. Sometimes we would play that nasty game two or three times a day and it must have been miserable for her and her husband. We did it often and we brought the knocker down hard.

We played 'knock down ginger' a lot. Sometimes we would tie string on the knockers of adjacent houses so that when the door was opened on one, the string pulled the knocker up on the other. As the first door closed, the knocker on the second would fall back to make a loud knock. The game could be self-sustaining, for a while at least. It was fun; it was a laugh. But what we did to the lady in 195 was nasty.

THE BEARDS

Mrs Beard and her family lived in 197. The Beards were the very best of East End people. Mrs Beard was the mother of Lily and, as Lily's husband's name was Levy, everyone in the house except for Mrs Beard was a Levy too. But that didn't stop people calling them the Beards. If a woman had grown up in the street, she was called by her family name even after she was married. So, my mum was always Nellie Powell to the neighbours and Lily was Lily Beard. All of the Beards were nice. Lily was friendly with my mum, and Doreen and I got on well with their children. Mr Levy was a lorry driver and he kept his big open-backed truck outside the house. Sometimes we would climb onto it and play in the trailer but he never minded. Once he even took me and Johnny Watton for a ride around the block with Johnny and me bobbing up and down in the back. The Beards moved away when their house became due for demolition and St Leonard's Road was the poorer for that.

THE HERRINGS

The Herrings lived next door to the Beards: Doll Herring, her husband Albert, their three children and Doll's sister, Mill. Mill was tough and hard to take. She was genuinely unpleasant; no one would dare to knock on her door and run away. She was not very tall but had a tough look about her that promised to take no prisoners. She told me off once for sitting on her airie. I wasn't doing any harm; I was just sitting there. The front door opened and Mill came out. For some reason she objected to me being there and told me to go: "Oi Joey Conley, clear off and get down yer own end!" Her outburst upset me and I went home almost in tears. Aunt Rose came along shortly after and asked me what was wrong. "Ooo's upset yer, Joey? Ooo was it?" "Old Mill, Aunt Rose." "What's she say?" "She said I 'ad ta go away and play down me own end." Rose was having none of it. She turned around and went back to confront Mill. Mill didn't know why Rose had knocked on her door and greeted her in her usual charmless way. "Yes? What do *you* want, Rose?" Rose was ready with her reply, "Do you like your nephews, Mill?" she asked in a matter-of-fact way. "Course I do," replied Mill. Then Rose's tone changed and she gave Mill full blast. "Well, I like my nephew too. You 'av a go at 'im agen and I'll come back and really sort you out!" Mill had met her match in Aunt Rose and she knew it.

Dolly Herring was small with lank dark hair and bulbous eyes. Albert was short, bald and gummy. Their two sons were like younger versions of their father but with hair. I think they all would have struggled at school; Mill was the brains of the family for sure. The Herrings had a baby daughter, Christine. One day she went missing: just disappeared from the house. Doll was distraught. A search was mounted and a group of us combed the streets and bomb sites to find her. In desperation, Doll decided to call the police. She hurried home to await their arrival but, before they got there, the baby Herring had turned up. When Doll entered her bedroom, she found her fast asleep under the bed.

One afternoon I was standing on our airie when I saw a motorbike coming along from the direction of the church. It wasn't going very fast and that was a good thing because, without warning, one of the little Herrings came sprinting out from his house and ran across its path. The bike hit the little Herring and knocked him to the ground but, thankfully, he wasn't too badly injured. Doll heard the screech of brakes and came running into the road. "You've killed my baby! You've killed my baby!" she shouted to the unfortunate rider. Luckily the boy wasn't fatally injured but it was a good thing for the rider that Mill wasn't around when it happened.

THE HONEYS

I cannot work out some of the complexities and connections that ran through the families in St Leonard's Road. My mum was related to the Kennys in 201 for example and Marie Kenny was her cousin. There was Big Marie and Little Marie and Big Marie, the mother, was married to Hughie Honey. Little Marie was known as Mary Kenny until she married Hughie's son, Pat, and became a Honey in her own right. Confusing?

Big Marie was heavily-built and unsmiling. She had a tough side that revealed itself in negative ways at times but she wasn't always like that. Hughie was friendly and quick to smile; a cheerful figure in corduroy trousers, white collarless shirt and cap to cover his baldness. Big Marie and Old Mill were very close; too close some people thought. Mill would stay overnight in Marie's house and there were rumours of a liaison between the two of them but Hughie didn't seem to mind. Whatever their relationship was, Hughie's easy-going nature allowed him to turn a blind eye. Young Marie had a sunny disposition; she was good-natured and fun. She was good-looking too and very much the girl of her times. She and my mum were close. They had great laughs together during the war and, when I was born, Marie was asked to be my godmother.

Marie married Patsy Honey in 1950. I went to the wedding and remember how good it was to be given a carnation buttonhole. Marie and Pat moved into a house across the debris from us in Woodin Street. Patsy Honey was a dodgy character; dark and swarthy with a look of Elvis about him. He was once caught under a neighbour's car syphoning petrol from the tank. He said he was looking for a chicken that had escaped from its hutch but he never explained why he needed a can and a length of rubber hose to catch it. Marie and Pat had two children and were settled for a while, but Patsy deserted the family after a few years and Marie never took another man. She moved to Dagenham but kept in touch with us and sent me Christmas cards every year until she died. I am so pleased that she was my godmother. She was sunshine and she stayed sunshine all her life.

OLD MOTHER JONES

Mrs Jones and Albert lived next door to Marie, with Rosie, Mrs Jones's daughter. There was a whiff of suspicion about

Lou Jones and Albert because it was said that they were not married and cohabiting was scandalous in the buttoned-up Britain of the 1950s. Mrs Jones was often disliked because of her fiery temperament. She was unpredictable and easy to fall into argument with, especially if she'd had a drink. We called her 'Old Mother Jones' most of the time or 'Bang Away Lu-Lu,' a nickname she earned because of her erratic character. She wasn't very tall, had a full figure and grey hair that fell naturally into waves.

Albert was a quiet presence, always in the background. He was like Hughie Honey in temperament but without Hughie's sunnier side. He had health problems too that restricted his mobility and Lou, always energetic and animated, looked after him well. She was such a presence in the street and unashamedly nosey. She'd spend lots of time at her front door looking up and down and wasn't beyond walking to the middle of the road to follow passers-by with her eyes as they went along. Subtlety was not a quality that Lou ever had to grapple with.

Mrs Jones had her kind side too and was fond of me. When I went to Roan, she would wait for me to pass her house on my way to catch the bus and give me an apple and two sweets. I hated her doing it for all sorts of reasons. I didn't like the feeling of indebtedness that these daily acts of kindness brought out in me and most of all I didn't like the apples. They were often greasy and shrivelled and, more to the point, I suspected that she hadn't washed them or washed her hands either. I tried to avoid her by leaving earlier or looking along the road to see if she was there; but most days she was and I was obliged to accept her apples and mint humbugs until I was in the sixth form.

Rosie Jones was about the same age as Uncle Henry and single like him. Sometimes they walked out together and Rosie was sweet on Henry. Neither had attractive looks but Rosie dressed well and wore lots of makeup. She arched her eyebrows in dark eyebrow pencil and powdered her face to a blemish-free pink. She wore bright red lipstick and kept her hair well-groomed in the scrolled fashion of the day. I liked Rosie. She was always friendly and pleasant to me. Aunt Rose was keen to see her marry Henry but Henry was always reluctant to commit. As the years passed and Rosie grew older, a desperation took over her; she wanted a man. Hers was not a humiliating form of desperation but an implicit and sometimes obvious one. One day she just upped and left. She found herself an older man and went to live with him somewhere south of the river. I saw her on the bus once on my way to school. She was sitting opposite me on the long bench seat by the stairs. She looked the same as ever; her make-up and hair as perfect as always and looking good in a belted gabardine mac. We talked together easily and I never asked questions. She had broken free of Lou and that wasn't a bad thing.

THE COUNTERS

Next door to the Honeys lived Mrs Counter; a short old lady with a shock of wild white hair. Her daughter, Ivy, was another close friend of my mum's and had been so ever since they were girls. Ivy Counter and Nellie Powell were quite a pair and got up to some tricks. They sat together in school, played together at home and sometimes got into trouble. When boys in their class tied their legs to the desk, the teacher, Madam Morgan, sensed something was up and challenged them: "Ivy Counter and Ellen Powell stand up at once," she said threateningly. What were the two of them to do? They couldn't disobey Madam Morgan and they couldn't tell tales on the boys, but they couldn't stand up either. So, they did their best and rose from their seats as far as they could and bent forward over their desktops. "What is wrong with you Counter?" Madam Morgan asked in her sternest of voices. "Our backs are hurting Madam, it's these desks," complained Ivy. "It will be more than your backs that will be hurting if you don't sit up and pay attention properly," Madam Morgan replied. My, mum was a nervous child, especially at school, but she liked a laugh too and Ivy's exchange with Madam Morgan made her rock with supressed giggles.

Mrs Counter once asked Ivy and my mum to go to Hedges the butchers to buy some faggots for the dog's dinner. The butcher weighed the faggots and wrapped them in newspaper. Ivy and Nellie both liked faggots and they were hungry. The thought of the lovely faggots going to the dog became too much of a temptation and eventually Ivy gave in. "Go on Nell, 'av one," she said, offering the opened package to my mum. "Go on, I'm 'avin one," she persisted. By the time they got home they had nothing to offer the dog but newspaper. "Have you got the faggots?" asked Mrs Counter as she came down the stairs. "Yes Mum," lied Ivy. The dog had already got the smell of the delicious cooked faggots and had raced to the door as soon as the girls were back. "Where are they?" asked Mrs Counter. "'E's et 'em Mum, look," said Ivy shuffling the empty pages of print in front of the dog in a way suggesting she was giving it the last crumbs of meat. Naughty girls.

THE SMITHS

Wally and Nell Smith lived with their grown-up sons, Benny and Joey, at 207. They were an unlikely family. Nell was frail, tiny and prematurely old. She had been ground down by the hard life she'd led: years of poverty, neglect and Wally's unrelating bullying. Nell looked 'down-at-heel'; literally down at heel because the backs of her shoes were trodden down and the soles worn with holes. I never remember seeing her without curlers in her hair and an overall covering her frock.

Nell was Wally's victim. He beat her and treated her with contempt. She coped with life by drinking; drink was her salvation but it was her burden too. She would often be seen swaying her way home from the pub singing as she went, apparently happy until the front door closed behind her and she confronted her fate. If she was lucky, she would get back before Wally and could pretend to be asleep. But Wally would still be there, badgering her to wake up when he came in, or complaining about her behaviour the next morning. Like all bullies, Wally could show a plausible side. He would give a nod of recognition when you passed and sometimes exchanged a few words. On days when the weather was fine, he would sit on the window sill reading his newspaper, an unshaven figure in shirtsleeves with gaps in his teeth and trousers belted at the waist.

Benny and Joey could never be taken for brothers. Benny was articulate and intelligent. He had a kind nature and his life was guided by principles of Christianity and Socialism. He was no radical but lent his weight to Attlee's Labour party and served as a sidesman in church. If he had faults, they were that he was soft, naïve and maybe too forgiving. Benny was friends with Uncle Henry and liked by my family. He was my godfather and I have a picture of him taken not long after I was born. He is in army uniform holding me in his arms. I am wearing what looks to be a white satin baby dress.

In the mid-1950s Benny married Joycie Bannister, the daughter of Bannister the fishmonger in St Leonard's Road. Joycie was a good match for Benny. She was open and friendly like him but maybe a bit cannier too. She wore her hair in the tightly-scrolled style favoured by Rosie Jones and like Rosie, she pencilled her eyebrows into thin black arcs and painted her lips bright red. After they were married, Benny and Joycie moved in with the Smiths and had their first baby there. It must have been difficult for them living with Wally and Nell especially after the baby was born. It wasn't a nice place to live either. The house was bare, there was no carpet on the floors, and it smelt of gas. Joey was still living at home when the baby arrived and he must have felt the strain too. There were only two bedrooms and I can't imagine how they all fitted in. Benny and Joycie found their own place eventually but Joey stayed living with Wally and Nell for another ten years.

Joey was a lorry driver and something of a mystery man. Although he never said much, he was likeable enough in his own way. The striking thing about Joey was that he was so unlike Benny in his looks and ways. Joey was wiry. He was shorter than Benny and more muscular. Benny and Joey didn't look alike either; Joey's looks were more rugged and he had a more defined jaw-line than Benny. The most obvious difference between the two was in their colouring; Joey was swarthy and darker than Ben. He had a Mediterranean almost south-Asian skin tone and that made me wonder sometimes if Wally really was his father or Nell really his mother. Joey was as private as Benny was outgoing. I never worked out the relationship between the two or how well they got on with their parents. I can only speculate that Benny and Joey had grown up in fear of their father and still feared him as adults.

Joey the 'mystery man' would go away for weeks at a time but he always came home. One evening he was stopped by the police outside *The St Leonard's*. He had no identification on him and the police became suspicious. Their suspicions grew worse when they asked him his name and he told them that it was Joe Smith. Then, to his relief, he saw that Nell was coming along so he knew he would be all right. "There's my mum, she'll tell you who I am," he said. "What's your name mother?" asked the policeman as Nell drew near. "Nellie Fackeral," she replied, giving the name she was born with. "Your name's not Mrs Smith then?" said the policeman. "No, I'm a Fackeral, always 'av bin," insisted Nell. For Joey things suddenly got a bit worse.

Joey brought a woman home once. To use an old-fashioned word, she could be described as 'comely.' She was older than him, in her forties and voluptuously attractive. She was as different to Joycie as Benny was to Joe. After a while she moved in with Joey but Nell didn't like it. There was gossip going around about Joey's woman: that she had a bad reputation and offered sex for money. As Joey was a lorry driver and a single man, I think it was not unlikely that she did take money for sex and that is how he met her. That she was penniless and had children adds to the likelihood; children have to be fed and the rent has to be paid somehow. "My Joey's going out with a prawsti-chewt, my Joey's going out with a prawsti-chewt," Nell complained when my mum and I met her up the road.

Nell outlived Wally but not by much. As time passed without him, she became more vulnerable and the drinking got worse. If I saw her coming, I would sometimes avoid her because facing her in drink was difficult. Benny and Joey kept an eye but she declined further into drink. Nell's ultimate indignity occurred late one night when I was in my teens. I heard a noise from the street and went into my mum and dad's room to look out from their bedroom window. "What's up?" asked my dad. "I don't know, I can't see anyone," I said. I looked up and down the street at the empty pavements and then I saw Nell in the gutter outside her house. "It's old Nell," I said, "she's lying in the gutter." My dad got out of bed, put on his clothes and went outside. He approached Nell and knelt beside her. Then he lifted her in his arms, carried her inside, cleaned her wounds and put her to bed. That was my dad. That was the man he was.

* * *

In 1996 we had a celebration for my parents' sixtieth wedding anniversary. We invited Benny and Joycie and Marie Honey too. They were like stars to me; lovely Poplar people who had kept their special qualities intact over so many years. Joycie was a special star that day, particularly to Alice and Joe though she never would have known it. She chatted to them incessantly in her old-fashioned cockney voice and her appearance was unaltered by time: the tightly-scrolled hair, the white-powdered face, the red Cupid-bow lips and the thin pencilled eyebrows.

"Joycie Bannister," said Alice after everyone had gone. '"We *loved* Joycie Bannister!"'

Benny kept in touch. He wrote to Doreen and me when my mum and dad died and two years later in 2003, we decided to visit him and Joycie before it was too late. I drove us to Poplar and parked by St Michael's church. We sat in the car eating our sandwiches and looked around at where we had once lived. Doreen hadn't been back since we moved away but, in 1971, I went to photograph what was left of it. It was a sad sight then: derelict land where houses once stood, shops that once saw queues now boarded-up and most of the pubs closed and neglected. It was a Saturday afternoon but I was struck by how few people there were. Eventually a couple came along from the direction of East India Dock Road. They stopped to ask me what I was doing. "I used to live here," I said, "I'm taking pictures." The couple were in their fifties. They'd 'had a few' and were happily disposed to passing some time with me. "What's yer name?" asked the man. "Joe Connolly," I replied. "Conlie? Conlie?" "Conlies out'a Space Street?" asked the woman. "Yes, my gran and grandad lived in Spey Street and some of my uncles and my Aunt Nell." "Nell Conlie out'a Space Street?" the woman asked. "I knew yer aunt Nell and yer grandad." "Old Bill Conley," said the man. "Used to get in The Hearts of Oak, didn't he?" They went on their way but I felt good about this encounter; the place wasn't there anymore but some of it still existed.

Doreen and I finished our sandwiches and went for a look around. Our houses had gone and all the ones that once faced them had gone too. A fence of railings stood where our airie once met the pavement and behind it the land ran flat to the railway across what was once Woodin Street and our debris. It was now Langdon Park: pleasant, flat and bland, offering space for recreation but without the abundant flora and unkempt landscape that we enjoyed so much when it was a bomb site.

The St Leonard's pub and St Michael's church had been converted into flats and the railway line where steam trains once ran to The West India docks was now the Docklands Light Railway. 'Chris Street' steps were gone and Langdon Park station now straddled the railway where the bridge had once been. A bus route ran past where our house had once stood. The kerbs were swept clean. So much had improved but the community was no longer there.

We left St Leonard's Road and drove over to see Benny and Joycie. They lived in a ground floor maisonette off Grundy Street on the Lansbury estate. Private ownership had blighted a few of the houses on Lansbury; the fashion for stone cladding had taken hold in the 1970s and a few of the yellow-brick houses were now covered in pastel-coloured slabs. But much of the estate had matured well and was greener and more mellow than it was when I was a boy. The concept of community laid out in the post-war plan for Poplar had endured too and Benny and Joycie lived happily and securely in their home.

THE PURTONS

It is hard to begin the story of the Purtons because they played such a part in my early life. George and Emma Purton lived upstairs in 209 with their children, George, Eileen and John. Downstairs lived Emma's mother, Granny Sims, and Granny

Sims's son Jack. Granny Sims was a small, old-fashioned lady with avian features and hair brushed tightly back into a bun. She wore long skirts and dressed in black like many widows did in those days. She never went far from the door but spent lots of time sitting on the window sill when the weather was fine. She was sociable and liked to chat, particularly to Nanny Powell. Like many old women who'd known each other for years, they called each other by their surnames: "Morning Powell." "Morning Sims." It was the convention in those days.

Jack Chambers was short like his mother and wore dark clothes too, but he had none of her chattiness and could be grumpy sometimes, particularly if he thought a child needed telling off. He kept racing pigeons and pigeons were his obsession. There was no space for recreation in the Purton's back yard because it was taken up with lofts and all the paraphernalia that went with keeping pigeons. On Friday evenings Jack would take his racers to a pub where they would be loaded onto a lorry with other birds and driven to a distant location for release. Then he'd spend Saturday afternoon in the back yard waiting for them to return. When one flew in, he'd grab it, put its leg into a timing clock and record its arrival. All pigeon fanciers had timing clocks and whoever clocked the first bird home got prize money. Sometimes the birds played the game and flew straight into the loft but often they didn't, preferring to perch tantalisingly on neighbours' roofs. Desperate to get them down, Jack would shake a tin of seed and call to them: "Cum on, cum on 'en, cum on, cum on 'en, cum on..." Then he would make a clicking sound with his tongue and start shaking the tin again. It could take hours sometimes: "Cum on, cum on 'en, cum on, cum on 'en, cum on..."

Mr Purton was taller than Jack but not by much. He had a large stomach that he kept in place with a wide leather belt and was rarely seen without a 'cheesecutter' cap on his head. I think he was quite intelligent and his children were bright too, particularly Georgie who went to grammar school. Mr Purton had a deep bellowing voice which he used to enforce his authority. He was definitely in charge of the family; his children wouldn't dare to cross him. He liked a drink and spent much of Saturdays and Sundays in *The Victory* on the corner of Bright Street. Sometimes he would go there on weeknights too and on Saturdays Emma would go with him.

Mrs Purton was delightful and when she was around, I always felt good. She was cheerful and straightforward and there was an earnestness in her manner that I found appealing. Her face wore a 'no-nonsense' expression that went well with her 'no-nonsense' ways. Apart from Georgie, all of the Purtons spoke cockney but Mrs Purton spoke it best. Once when she was asked if she had paid the bill for her council rates she said, "Good gawd no! I ain't payin' 'em yet. They ain't due 'til Octa-bleedun-tober." I don't know how well George and Emma got on together. He was a tough man used to getting his way and she was a soft easy-going woman, but the morning she died I heard him roar like a lion: "EM..EM..EM!!!"

Georgie Purton was like his dad in some ways; there was none of Emma's softness and humour about him. When he was young he moved out of the family home to live with Mrs Purton's sister Mary a few doors down. The move was a good one: it eased the overcrowding for the Purtons, gave Mary the experience of bringing up a son and offered Georgie a quality of life that helped him into a good career. When I think of Georgie, I see him in uniform: the black blazer and grey flannels of George Green school and the bluish-grey of the Royal Airforce. He was tall, dark and I think, good-looking. He'd nod or say hello when I saw him but mostly he kept himself to himself and seemed detached from his family. He played cricket, dressed well and was a cut above other boys of his age. When his national service was over, he got a job with an insurance company, met a girl, married and moved away.

Eileen inherited her mother's ways and had her same attractive disposition. She had lots of commonsense and was quick to jump on anything she thought pretentious. If someone used a fussy or unfamiliar word she'd say "…Oo's 'e when e's at 'ome?" Eileen was pretty and her looks added to her charm. She was fun to be with too and Doreen and she were good friends. When she was in her teens, she met Stan and soon they were 'going serious.' Before long she and Stan were married and expecting a baby. They got rooms upstairs in a house in Cobden Street. Below them lived Laura Fry, an old lady whose sparse home was even more basic and Victorian than Nanny Powell's. Laura was tall and thin with a long face and sunken eyes. She wore black and her black stockings and enormous black slippers gave the impression of a giant spider. Laura had nothing; she was the poorest person I ever knew and lived in the poorest home I ever saw; just bare boards, a few pots and pans and an old black stove, but she was kind and I think that she and Eileen got on well.

Johnny and I would visit Eileen when the baby was born. Sometimes we'd push the pram up and down the street while she spent some time with her mum. Stan was rarely there. He had been called up into national service and was in the army.

One evening when Johnny and I were playing outside Eileen's house, an army lorry full of soldiers pulled up and Stan went inside to see her; he had got the driver to make a detour on their way back to camp. Stan crossed swords with the army once and Eileen didn't see him for a while. "He's confined to barracks," she said.

I imagine it was physical attraction that brought Stan and Eileen together. They were both so young, only eighteen when they married. Eventually they moved to Silvertown to better accommodation in the same street as Stan's parents. Silvertown was a depressing place of docks, railway lines, factories and terraced houses. Rhea Street where they lived was a cul-de-sac. Cutting it off at the far end was the wall of the King George the Fifth dock, above which the decks and funnels of cargo ships were always to be seen. Eileen and Stan had three children together but, in time, Stan left and set up home with someone else. Eileen survived though. She met Lenny, an Irishman who liked his beer, stayed in Silvertown and had four more children.

* * *

Johnny Purton had been my friend ever since I could remember. There was something about being with him that I liked. He had the charm of Eileen and his mum and, even though he could be grumpy sometimes, it was good to be with him. Johnny was one of the little brothers on the debris; wherever I was, whatever I did, Johnny was there too. He knocked on doors and ran away, had his hair cut by Percy Palaver, went to The Five Ways mission, made traps to catch baddies on the debris, played cowboys, climbed the stairs in the bombed-out house, joined in the wars with Jackie Painter's gang, made swords out of sticks, dug graves for dead birds and gave them a Christian burial.

When he was very young, four or five years old, Johnny invented a pigeon game. He would call for me with a little brown attaché case and we would go to Nanny Powell's. Inside, he'd go into the kitchen, get under the table, select some of the boots and shoes that were kept there and put them in his case. These became his pigeons and we had to release them to fly home. "Cum on, we gotta let 'em go now," he'd say and he would go into the passage, open the case and throw the boots up into the air. My job was to help get the pigeons home. "Cum on, cum on 'en, cum on, cum on 'en, cum on..." Johnny would call, just like Uncle Jack.

I owe my introduction to football to Johnny. Ours wasn't a footballing community and professional football never featured much at Susan Lawrence. I knew that someone called Harry Hooper played for a team called West Ham and I always watched the FA cup final on television and evening games when Wolverhampton Wanderers played foreign teams like Spartak Moscow. But it was Johnny who told me about the Busby Babes, the outstanding young players of Manchester United who played magnificent football and were winning everything they went for. Johnny and I became supporters. We followed United and started our own team: Manchester United Schoolboys. We played on a cinder pitch at Glaucus Street in Devons Road. Someone gave me a pair of boots; high-ankled heavy old things with toecaps and nails from the studs that dug into my feet. For Christmas I got a United shirt; a V-necked classic in the perfect shade of red with white trimming. So shoddy were the clothes in those days that the red dye turned the white trimming pink the first time the shirt was washed and I was heartbroken.

Johnny and I knew all of the *Babes* by name. I collected pictures of them from newspapers and magazines and started a scrapbook. My idol was Bobby Charlton. He was barely out of his teens then, but already a wonderful player. He meant so much to me that I mentioned him every night in my prayers:

"God bless Mummy, God bless Daddy, God bless Doreen, God bless Aunt Rose, God bless Uncle Charlie, God bless Uncle Henry, God bless all the soldiers and sailors and airmen and keep them safe, amen. And please God, let Doreen marry Bobby Charlton."

Whereas my memories of friendship with Billy Mac and Johnny Watton run into my teenage years, Johnny Purton gradually withdrew from our lives and I remember doing nothing with him after the age of twelve. More often than not when I knocked to ask if he wanted to come out, he'd say no. It was such a shame because it was always good doing things with him. Gradually Johnny's life was focused on Jack and the pigeons. The Purton's backyard was only a few feet from ours and I would often see him on the shed rattling the seed tin and calling to the pigeons just like Uncle Jack did: "Cum on, cum on 'en, cum on, cum on 'en, cum on..." We would acknowledge each other over our garden walls and we would talk sometimes, but he never said much. When I saw him in the street, he would pass me by with just a nod of the head by way of acknowledgement. As Johnny Watton and I grew to become teenagers together: going to West Ham, buying records, liking clothes and being curious about sex, Johnny was nowhere to be found and that was a shame because we missed him.

THE BROWNS

The Browns were our next-door neighbours, three unmarried sisters: Emmie, Dolly and Tiddles. They'd grown up in the house and never moved away. Emmie was the eldest and, although she was the least attractive in both looks and character, she was the only one of the three who had a man. Emmie's 'beau' was Alf Allen who lived a little further down the street. Dolly Brown was the middle one of the three; she had a friendly face with a permanently furrowed brow that gave the impression that she was always about to ask a question. Dolly was friendly and, unlike Emmie, had a cheerful way with her. Tiddles was the youngest of the 'girls.' She resembled Dolly in looks and had her pleasant ways, but she was less self-assured than Doll, maybe because she was the youngest and had been protected by the other two. Em, Doll and Tids had a married brother called George and George had two children, Brenda and David. George came to visit fairly often and David and I and would chat together across the garden wall.

The Browns were good neighbours. Even Emmie with her occasional grumpy ways wasn't that bad but, although we got on well with them, we never socialised. The Browns put up with a lot from me when I started playing football, because I would spend hours in our backyard practising goalkeeping catches and shots on the volley against their wall. My dad kept our backyard looking nice. The walls by the scullery were whitewashed and our small patch of garden was planted with flowers, runner beans, Cos lettuce and tomatoes. Ours was the only planted garden in the street; the other neighbours just left theirs to the weeds. The Browns never went into their garden except to hang out washing. In the summer it became a mass of tall stalky weeds and I dreaded having to jump the wall and wade through them to get my ball back when it went over.

Em, Doll and Tids led a good social life. From time to time, they held parties and, when they did, they would let us know in advance. They never had enough chairs to seat their guests so Emmie or Doll would knock on Nanny Powell's door to borrow the two wooden benches she kept in her scullery. The Brown's parties were knees-ups with plenty of singing and 'thump, thump thumping' on the floor. We never minded, even though they went on well into the night. On Saturday nights, the three of them would go to the pub with George and Emma Purton, Emma's sister Mary, her husband George and Alf Allen. When I slept in the front bedroom, Saturday nights were all about the pub. From nine o'clock onwards, when the drink had taken effect, the singing would start: old songs belted out in unison in that unmistakable drinkers' voice of those times:

"....ho, we ought not to part-ah
I've-a said frohm the stahrt-ah
You're the whun rowes that's-a left in miiiya haaaaart-ah."

There would be cries of encouragement: "Go on Lil, giv us annuvver." Once the pubs turned out, my neighbours made their way home and before 'turning in' they would stay talking under my window. When the chatting was over, the 'good-nighting' would begin. 'Good night' was a ritual; something of a social obligation. Everyone was obliged to 'good night' everyone else, so each of the eight neighbours had to 'good night' each of the others in turn. Eight people saying good night seven times, made a total of fifty-six 'good nightings.' Fortunately, they often 'good nighted' at the same time and sometimes Mr Purton would cut it all short by playing his trump card of "good night, all."

The Brown's coal cupboard was on the other side of our living room wall. When coal was delivered, we'd hear it fall like thunder as the coalman tipped his load into the dark space under the stairs. Sometimes we heard scratching coming from the other side. We would dismiss it at first and hope it would go away, but if it persisted, we knew that a mouse or a rat was gnawing away in the Brown's coal cupboard. Mice were often a problem for us. We controlled them by having a cat and using mousetraps. We often saw them in the scullery but sometimes they ran about upstairs too. Before going 'down the scullery' my mum would throw a shoe to frighten any mice away. We never had rats but the Browns were less fortunate than us and had rats and mice. We could tell the difference between the two by the sound of the gnawing; rats were louder. Once the gnawing was so loud that we thought a rat was coming through the wall.

Vermin were just one of the challenges faced by people in houses like ours along with: no bathrooms, outside toilets, leaking roofs, dangerous wiring, unsafe gas pipes, loose floorboards, damp walls, lack of hot water, windows that wouldn't close and very little space. However much they tried, families could never overcome the difficulties of living in old shoddily-built houses that had been recently battered by war.

The Browns moved away when we did; their house was earmarked for demolition at the same time as ours. They left Poplar and took a flat not far from the house we moved into on the Hainault estate so we saw them from time to time. I never knew who the surviving sister was, but I imagine it must have been a dispiriting experience to be the last one of three who had lived together all their lives. Whichever of them it was, that end had a sad inevitability.

THE MILES FAMILY - 215 AND THE HOUSE OPPOSITE NANNY POWELL'S

Until I was eight, our next-door neighbours on the other side were a very different kind of family; Ernest and Joan Miles and their daughter Sheila. Ernie Miles was the son of the Mr and Mrs Miles who lived opposite Nanny Powell with their adult children Douglas and Joan. The Mileses were lower middle-class; Dougie and Ernie wore suits to work when other men in the street went in overalls. They carried briefcases too and Ernie always held a pair of yellow kid gloves in his left hand. Joan was very much the middle-class housewife of her day and would not have looked out of place on the cover of *Woman's Own*.

The older Mr Miles drove a black Wolseley saloon which he polished to a mirror shine every Sunday morning. He and Mrs Miles had a telephone too; they were the only people I knew that owned one. They voted Conservative and put Conservative posters in their windows at election times.

Everyone else voted Labour. In the 1945 election 'old Bill Guy' the Labour candidate received an astonishing 89.2% of the vote. Given the deprivation the people of Poplar had suffered over so many years, perhaps it was hardly surprising.

Dougie and Ernie were heavily built, ponderous and dull. Dougie resembled his father in looks and had shiny black hair which he wore heavily Brylcreemed and combed back from his forehead. Mrs Miles was stout and short. She wore long dark clothes that gave just a glimpse of bandaged leg under her thick lisle stockings. Joanie was ugly. Perhaps it would be kinder to find another word to describe her, but it would still amount to the same thing. Her most unfortunate feature was her left eye which turned in so badly that the eyeball almost disappeared at times. She was quaint, earnest and unfailingly sociable. Like her mother she spoke with a particular kind of London accent: neither cockney nor posh. It was a way of speaking that might be considered an attribute today, but it wasn't in those days when 'cut glass' pronunciation was the mark of a person's status.

We never really disliked the Mileses. Joanie was something of a comic figure to us in private, but we liked her for all that and we never showed her anything but our best sides. Dougie and Ernie were 'stuck up' but they were polite enough in their stuck-up way. Mr Miles was aloof, but he was never unpleasant or rude and Mrs Miles praised our successes like when I gained a grammar school place or when Doreen got into college. All in all, the family stood out like a sore thumb in St Leonard's Road but they were given respect and fitted in in their own way.

The older Mileses lived next to Appletons, a removal firm, and their house extended over its entrance. Joanie worked for

Appletons. She took care of administration and was responsible for issuing quotes for house removals. The firm had three vans, each one painted in brown and cream company livery. Across the front of them were the words: *Our motto – keep moving*! Reversing the vans into the narrow passage and along into the yard was a difficult manoeuvre but the drivers were well practised and never seemed to scratch or damage their trucks. My grandfather James Powell worked for Appletons as a cartman for many years until he died. He was held in high regard there and because of that, there was an affinity between Nanny Powell and the Mileses that had endured over years.

In 1953, Ernie and Joan moved away. They had saved enough to afford a house out of the East End and were on their way to Bexleyheath, a suburb in Kent. Without doubt, a Kentish suburb suited them better than bombed-out working-class Poplar.

THE JACKSONS

The Jacksons lived next door to Nanny Powell in 219. They were a quiet, refined family of four. Because she had lived in St Leonard's Road since she was a child, Mrs Jackson was known by her family name of Kitty Sharp. Frank Jackson was quietly-spoken and pleasant like Kitty. He walked with a limp that may have been caused by a wartime injury or perhaps an accident at work; disabilities like his were more common in those days. Their children, Maisie and Frankie, were outdoor types in their twenties. They had been to grammar schools and, although they were older than Doreen, they took an interest in her because she went to one too. Maisie and Frankie were cyclists. They had drop-handlebar racing bikes and wore cycling shorts. Frankie looked older than his years and was very much a man of the fifties; serious, bespectacled and dull. Maisie had a healthy, open-air look: her eyes were bright, her hair shone and her arms were brown from cycling in short sleeves.

At weekends, Maisie and Frankie went on long bike rides into the country with their friends. In spring they would return from Epping Forest with huge bunches of bluebells tied to their bike racks. They lived with their parents well into their twenties and I was in my teens when they married and moved away. When the Jackson's house was earmarked for slum clearance in 1965, Kitty and Frank moved away too and another domino had fallen. They had been good neighbours.

ALF ALLEN AND THE BUTLERS

Alf Allen lived next door to the Jacksons with his sister Ethel. Alf was a thin, upright man in his fifties. He never said much as he passed by in the street but there would always be a nod of recognition. Alf 'walked out' with Emmie Brown and they had been walking out together for years. They went to the pictures once or twice a week and Alf would call for Emmie to take her to the pub. Ethel had been born with Down's Syndrome and had a limiting form of that condition that didn't enable her to enjoy the quality of life that many people with Downs have today. Ethel was like a child. She would say "hello" but little else. She was accepted by the community and I can never remember anyone being unkind to her. Ethel wore frocks, little girl dresses in yellow or blue that came below her knees. She wore children's buckled sandals too with white ankle socks; although she was an adult, she was always dressed like a child.

When I worked for the education department in Suffolk, I had responsibility for a group of the County's schools. One of them, Belstead School, provided for children with a wide range of learning difficulties. The Headteacher, Hillary Birkin, was a charismatic no-nonsense lesbian with an outstanding ability for getting things done. She told me that when she took over the school from the health authority, the pupils were kept in cots. "They ran it like a hospital," she said. "And bloody ankle socks. The girls wore frocks and white ankle socks and they dressed the boys in short trousers. I threw the lot out and put them in tee-shirts and jeans; our kids are teenagers for God's sake, they want to dress like any other teenagers."

Alf and Ethel shared the house with the Butler family. When the Butlers moved in, they were a family of six but before long they had a little girl and were up to seven. Doll Butler was a confident working-class mother, large rather than fat and taller than most of the women around. George, her husband, was taller than Doll and fair with blonde hair. Their eldest daughter, Maureen, was a couple of years older than me, and Babsie, the next one down, was a year my junior. Then came Georgie, Frankie and the little girl whose name I forget. Frankie and Georgie favoured their father in looks and Frankie had his blonde hair. Maureen and Georgie were ginger and Maureen had freckles. Babsie's name was Raymonde but everyone called her Babsie or Babsie Beano. Maureen Butler was fun. From the moment she arrived she was a leader and we had great times with her playing on the debris. Sometimes she called herself *The Secret Sign* and we'd follow her across the bomb site searching for criminals and evil doers who, fortunately for us, never materialised.

Babsie was nice. One summer's day when I was seven, she and I were sitting on the bomb site together. It was rare to be alone and so close to a girl. There was no one around, so I gathered my courage and offered to show her my willie in exchange for a glimpse of whatever she had to show me. "Go on, Babs," I said, revealing mine. Willies held no interest for me, all of ours were the same; what girls had, though, was more of a mystery. "Go on Babs, please," I pleaded but Babsie was resolute. "No," she persisted. Her resistance was no doubt due to the fact that she had been told that it was wrong to show herself to boys. It was also likely that she had no curiosity about what boys had either; she had two brothers after all, and boys in the street weed in the kerb whenever they wanted to, so Babs had seen plenty.

George Butler took over *The Victory* for a while but I don't know if he had much success with it. George enjoyed a drink himself and that can be a disadvantage for a landlord. He was a quiet man too, so maybe he needed to assert himself more. It didn't help that he had been a regular in *The Victory* and had lots of pals on the other side of the bar.

I don't remember when the Butlers left or where they went. I never knew Maureen as a teenager, so presumably they had gone by the mid-sixties. Neither do I remember anyone moving in to share the house with Alf and Ethel. They lived on there until it was demolished in 1967 so maybe that's when the Butlers left too.

AUNT MARY

Aunt Mary lived in 223 with her husband George and Georgie Purton her nephew. Mary was Emma Purton's sister and the two were close. "Hello, sis," Mary would say when she saw Emma coming along. "All right, sis?" Emma would reply. Mary had Emma's chirpy personality coupled with a huge dollop of common sense. She kept herself smart and her home was well-furnished and tidy. George was tall, upright and well-turned-out, but I never remember him saying much.

Having no children gave Mary and George more money and enabled them to give Georgie a good home. Taking him in was a big commitment and he owed a lot to his aunt. She gave him the attention, care and quality of life that George and Emma could never have afforded him. She was good to Eileen too and Eileen thought a lot of her. Doreen and I called her Aunt Mary but Eileen just called her Aunt. "Ooo-oo, Aunt," she'd say with a wave if she saw Mary in the street. Mary disapproved of Jack's influence on Johnny Purton and all the time they spent on pigeons. Sometimes she would admonish Johnny but, however good her intentions, it seemed like nagging to him and he didn't like it.

When the time came for their house to be demolished, Mary and George moved to Ilford. I visited her there once. She was well into her eighties then and George had died. The house was very nice. She had been fortunate to have known someone who offered it to her for a low rent. My impression is one of lightness, polished glass and wispy net curtains. Eileen kept close to Aunt Mary until she died and Mary lived independently and maintained her high standards until she died.

THE WOODYARDS

There was a small debris that separated Aunt Mary's from the houses further along, because three of the ones that once stood there had been taken out by bombs. The gap led from the street through to the big bomb site behind our houses. Across the gap were the Woodyards a family of about ten who lived in total poverty. Albert was the oldest boy, next came Pauline and then Brenda, a girl near to me in age. Then there was 'Spanner' but I can't remember the names of the others. When the last child was born, they named her Wendy. It was a name we had never heard before and everyone mistook it for 'Windy.' "They've only gone and called it 'Windy'," said Mrs Purton in disbelief. "All the kids'll laugh at it when it goes to school."

The Woodyards were often ridiculed by their neighbours. They called Mrs Woodyard 'Sookie.' Her husband, a hefty sallow-looking man, was mocked for having a bad back that kept him off work but allowed him to produce children seemingly at will. In truth, the Woodyard family was down-at-heel and, at times, unwashed too. My family was relatively poor, but our lives were nothing like as hard as theirs was.

Like Nell Smith's and Laura Fry's, the Woodyard's house was neglected and bare. Sometimes a bedsheet would hang at the front window to give some privacy but they had nothing much to hide. Once, when workmen came to do repairs, Mrs Woodyard gave them tea in jam jars. Although they had so little, one day to everyone's surprise, they bought a car. It was a big old thing like a London taxi and Mr Woodyard painted it blue. Several attempts were made to get it going but it never moved from outside the door. George Mitchell who did car repairs in his shed on the corner offered to help. Eventually he got it going and with Albert beside him and several children in the back, Mr Woodyard went for a ride. The Woodyards had taken a fancy to Nanny Powell and one Saturday afternoon Mr Woodyard invited her to go for a drive. Being the woman she was, she accepted. I don't recall if the car and Nanny Powell ever left the kerb but, if it did, it couldn't have gone far.

Spanner Woodyard was younger than me and a well-meaning little boy. He was small, dark, and slightly bent-over, with feet that turned inwards like his brother Albert's. Spanner often kept his head slightly bowed so his eyes seemed permanently to be looking up and there was an earnestness about him that added to his vulnerability. He was a sociable boy and always said hello when he passed by in the street. He was a grafter too. When he was older, he would be out and about trying to make a little pocket money for himself. He ran errands, cleaned cars and helped the stallholders in Chrisp Street market. Sometimes he would pass the door with a crate of cabbage leaves, carrots and other discarded vegetables for the family to have for their tea. Spanner was an unlikely hero but he brought a lot to his family.

The Woodyard children were lacking in education and wanting in the qualities they would need to get them out of poverty, but like Spanner, some had a little more about them and may have made it to a better life in time. I certainly hope so. Poverty is a terrible thing; ugly and horrible.

THE STRECKERS

Mr and Mrs Strecker were quite tough. Alf Strecker was quiet, steely and argumentative; it wasn't good to get on the wrong side of him. Mrs Strecker was sociable with the women in the street but she could be unpleasant too and often fell out with them. The Streckers had four children. Julie and Danny, the older two, were in their late teens and Terri (Theresa) the other daughter, was a few years younger. Tony was the youngest. He was a year older than me and a difficult boy to like.

Julie and Danny were nicer than their parents. Julie had a job and money to spend. She dressed in the fashion of the times with full-skirted dresses and accessories like buckled belts and 'fully-fashioned' stockings. Danny's appearance had something heroic about it and not just because of his Viking-like features. He had a BSA motor bike, wore a thick sheepskin flying jacket and looked good. Terri was plain, heavily built and freckled. She had few of the social skills of Danny and Julie and it was difficult at times to work out if she was being sincere or not. Her position in the family made things more difficult for her. The older two had their lives sorted out and Tony had boys of his own age to play with but Terri seemed left high and dry.

Tony was a tough, unpredictable curly-haired boy and a bully. Johnny Watton, Johnny Purton and I called him 'Mad Mulla' and we dreaded him being around. If he found us playing in the street, he would take over and disrupt our game. He picked on Johnny Purton and used his strength to overcome him. Johnny was physically and mentally abused by Strecker; mocked for his love of pigeons and pinned to the ground and pummelled under Strecker's bigger, weightier body. Johnny was a good boy in many ways and he didn't deserve that, but there was nothing that Johnny Watton or I could do to stop it and there were times when we got similar treatment ourselves.

One day my mum said that Mrs Strecker had cancer. It was the first time I recall hearing that word and yet all that it implies was there in her voice when she said it. From the outside, it isn't possible to know what goes on within a family, so I don't know how the Streckers coped after she died, but they survived. Terri took on a bigger role, Julie and Danny paid their way and Mr Strecker carried on, though with less of the swagger that he once had. I don't know what happened to Tony. I was just glad when he moved away.

THE WARDELLS

Like the Beards, the Wardells were the best of Poplar people. I remember Mr Wardell as a slim man in his forties in white shirt, dark waistcoat and black trousers. He was known as 'Punch' but his real name was Matthew. People spoke highly of him and of his wife Nell and their family bore witness to their good qualities as parents. Punch died of cancer about the same time as Mrs Strecker and Mrs Wardell was left with a large family to look after. Nell Wardell was a woman of quiet grace. She had fair skin, golden hair and a friendly face. In company, she would wait her turn to speak but when she spoke, people listened. The Wardells had six children: Nellie, Violet, Margaret, Kathleen, Patsy and Carol. Patsy was the only boy. They were a close family and stayed that way long after their house was gone and they went off to lead their own lives.

Doreen and Margaret were best friends and Margaret stayed overnight at our house sometimes. She and Doreen got married once; one of them wore a nightdress and the other was in pyjamas. I can't remember which one was the bride, but when I was asked to be the pageboy, I was pleased. Margaret was a clever girl and went to a grammar school. Being Catholics, the Wardells chose St Victoire's, a convent school near Victoria Park in Bow.

Of the older Wardells I remember Nellie and Violet best. I went to Violet's wedding in 1956. Nellie and she had moved out by then and the wedding was in Dagenham. Kathleen was the most unlikely Wardell of them all. She got into scrapes as a girl and always seemed to have a runny nose or jinked knee. For a while Carol was in my class at Susan Lawrence. She was intelligent and pretty too.

In the mid-1950s the Wardells moved to a bigger house in Poplar High Street. Not long after that, Mrs Wardell died of cancer. Gradually the family was dispersing and in 1956 Margaret found her life partner in Terry Blancke. Terry was a young docker who lived in Byron Street, a turning off St Leonard's Road. He was a perfect match for Margaret and shared her easy-going ways. People spoke highly of Terry but thought it unusual that he didn't smoke; Terry was the only non-smoking man I ever knew in Poplar.

When Margaret and Terry married, they rented upstairs rooms in a house in Sabbarton Street by Stinkhouse Bridge. I visited them there a few times and I got on well with Terry. He was an Arsenal supporter and he offered to take me to see them play at Highbury stadium. I was twelve and I had never been to football before, so I was really pleased. I went to Arsenal with Terry a few times and he encouraged me to support them, but it never stuck. A few years ago, Joe asked me about my first football match and I told him about Terry and going to the Arsenal. West Ham were facing relegation at the time. Joe thought for a moment and said: "Dad, you know I'm a Hammer and I'll be a Hammer until the day I die, but sometimes I wish you had listened to that Terry." Unfortunately for Joe, I listened to Johnny Watton instead so his fate was sealed nearly seventy years ago.

* * *

I remember little of the couple that lived next door to the Wardells other than that they had no children and the lady was young and always gave me a pleasant smile. The house that would have completed our block had been destroyed in the bombing and George Mitchell's improvised garage stood in its place. From Percy Palaver's to George Mitchell's was the run of St Leonard's Road on our side. Over the road the houses were better and the pavement was planted with trees.

A WALK ON THE OTHER SIDE

THE KILDUFFS

Across from Percy Palaver's barber shop, St Leonard's Road made a sweeping hairpin curve into Ullin Street. The corner where the streets met was planted with huge trees that stood in an open garden behind a low rounded wall. The large bay windows of the houses behind looked out beyond the trees to the Gothic façade of St Michael's church. The junction was spacious and uncluttered; the war hadn't touched it and the combination of trees, church and space made this a pleasant place to be. A wall ran from the corner with Ullin Street as far Nell and Wally Smith's on the opposite side. From there a terrace of houses stretched along St Leonard's Road to a small bomb site on the corner with Zetland Street. Sometime after 1919, Maple trees had been planted at intervals on that side of the road and from April to August their branches were filled with chirping sparrows.

The first house along had two flats. Mr and Mrs Farnham lived downstairs with Peggy their big Alsatian dog and upstairs were Jean and Bennie Kilduff and their daughter Linda. Jean was the Farnham's daughter. Linda adored Peggy and the two were inseparable. I loved Peggy too. She was large and docile and I played with her whenever I could. Linda took her for walks and in the summer of my twelfth year, I started going with her. Linda and I became close because of that and we developed a special friendship unlike any other in my young life.

Linda wasn't particularly pretty but there was something indefinably attractive about her. She had lovely skin and fair hair that was cropped and bobbed in a way that suited her face. Her complexion was neither pale nor dark; olive perhaps describes it best. Her eyes were narrow, almond-like almost, and her mouth was wide. There were little dark moles on her arms and face; not many, but enough to add interest to her skin. She had a slight slur to her speech and when she spoke, some words came out with a 'schushhh' that added to her appeal.

My friendship with Linda ran in parallel to my time with Johnny Watton and the boys, though I was with them more. What was different about being with Linda was that we both wanted to 'do stuff,' to be active in the real world like grown-ups. We wanted to solve mysteries and thwart criminals. We wanted adventures, real ones not made-up games from our imaginations. We got the chance to do that when we discovered that Cyril the paper boy did more than just deliver papers.

However old they were, the people who delivered newspapers were always called paper 'boys'; Cyril was in his forties but he was still a paper *boy*. He delivered to several houses in the street and brought Nanny Powell her *Star* every night. Cyril had been her paper boy for years. She liked him; everybody liked him. He was upbeat, cheerful and friendly. People would wait on their doorsteps for him to arrive and he would chat with them for a while before moving on. We'd hear Cyril before we saw him; whistling his way along or calling out "Star, News, Stan*durrrred*, Star, News, Stan*durrrred*."

Because we saw a lot of him, Linda and I began to notice that Cyril spent more time at some houses than others. At Flo Woodford's and Mrs Stock's he would linger a while and slips of paper and money would change hands. We suspected him of being a 'bookie's runner.' Betting was illegal except at race tracks and bookmakers used people like Cyril to take bets on the street. Being a bookie's runner was illegal and there were serious consequences for those who got caught. Linda and I kept an eye on Cyril and found out quite a lot about him. We were playing detectives. It was a good game and it began to take up more and more of our time. It got even better when we discovered that Cyril had a female accomplice. She was in her forties; ordinary but in an attractive way. At first, we didn't give her a second look as she went about her round, but in time we noticed that she too lingered on doorsteps just like Cyril did.

Linda and I became good at being detectives and followed Cyril and the lady around without arousing their attention. We took turns at eavesdropping, became adept at stepping back behind corners when one of them turned around and pretended to play ball whilst really keeping watch. We got to know their separate rounds too and, best of all, we learned that the woman was called Vi and that she lived in Layfield Place. We had seen money change hands, heard talk of gambling odds, plotted the routes of two bookies runners and knew both their names. We also knew where one of them lived. We had all this evidence and no idea what to do with it. That didn't matter though, because the fun was in being detectives not in prosecuting criminals. Besides which, we liked Cyril and Vi and we certainly didn't want to see them come to any harm.

Linda got me to join The Canine Defence League because she'd learned that too many dogs were treated cruelly; there was always a streak of idealism in Linda. Sometimes she and I talked of deeper things like evolution and the nature of stars. We climbed into the emergency water reservoir on Tapley Street bomb site once and searched for creatures in the water. Linda found a small gelatinous grub and I suggested it was probably one of our predecessors so she called it 'Preedie.' In the long summer holiday we sometimes stayed out late into the evening. One night we lay on our backs on the Brown's airie looking up at the stars until nearly midnight. Our parents checked on us from time to time but we managed to stay there looking up and speculating on what it all meant. How was this possible? I could never have spoken like that with my mates. We were so young. Was it because Linda was a girl, or that she was intelligent or were we just soulmates? Two little ships passing in the night.

THE BROMLEYS

When I think of Charlie Bromley, my heart warms and a smile comes to my face. Charlie Bromley, 'Old Brum,' was a short, slight man in his eighties. He had the look of a soldier: straight-backed and with the soldier's moustache of the trenches. My father thought the world of Charlie and they were mates despite them being over forty-years apart in age. Old Brum was good-natured and funny. He never left you without making you smile and as I think of him, I am smiling now. He sparred with my dad sometimes; raising his fists and challenging him to a fight. "Come on then, let's av ya or are ya too scared to take me on?" Brum's humour was delivered with guile; a story kept you engaged until it reached its unlikely conclusion and you realised that he'd been pulling your leg all the time. He never admitted to the unlikeliness of his stories however far-fetched they were. "I bin up the fire station today, Joe," he told my dad once. "What did you go up there for, Brum?" "I'm out a' work, Joe; I need the money. I arst 'em for a job as a fireman." "What did they say, Brum?" "No luck, Joe. They said I weren't old enough so come back next year."

Jeannie Bromley, Brum's wife was small, thin and never without a cigarette in her hand. She was a chain smoker; that she lived into her nineties lends weight to the view that it is the exception that proves the rule. The Bromleys never had much money, just enough for food, tobacco and rent, but their house was well-kept, adequately furnished and they got by.

One winter's evening in 1964 a man knocked on our door and asked if he could talk to us about Jean and Brum. He was a reporter for the *Evening Standard* and was on assignment to write articles on poverty. His brief was to live with the Bromleys for a week and get by on the same amount of money that they had to live on. Brum and Jeannie only had the state pension of six pounds ten shillings a week, so for a well-paid London reporter it was quite a challenge. I thought he had taken on a lot; not just the frugal existence, but sleeping at the Bromley's and sharing the sink to wash in and having to use the toilet in the backyard. And I wondered too how he would pass the time. Jean and Brum didn't have a television and, if he stuck to the rules, he wouldn't have much cash to spare for trips to the pub.

Unsurprisingly, like many others, he found us. At first his visits were for research. He would sit in our front room asking questions and jotting down answers in his notebook. But my mum and dad couldn't let anyone come to our house without feeding them and giving them a cup of tea. So, inevitably, what was to have been a one-off enquiry about Jeanie and Brum became a nightly social. I loved his visits. He was so interesting and he had an engaging personality that kept me wanting to hear more. Without doubt he was bending the rules by coming to us but it suited him and it suited us too. Then there was the bonus of reading his articles in the paper. He even quoted my dad once or twice.

In 1962 the Queen visited the East End and, on her way to the Bryant and May factory in Bow, her car drove slowly past our house. I was at school at the time so I didn't see her, but my mum told me that Old Brum was waiting outside all morning for her to come by; smartly dressed and wearing his full set of medals. When, at last, the Queen's car approached, Brum marched to the edge of the kerb, straightened his back and gave her a stiff soldier's salute.

Brum died not long after that. His illness was protracted and Jeanie struggled. I was sixteen and his demise saddened me because I liked him so much. I went across to see him not long before he died. His breathing was poor when I was there and it was obvious that Jeanie was finding it hard to cope. My dad never left Charlie to a neglected death. He would go over to see him in the evening after work or in the morning when he came off night shift. Like I said about him when he lifted Nell Smith from the gutter: that was my dad, that was the man he was. And Old Brum is still there in my heart and still making me smile.

THE MEADS

Next door to Brum and Jeannie lived Mr and Mrs Mead with their two grown-up sons. They were a quiet, reserved family and, although their house was opposite ours, we didn't know them very well. The sons looked alike and maybe they were twins. They would often be seen together: coming home from work or setting out side-by-side on some errand or other. Mr and Mrs Mead were an unremarkable couple. They lived their lives privately as neighbours without fuss or annoyance to anyone, but one remarkable thing happened to this unremarkable family when, out out of the blue, one of the brothers brought home a wife. Neither of the sons had been seen with a woman before, even though they had spent their teenage years in the same house and were now in their thirties. More remarkable was the fact that the woman he married was French. How he found her is a mystery. The most likely explanation is that he had served in France during the war and met her while he was there. I can't imagine how else a local man would have found a French wife in 1950s Poplar.

Tongues wagged when the news was known and the couple became the talk of the street; when they walked out together, curtains twitched. I saw them a few times though not through twitching curtains. They struck me as a vulnerable pair: he attempting a manly protective presence and she slight, apologetic and shy. Was she from Paris? A Breton girl maybe? Had they met in Normandy when the British Second Army swept south from Arromanches? I will never know. I do not even know if the Mead brother was in the army at all, but what I do know is that his wife didn't stay long. How difficult it must have been for her to come from France to Poplar, from a country with different food and a different language, into a poor part of London to live in a small rundown house with a quiet working-class family. She left. "She's gone and he's trying to trace her," my mum told Aunt Rose. I wasn't very old and I couldn't understand why the Mead brother wanted to trace his wife. I just imagined him running after her with a huge piece of tracing paper.

THE MASSERS

Life wasn't easy for the Massers. Mr Masser had been profoundly deaf since he was a child and his deafness affected his speech. He also had a physical disability that made it difficult for him to walk and his left leg was supported by a metal calliper. But despite these setbacks, Mr Masser was cheerful and optimistic and never let his disabilities get the better of him. Mrs Masser was a lovely person. She had a quiet dignity and a reassuring presence. She was generous and helpful and the support she gave her husband enabled him to play a full part in life like any other working man.

The Massers had three children: Artie and Bessie who were a little older than Doreen, and Valerie who was my age. Artie was the kind of young man that boys like me could look up to. He was friendly, he always looked smart and he rode a motorbike. When he did his National Service, he would come home on leave wearing his army uniform and that was such a good look. Bessie was like a female version of Artie. She looked good too and she was friendly like him. Both were clever and Bessie had a good job. When Artie left the army, he lived at home for a while, but before long he was courting and married. Bessie followed suit and Valerie was left with her mum and dad.

Valerie was a chubby girl who wore her hair curled in ringlets and topped with a large bow. She had nice clothes and she was friendly. She was bought lots of comics and, every Sunday morning, Mrs Masser brought me over the ones that Valerie had read the week before. It made Sunday mornings the best part of the week for me and I spent blissful hours in the company of Desperate Dan, Minnie the Minx and Dennis the Menace. Comics were such a pleasure and there were so many to enjoy. Valerie's weekly 'stash' included *The Beano, The Dandy, Knockout, Radio Fun* and *The Eagle.*

The Massers were the first family in the street to have a television and on Mondays Mrs Masser would ask me and Johnny Purton over to watch cowboy adventures with Valerie. She would give me a cup of tea and a plate of biscuits and I would sit engrossed as the Lone Ranger, the Cisco Kid, Roy Rogers, Hopalong Cassidy, Tex Ritter and Tom Mix triumphed over their adversaries. In 1952, Uncle Henry took me to see Tex Ritter in his spectacular wild west show at the Harringay Arena. During a break, Tex came forward to meet the crowd and I saw him close up. He was chatty and friendly and he gave me a sheriff's badge with a picture of his face in the middle. To my amazement, Tex was wearing green mascara.

Valerie never played much with the children in the street but she and I got on well enough. Some of the others thought that she was stuck up but she wasn't. When she was chosen to be the Coronation Beauty Queen, there were accusations of favouritism but with decisions like that there will always be disappointment. As she grew older, she had a fairly troubled adolescence and changed from a shy withdrawn girl to a more problematic teenager. She seemed to disappear for a while but sometimes I saw her in a car with an older boyfriend. We barely acknowledged one another then, and we rarely spoke in our teens. But eventually she found herself again and grew to became a friendly, likeable young woman. Growing up isn't easy.

THE STOCKS

There were five Stocks: 'Old mother Stock,' her daughter Sarah, her son-in-law Arthur and their girls Mary and Pam. Arthur's family name was Cos, but Sarah was always known as 'Sarah Stock.' Old Mrs Stock was a short peppery woman with a stern-looking face and dark-framed glasses. She spent hours at the front door, smoking and looking up and down the street with her right arm raised against the door frame and her left hanging loose at her side. She was a plain woman. Her glasses accentuated the severity of her features and her hair was tightly packed into a hairnet so it never softened her jaw.

When Old Charlie Johnson gave up his little general store in Cobden Street, Sarah and Arthur took it over. People said it was a little goldmine and they were probably right. Charlie was cheerful, efficient and knew his customers well. We used to call him 'Old Singer' because he would often be humming a tune when you entered the shop. Uncle Charlie thought that his name actually was 'Singer' and called him by that name much to everyone's amusement. Sarah and Arthur didn't have Charlie Johnson's warmth and sometimes treated their customers dismissively; after Charlie left, visits to the shop became less light-hearted encounters. It wasn't just Sarah and Arthur's manner that made going to the shop a bit less pleasant, but the fact that they were both given to making loud burps. Mary Stock sometimes served in the shop too but, fortunately for the customers, she didn't suffer from the same belching affliction as her parents. Mary was about the same age as me. She had a plain, freckled face and dark hair that she wore in plaits. Her sister Pam was younger and more easy-going. I didn't play with Mary and Pam much but I liked the way they always joined in when we had stone fights. Mary could throw stones like the best of us and she was never scared.

Not long before Aunt Rose moved away, a strange phenomenon began that concerned us all and went on for weeks. One night I heard the sound of shattering glass in the street. Uncle Charlie heard it too. In the morning, the road was covered in glass fragments. With no obvious explanation, we put it down to vandalism but vandalism was unheard of in St Leonard's Road and there was no other noise either; no shouting, or calling or sound of fleeing footsteps.

Nothing happened for a few days until, what started as an isolated incident, became more frequent and the glass breaking occurred two or three times a week. No one witnessed these episodes because they took place in the night so the culprit was never seen. Most of the glass came from milk bottles but sometimes there were brown fragments from beer bottles too. That the wrongdoer was a tea drinker who liked beer may have been a reasonable deduction to make, but it wouldn't have narrowed the field much in the Poplar of those days.

As the glass-breaking continued the problem became more serious. Although neighbours were quick to sweep the road, it wasn't possible to clear the smaller flakes of glass that accumulated where children played and the glass was dangerous for motorists too. More to the point, it was a strange and unpleasant thing to experience, particularly for Aunt Rose because the glass usually landed outside her house. Suspicions were aroused. We concluded that it must be a neighbour who threw the bottles; but who? In the end it came down to two: Flo Woodford and Mrs Stock. My money was on Mrs Stock. She was more unpredictable than Flo and spent a lot of time peering out into the street. More to the point, the glass shattered opposite her house and, although glass landed opposite Flo's house too, Flo wasn't the kind of woman to throw bottles around. No, it had to be Mrs Stock. Nobody accused her, but after some measured comments directed at Sarah and Arthur, the bottle throwing stopped. Not long after that, Mrs Stock's mental deterioration accelerated.

THE WOODFORDS

Like several people in the street, Flo Woodford and her husband shared their house with their grown-up children. They had two daughters: Eileen and Joanie. Flo was a short, fat, barrel of a lady with a round face and a belly to match. She could be belligerent and it didn't do to cross her but she raised two lovely children in Eileen and Joan. Because of her tetchiness and her rotund form, she earned the nickname 'Belly a' pups.'

Mr Woodford was quieter and more placid than Flo and I fancy he may have been henpecked by her.

Eileen and Joan both married. Joanie and her husband moved upstairs in Flo's house after their wedding and lived there for several years. Joan was open, sociable and friendly and her husband was a nice chap too. I particularly liked the way he dressed: he wore checked shirts, blue jeans and styled his hair into an impressive quiff that flopped down onto his forehead. Doreen met one of Flo's granddaughters recently and she asked her what she remembered of her parents and their life in St Leonard's Road. I said to Doreen, "When you see Flo's granddaughter again, tell her that I think she had a very nice mum and dad."

THE CABLES

Next to Flo were the Cables: Mr and Mrs Cable and their three grown-up children: Evelyn, Kenny and Ernie. Evelyn was small, dark and attractive. She was a smart dresser and had a stylish 1950s look that she carried off well. The Cables were nice people but Evelyn was sometimes accused of being snooty. Perhaps this was because she was shy and didn't have much to say or maybe her name had something to do with it; Evelyn was an uncommon name in Poplar and sounded posh. People never got used to pronouncing it either and called her 'Ever-lean.' Saying it that way made it sound like she was perpetually slender. Evelyn had a boyfriend. He was small and nattily dressed, like a male version of Evelyn herself. Something about him struck us as funny. Maybe it was because he wore shoes with very thick spongy soles. They gave him extra height but looked just a bit ridiculous. They didn't go unnoticed by Uncle Charlie, either. "I think I'll get a pair of them brothel creepers like Ever-lean Cable's boyfriend's got," he said.

Mrs Cable was a nice lady; the kind that would help you out and expect nothing in return. Her husband was much the same. The brothers, Kenny and Ernie, were friendly too, a seemingly uncomplicated pair but these are views of a family seen from the outside. Not long ago, Doreen learned that Kenny Cable was alone and suffering from dementia. She tracked him down and found him living in squalid conditions surrounded by years of accumulated clutter. She intervened, got the house cleaned and Kenny was admitted into care. Because of Doreen, Kenny regained some dignity at the end of his life; her father's daughter if ever there was one.

THE WATTONS

Johnny Watton lived in an upstairs flat next door to the Cables. Fan, his mum, was Dolly Herring's sister and Johnny had Doll's swarthy complexion. Fan was friendly, energetic and always on the go. She and my mum were friends and she was one of the mums who 'went for a walk' on Pastor Thomas's ill-fated outing to Chalkwell. John, her husband, was a gentle man, small and inconspicuous but a good dad to Johnny. Like many Poplar people, Fan and John were not well-educated and struggled to express themselves particularly when dealing with authority. They were a plain-looking couple but Johnny had not inherited their looks and, when he was older, he grew to be tall and good-looking.

Fan and John both had jobs and when he was young, Johnny was looked after by his nan. As he grew older, she kept an eye on him but he was left to himself for much of the time. By the time I was twelve, Johnny Purton never came out with us anymore and I spent my time with Billy McAvennie or Johnny Watton. My relationships with them were different: Johnny and I set off towards adulthood together but Billy and I stayed boys. My life was becoming more complex by then; the innocence of my boyhood friendships had become complicated by fractures in our lives. Billy and the others left Susan Lawrence for a new school in Wyvis Street and Johnny Purton had gradually withdrawn to the pigeon shed. When we all transferred to secondary schools, he and Billy went to Hay Currie around the corner in Bright Street while Johnny Watton and I went further afield: Johnny to Bow Boys' and me to the Roan in Blackheath. And although the boys in the street were still important to me, I now had friends at Susan Lawrence and Roan was about to give me more.

Billy Mac and I did some good things together but, although we kept on good terms, our friendship gradually petered out. Johnny Watton and I stayed mates for longer because we had teenage things in common. Music and football were the main ones. I was fourteen when I bought my first record. It was *Til I Kissed You* by the Everly brothers. I played it constantly and never tired of it. I took it to Johnny's one afternoon and played it to him. Then he played me *It Doesn't Matter Anymore* by Buddy Holly. At the end of the afternoon, I offered to swap and I came away with my first Buddy Holly record.

My friendship with Johnny endured longer because we were growing up together and nature was establishing our new identities. We rejected the music of our parents for music of our own, we talked about clothes and shoes, and we got good haircuts. We started playing cards and then played cards for money. We loved football and played it a lot; Johnny was an excellent footballer and played for East London. We went to West Ham together. We listened to records in Johnny's flat and we shared a few secrets.

When I was fourteen, I became aware of a girl who passed my door almost every day. She was so lovely that I couldn't resist looking at her. When I saw her coming, I knew that I shouldn't stare but, however hard I tried, I just had to look at her. Nothing passed between us and, like *The Girl from Ipanema,* she 'looked straight ahead, not at me.' I don't think she even knew I was there. But I ached for her and wished I could know her and be with her. The power of my feelings for her was something I had never experienced before; they hurt me and diminished me in my own eyes. And that was the pain of adolescence: the unrequited lust, the frequency of desire, the misery of spots on the chin, the embarrassment of unwanted erections, the romantic fantasies and the constant self-doubt. I knew that Johnny experienced all of these things too. He felt them as implicitly as he felt the joy of rock music or the elation when a goal went in at their end at Upton Park. We never talked about our feelings very much but we didn't ignore them either and knowing that Johnny felt as I did, helped me to deal with it all.

Johnny and I never fell out and we never ceased being friends but in time we just drifted apart. One summer's evening in 1964, he came by my door. I hadn't seen much of him over the past few years but we were still easy with one another. He'd grown taller and broader and it suited him. He told me that he was working as a tiler. "I get seventeen pounds a week laying floors, more with overtime," he told me. Seventeen pounds was a very good wage. In a week, Johnny was getting nearly half my student grant for a whole term. "It's good money but your knees go," he said. "I wear pads on me knees and they still hurt." "Can you get me a job?" I asked. "You interested?" he asked. "I think so," I replied. "I could speak up for you if you like," he said. We chatted some more. He had got himself a girlfriend in Wales and went there to see her whenever he could. He hadn't spoken to any of the boys we used to know and he wasn't playing football anymore. "My knees are going," he said. He was just eighteen and his knees were going.

THE REST OF THE STREET

There were two more houses on Johnny's side but I don't know much about the people who lived in them. The picture in my mind is of well-kept places, with big windows draped in net curtains. A lady called Mrs Besant lived next door to the Wattons and I used to think that she was a relative of Annie Besant, the campaigner who led the match workers' strike at Bryant and May in 1888. The Bryant and May factory was not far away in Bow and I made a connection that wasn't there. From what I've read about Annie it seems very unlikely that she would ever have had a relative in working-class Poplar.

I was not quite five when the Korean War began in 1950, so I do not remember much about the suicide of Mrs Lay in the end house other than that it was spoken of in hushed terms. She was found hanging by the neck from her staircase bannisters, one of the war's earliest victims. It seems that she could not face the prospect of living through another war having experienced the horrors of the Blitz, so she took her life.

BILLY MAC

Billy McAvennie was a bright-eyed, apple-cheeked boy with thick black hair and a look of the Artful Dodger about him. He spoke cockney better than any of us and he swore quite a lot. Billy was the only boy in his family and the youngest of five, so perhaps the McAvennies had kept trying until they got a son. Billy's sisters: Nellie, Rosie, Annie and Joycie, all spoke strong cockney like Bill. Although they were all different from one another, there was something uniquely 'McAvennie' about them all. Mrs Mac was small and busy; a nice little lady who it would be hard not to like. She was even more cockney than Billy and his sisters if that was possible.

Mr McAvennie was in charge of everything, including his wife. He was short and stocky with Brylcreemed hair like the cricketer Denis Compton. He was a messenger in the City of London. Banks and other companies employed men to take documents from one building to another in those days, because it was cheaper and quicker than posting them. Messenger work was clean but it was heavy on the feet and didn't pay much. Like Mr Purton, Mr Mac was often in the pub so there couldn't have been much money left over to spend on the family. He was a tough little character too and could be harsh on his wife and children, but the home ran well and they were a good family.

The McAvennies lived in Radford House; a small block of flats on the corner of St Leonard's Road and Chadbourne Street. It was built in 1920 by Poplar Borough Council to provide good accommodation on a human scale. There were three floors and nine flats. The building was enclosed by walls with huge iron gates that opened from the street into a forecourt. It was nice being at Billy's on days when we had the flat to ourselves. It was a quiet, tidy place. The living room had two large windows that looked onto St Leonard's Road so it was never dark. On Saturday afternoons Billy and I would sit at the big square table playing cards or building model aeroplanes. The McAvennies had a dog called Flossie and we would play with her on the floor or take her out for walks. Flossie was a black Labrador and, true to her breed, she was soft, perpetually hungry and an eternal pup. In these respects, Flossie and Billy were quite similar.

Radford House was a great place to play. The stone staircases and set-back porches were perfect for playing 'hide and seek' and cowboys. We played cricket in the forecourt too; the walls were our fielders and stopped the ball from running away. The best thing about Radford House was that we could get onto the roof and, although we were often told off for being there, it was a terrific place to play. When he was twelve, Billy got an air rifle and we would lie on our stomachs like soldiers and fire lead pellets at the dustbins. He also got a bike;

a Raleigh Roadster with straight handlebars and *Sturmey Archer* gears. I had a bike already. My dad had bought me a Triumph Palm Beach. He said it was for being successful in the Eleven-plus exam but I think he would have got me one anyway. I loved my bike. It gave me independence and it got me fit. Not long after I had it, I stopped being a chubby little boy and started feeling better about myself.

I never went very far on my bike although sometimes, Johnny Watton and I would cycle to the ponds at Whipps Cross. We had great sport there scrambling over the gravelly hills and doing fast braking skids. As my thirteenth birthday approached, I asked Billy if he would like to do a proper bike ride with me; go off into Kent or something like that. Billy was biddable and he never thought things through, so he agreed straight away. On the morning of the twentieth of August 1958, my thirteenth birthday, we set out together with the intention of getting as far into Kent as possible. In my mind Kent was 'the country' and I thought it would be nice to spend my birthday in the country. However, it took miles of urban roads and dual carriageways before the first field could be reached. The worst roads were the first ones: the manic traffic-laden gauntlet of Brunswick Road and the narrow dangerous fume-filled tube of the Blackwall Tunnel.

In Greenwich, we pushed up Vanbrugh Hill, crossed Blackheath and cycled on though Lee Green. We kept pedalling and it rained; it rained and rained. So, we put on our cycle capes and sang to keep our spirits up, Lonnie Donegan's Grand *Coulee Dam* and other hits of the time. The rain trickled through our capes and down our backs. Still, we kept pedalling until, gradually, the A20 started to look greener and we were in the country. The rain stopped and at Swanley we sat down to eat the last of our sandwiches. It was mid-afternoon by now. "I think we should go home, Bill," I said. In my heart I wanted to go on but, in my head, I knew it wasn't a good idea. Billy didn't agree or disagree, he just said "all right." He would have said "all right" if I had suggested we kept on pedalling to Dover.

We did well on the way back until we got to a big junction near Sidcup. It was a dangerous place to cross on a bike. For much of the day I had cycled behind Billy so that I could keep an eye on him, but I paid the price for that when his nervousness at the junction caused him to brake sharply. I couldn't stop. My front wheel tipped lightly against his back one and knocked him off balance. He took a heavy tumble, cut his knee badly and started to cry. He lay in the road next to his bike with cars passing close by. It was a dreadful situation and I knew that the first thing I had do was to get us out of the road and onto the pavement.

Billy sat on the kerb still crying and I looked at his knee. It was badly cut and bleeding. I took out my handkerchief: "Go on Bill, spit on that," I said. Billy complied. "More spit, Bill, we need to get it wet." I dabbed the wound and wiped away the grit, then tied the handkerchief around his knee like a bandage. Inside I was desperate. We were miles from home and needing help. Then I saw that Billy's bike was damaged. The front light had broken and the back wheel had buckled. When he saw the damage, he started crying again "Me dad's genna kill me when he sees it," he sobbed. "And 'ow am I genna ride it?" "I'll ride it for yer Bill and you can ride mine," I said and Billy stopped his sobs.

The best thing about this bad situation was that I knew where we were. I had visited some woods nearby with a few of my classmates from Roan in the Easter holidays. We had called for Keith Valentine at his house in Wynford Way that day and the area was familiar. "We'll be all right, Bill," I said "Get on my bike and I'll show yer where to go." I pushed off on Billy's wobbly bike. It was tricky to ride and the front brake wasn't working properly. I found Keith's house quite easily, knocked on the door and told his mum our story. She patched Billy up and made us a cup of tea. I was grateful of her kindness and I shall never forget the sense of relief I felt when she took the problem from off my shoulders.

Billy's bike was hard to ride but the pedals still turned and it was possible to make progress. The worst thing was that the brakes had been damaged and it was only the rear one that worked properly. We still had some way to go and some difficult roads to tackle. At Blackheath we passed my school and started down the steep, steep incline of Vanbrugh Hill. "Don't let it run away with yer, Bill, keep breaking gently," I said as we approached the great incline by the nurses' home. I have cycled down Vanbrugh Hill a few times and it is a tricky thing to do. The one-in-four incline slackens a little and then the hill sweeps sharply left to run straight down to an abrupt halt by the traffic lights in Greenwich High Road. Billy got down safely and so did I, though my left hand was pained from constantly having to pull the lever for the back brake. We got through the Blackwall Tunnel all right too and I left Billy to face whatever fate awaited him in Radford House.

FAITH OF OUR FATHERS

When the Mileses moved out from next door, Albert and Aileen Robinson moved in downstairs and Rory and Betty Clery took the flat above. After the stilted conservativism of the Mileses, the two couples were a breath of fresh air. Aileen was small and mousey with a quiet voice and broad Manchester accent. She had a dry humour that came over well when Rob her husband chose not to intervene. Rob was rattish, beady-eyed and shifty; a small, and almost-likeable rogue. That he was a rogue was proved beyond doubt over time. He was likeable too, but his 'likeableness' was often absent. Rory and Bet were a handsome pair; open, friendly and full of Irish charm. They were Dubliners, newly-married and looking for work in England.

My parents were welcoming to the newcomers and helped them to settle in. Rory and Bet were the more friendly pair and took to us from the start. Bet got a job in the office at the McDougall flour company on the Isle of Dogs and Rory found work as a fitter at the gasworks in Bow Common Lane. Before long they began to spend time with us. Betty would call in for a cigarette and a cup of tea every night after work and Rory often came too. Sometimes they stayed until seven o'clock or later. Rory got on well with my dad; he respected him and took his advice. The two had things in common. They were both Catholics, though dad never went to church. They had both been at sea; Rory was an engineer on merchant ships and dad an Able Seaman in the Royal Navy. Both worked in local gasworks and could talk shop together about things like 'retort house blow-outs' and 'pressure losses.'

Rory and Bet were good to me. Rod called me 'Buster' and I liked that. On Christmas night that first year, they invited us up for supper and Bet gave me a lovely picture book called *Great Events of the Royal Year 1953*. It was full of photographs of British achievements: Roger Bannister collapsing under the strain of running a mile in under four minutes, a page of jet planes with the caption 'Britain leads in the air,' pictures of 'Britain conquering Everest' and lots of shots of the Queen's coronation.

As time went by, Bet became loose-tongued about office life at McDougalls and told stories about escapades with managers in the broom cupboard. She never included herself in the stories and my mum and dad passed them off as gossipy fun, but the reality was that Bet was having an affair with her boss. Her secret came out one day when she took the day off to go to the *Ideal Homes* Exhibition in Earls Court. She came home about eight that night with an exhibition catalogue as evidence to show that she had been there. Even as a child I knew this didn't seem right because when people went to the Ideal Homes Exhibition, they brought back lots of leaflets, booklets and samples. The truth came out. Rod told her to leave. She pleaded for a reconciliation and a meeting was arranged with the lover to sort things out. Rod asked my dad if he would take part too, so he did.

On the night the meeting took place, my mum and I looked though the landing window into Rod's flat to see what was going on. We could see the lover quite clearly. With his combed-back wavy hair and David Niven moustache, he looked every bit the 1950s cad. With casual arrogance he said to Rod, "It's just one of those things, Old Boy. You read about it every day in the papers." Mum and I watched on until the room emptied. Then they were all downstairs in our passage. Voices were raised, the street door slammed and Bet was gone. It was a nasty business. Bet got in touch with my dad to see if he could persuade Rod to take her back but that was never going to happen. Then Rod received a series of anonymous postcards, children's picture cards with nothing written on them. They must have been from Bet and if they were, it was a silly, vindictive thing to do. For a while she lived at the Angerstein Hotel in Greenwich and then she disappeared.

Rod was shattered by what had happened and leaned heavily on us for support. My mum and dad were so good to him, especially my mum who cooked his meals and did his washing. He spent hours in our house; he came home to eat at lunchtimes and ate with us in the evenings too. When we'd had our tea, he would stay on talking about world events and the evils of freemasonry and communism. The breakup of his marriage had shattered him and he turned to his Catholic faith to help him through. He went to mass, gave his confession and made a small shrine for prayer in his bedroom.

Rod's presence began to have a big influence on our lives and, particularly on my dad, because it rekindled his Catholic faith and he started going to church. The parish church of *St Mary and St Joseph* in Poplar was bombed in 1940 and a new church was built in Canton Street to replace it. I could see it going up from my classroom window at school. It struck me then as a heavy, lumpen building and nothing like a church ought to look. Over seventy-five years later, I still can't decide whether I like it or not, but it has been given grade two listed status so it must have some merit. Building the new church was expensive and members of the clergy were sent into the parish to raise funds to help pay for it. My dad's name was on the parish list and priests came every month to ask him for half a crown to buy a brick.

Decades of Irish emigration brought many Roman Catholics to our part of London and Catholicism proclaimed itself with schools, street processions and new churches. The processions were huge. The Poplar one started in Cotton Street, followed along East India Dock Road as far as Upper North Street, turned right and came to an end outside the church. It was led by Irish pipers in green woollen jackets and snuff-coloured kilts, swaying along as they wailed out hymns like *Faith of Our Fathers* and *Hail Queen of Heaven*. Following them came a succession of parishioners and clergy: the Children of Mary in white and pale blue, the Sacred Heart 'abstainers', the Catholic mothers, boy scouts, girl guides, a second pipe band, men in groups of four carrying statues of the saints on their shoulders, then more ribboned banners before a group of incense-swinging clergy brought up the rear. The processions were popular and attracted good crowds. When a procession was over there would be mass in the church followed by the blessing of street altars when priests went from door to door flicking holy water over the highly-decorated altars that Catholic families had erected outside their homes. I loved it all. How much better this was from the dull old Church of England who never came out to play.

Inevitably, I was asked by my dad to start going to mass. I don't think I had much choice and I agreed. So, by the age of twelve, my path to heaven had seen me go from non-conformist Evangelist to Roman Catholic via High Anglican. Attending Catholic mass was just as tedious as attending The Five Ways and St Michaels, but I'm glad I went because it allowed me to witness the Christian divide at first-hand. The English establishment had still not got over the Reformation when I was young and suspicion of Catholicism was widespread. There was a fair degree of prejudice too, but there is nothing better than inside knowledge for exposing prejudice and I think that I was fortunate to have known both sides.

At St Mary and St Joseph's I was even more of a spectator than I had been at St Michael's. I wasn't baptised a Catholic and hadn't been confirmed, so at best I could only be a passive observer. I hadn't been to Catechism class either, so I had no idea what was really going on. Why did the Catholics have a Missal and not a Bible? I wondered. Why was everything in Latin? How come they had statues to saints everywhere when Jesus was supposed to be in charge? Why did the priest include 'Prayers for the Conversion of England' in his prayer list? Why did they all love the Pope so much? Why did they worship Mary like she was God?

I timed my arrival at church carefully so that I could slip in just before the mass started, sit at the back and get away quickly when it was over. I never participated in the service but was polite enough to stand and sit when everyone else did. I liked some of the hymns and learned the sequence of the mass from the first 'Dominus vobiscum' to the end when the priest sent us off with 'Benedictat vos omnipotens Deus, Pater, et Filius et Spiritus Sanctus. Amen.' I would watch the stream of people making their way to the altar for Holy Communion and wonder how they could believe that they were actually swallowing God's body and blood. I got to know the faces: the tall pious Mr Mudge with his head permanently bowed, Ann the devout teenager who we later called 'The Singing Nun,' Mary Driscoll who everyone fancied, various members of the O'Mahoney family from Three Colt Street in Limehouse, Denis Barnes and his mum from Cobden Street round the corner to us and more. I got to know the priests too and liked them all: Canon Wright (dignified and saintly), Father Haines (dignified and dull) and Father Ellis (rakish and a bit 'London cool.') What I particularly liked about the Catholic clergy was their apparent classlessness. It was never easy to tell what social class a priest came from; they were so unlike the Church of England clergy who were always posh.

Being the passive observer didn't bother me that much when I started attending mass, but later, my self-consciousness became acute and I wondered what everyone made of me; the boy at the back who never took part. In reality I don't suppose it mattered to anyone, not even the priests; when Canon Wright saw me coming or going, he would greet me politely and never ask questions. The congregation was large and there were three masses on Sunday but the priests knew all of the parishioners so they must have known me.

I got more involved with the church when my dad became a collector for the football fundraising scheme. Every week, people paid for numbers that corresponded to football teams and, depending on the football results, they could win money prizes. On Sunday mornings after the eleven o'clock mass, the winnings were laid out on tables in the parish hall for collection. Each collector had a round and when my dad was at work,

I would do the round for him. Getting winners was good, because the recipients gave the collector a proportion of their winnings 'for a drink' and sometimes the collector was me. Because of this, I became better known in the parish. People were nice to me and, as no one ever seemed to challenge my passive observer status, I began to feel more relaxed about going to church.

But, when I was younger, there was another side to Catholicism. Rod's constant promotion of its cause, the zeal of his faith and all the rigmarole that went with it influenced my young mind and, for a while, I became ensnared by the church and its trappings. I bought a small statue of one of the saints and kept it in my bedroom. Rod gave me a set of Rosary beads and I tried saying the Rosary. Reciting the Rosary is a fundamental part of Catholicism. It is intended to focus the mind through prayer on the mysteries of Christianity and the sequence of prayer is guided by beads. I attempted my recital with the best of intentions but I couldn't find anything in it; it just seemed mechanical and repetitive to me. It had been the same a few years before when, under the influence of Five Ways missionaries, I tried to study the Bible. "The answers are there if you study the scriptures," I was told, so I chose a chapter from the Old Testament and read it several times in search of meaning but nothing came back. I do not doubt the value of prayer for some people or the solace that they find in the Bible, but that is their business and it is not for me.

On some Sundays Rod took me to mass at Westminster Cathedral. I went along compliantly without knowing if I wanted to go or not. I must have attended mass there three or four times when I was twelve and thirteen. Westminster

Cathedral is vast; a huge building in the Byzantine style set back on a piazza near to Victoria station. It was unfinished then and is unfinished now, with its interior an unlikely mix of dirty unadorned brick and colourful mosaics. It is a dark and interesting place and one that I have come to appreciate more over the years not least for the perfection Eric Gill's *Stations of the Cross*. The fourteen bas-relief carvings depicting the sufferings of Christ are perfectly designed and artfully executed each within the confines of a square. That Gill indulged in the most gross acts of depravity during his lifetime throws up the moral dilemma of separating artists' lives from their work but, for me, nothing can detract from the magnificence of Gill's *Stations.* Westminster Cathedral played a significant part in persuading me of the superiority of Catholicism; but perhaps the first function of a Cathedral is to impress.

When I was young, most people believed in the existence of God and I believed that too and all that went with it. I believed that Christians were good people and that they cared for others and looked after the poor. I believed that God was everywhere, and that he could see everything I did. When I committed my own little sins, I felt guilty because I thought that he was watching me. People talked of 'the fear of God' and God's fear was a parental threat; "I'll put the fear of God up you if you do that again." I stopped believing in God when I was fourteen because supernatural belief seemed so unlikely to me. By then I had concluded that, although some Christians were good, caring people, others were cruel and uncaring; history gave plenty of examples of that. It didn't take much for me to link good and bad Christians with good and bad people. Christians were considerate or vindictive, generous or grudging. All people are like that and Christians are just people. Devoid of any belief, I had no reason to attend church anymore other than to please my father and I had no wish to upset him or to fall out with him.

What the church in Canton Street offered to its faithful believers was a sense of togetherness; a confederacy of mutually-supportive people who had something in common. That was, without doubt, a good thing. The church provided social activities and they were popular. Every Sunday night there was a social club in the parish hall and it was well-attended. My mum and dad went with their friends and Aunt Rose, Uncle Charlie and Uncle Henry were regulars too. The few times I went, it struck me how like an East End wedding it was with beer, music and inter-generational mixing. On some nights Mr O'Mahony played his bagpipes to much cheering and applause and private asides of "Oh, no, not old Jim on them bagpipes again." There was Irish dancing too and some people did 'turns.' The priests came along and were sometimes persuaded to join in the dancing, though Canon Wright politely declined any invitation to take to the floor. The priests were popular and seemed at ease in the jolly and sometimes boozy company of their parishioners. Sister Pat, a remarkable nun who gave sixty years of her life to the people of Poplar, also turned up occasionally too.

Sister Pat was a legend in Poplar and her influence went beyond the Catholic community. She arrived as a young nun in 1935 and stayed until she died. Her mission was to be like Robin Hood, taking from the rich to give to the poor except that nobody was rich and there were plenty of poor. Sister Pat could turn up anywhere and never shied away from going where she might not be welcome. She had charm, humility and outrageous confidence. She disarmed tough stallholders with her soft Irish voice, requiring rather than requesting of them. "I need carrots Alfie, and cabbages too and flowers," *"SISTER!!"* "Alfie, I wouldn't ask if I didn't need." "Go on then…'ow many d'ya wont?" She was no modern nun; she wore a long old-fashioned habit trimmed with white and the most enormous winged headdress. Her face was soft and Irish with eyes that could narrow into something expressive of a smile. She had a wonderful way of persuading. She never showed irritation and never gave up on insistence. I never knew anyone with such a beautiful authority.

THE CONNOLLYS

Hold on to your hat...this could be a bumpy ride!

My great, great, grandfather Thady (Timothy) Connolly was born in 1828 in Baltimore, a village on the south-western tip of Ireland. The West of Ireland was poor and agricultural and like many Irish people, Thady's family would have existed on a diet of potatoes. In 1845 the potato crop became diseased, the food rotted in the earth and people starved. Over a million died of starvation and well over a million left Ireland in order to survive. Thady was one of them and it is because of the potato famine that the Connollys came to East London.

My father was one of seven brothers and four sisters. Together with my grandparents, there were thirteen living in their small over-crowded terraced house. The boys slept head-to-toe in cramped conditions and the girls shared a room between the four of them. My grandfather was the sole wage-earner and there was very little money. For a while my grandmother scrubbed the decks of ships in the East India Docks but that would not have brought in much.

The Connolly boys were tough and unruly. They were often flogged and beaten and my grandfather controlled them with a sharp tongue and a leather belt. On Sundays, my great-grandfather, Patrick Connolly, would come back from mass with a list of the boys he hadn't seen there. He wore a suit to church with a 'dicky' front and false cuffs to give the impression of a shirt. During mass he would write the names of absentees on his left cuff and hand it to my grandad when he got back. Those whose names were on the list were given a belting.

The Connollys were 'piss takers,' they enjoyed winding each other up. They were boisterous and argumentative; it only took two in a room to set things off. There were rows and fights but they had a clannish loyalty too and would take on the world together if one of them was threatened by an outsider. Poverty and toughness were the hallmarks of my dad's childhood and they are both evident in a story he told me about being sent to buy bread. He had no shoes of his own so he searched the house for a pair to wear, but there were none. "Go in mine," his mother told him so, rather than go barefoot, he went to buy bread in his mother's shoes. When a group of boys saw him wearing them, they ridiculed him, so he chased them, caught one, took a shoe and hit him hard on the head with it. The tough, harsh childhood they experienced may explain the weaknesses that some of his brothers displayed in later life. I have described the Connollys as piss takers. It is not a pleasant term, but it is the right one to use because alternatives like 'leg pullers' or 'mickey takers' do not express adequately the victimisation and cruelty that sometimes accompanied their banter.

GRANDMA CONNOLLY

Elizabeth Connolly, my grandma, was sixteen when she had her first child. She married my grandad when she was pregnant and spent the next thirty years bearing children and bringing them up. She was short with dark button eyes, a distinctive nose and the thick black hair of a younger woman. Years of childbearing, poverty and obedience to her husband took their toll eventually and by the time she was in her sixties, she had begun to lose her mind.

To the family she was 'The old lady.' East End mothers were often referred to that way in those days; my grandad was always 'The old man.' Although it was he who got most of the attention, Grandma Connolly was not neglected by her family. My aunts styled her hair and sometimes gave her clothes. In family photographs she can be seen in the centre of the group and her children never left her short of money.

My grandad never came to our house but Grandma Connolly often did, although she never stayed for long, fifteen minutes maybe and then my dad would give her a couple of shillings for a drink and she would be on her way. I felt uncomfortable when she came because I didn't know her very well and she never had much to say to me. Once when she came, my dad killed a chicken for her. He took it from the shed, wrung its neck and put it in a bag. "Murderer!" I shouted from my bedroom window when I saw what he had done. I was eight.

As she became increasingly bewildered, Grandma Connolly would forget that she had visited already and come back the same day. "Is Joe in?" she'd ask. If he was there, my dad would be patient with her and walk her back home. If he wasn't, my mum would have to deal with her and this could be difficult because her behaviour was sometimes challenging. To avoid difficult encounters, we took to looking out of the front window when we heard a knock and, if it was her, we sometimes pretended not to be in. One day things got so difficult that my mum sent me into Nanny Powell for help. "Go home, Liz, he's at work," she said. "I'll walk you to the corner." Grandma Connolly's condition deteriorated so much that, eventually, she was admitted to a psychiatric hospital. I felt sad for her because the hospital was miles away at Epsom in Surrey and she was so far from her family. But she wasn't neglected; the family took turns to visit her and she was rarely alone on visiting days. After some months her condition improved and she was allowed to come home but her return to normality didn't last long; she suffered a relapse and never recovered.

Grandma Connolly died in May 1954; she was in her mid-sixties. I can remember being at Aunt Nell's on the day of the funeral. "Do you want to see your grandma?" someone asked. I did, out of curiosity as much as respect. I gazed at her looking up from the coffin, fascinated by the reality of her face; that she looked so much like herself but was no longer alive. I do not remember the funeral; I probably didn't go, but I can recall the meal after it. When Aunt Nell came in with a big silver teapot, Uncle Will shouted, "Look out. Here comes Tom Finney with the FA cup!"

GRANDAD CONNOLLY

My grandfather, William Connolly, fathered eleven children and had twenty-four grandchildren. He served in the army in the First World War and was wounded in the leg by rifle fire. He was in his thirties then, married and a father of six. For much of his life he worked at Lusty's Lloyd Loom factory in Bromley-by-Bow and, like other men who'd worked there, he'd lost the tops of some of his fingers by coming too close to the electric saw. He was a big man, or at least he seemed so to me, and he spoke in a deep voice; not with the broad cockney of other Poplar men, but in a refined, clipped tone that seemed to emphasise his authority. He was known and respected in Poplar and respected and feared by his family. He was always there when I was a child, but not close; someone important but in the background. When I was fifteen, I decided to get to know him and I am glad that I did.

Grandad Connolly lived in Spey Street just a short walk away from us. I was wary of him on my first few visits but, as I got to know him, I became more relaxed around him and it was clear from the start that he was on my side. I was, after all, a Connolly and in the ways of the East End, family was everything and family came first. As a Connolly I could do no wrong in his eyes. And then, of course, I was a grandson and not his child. He had ruled his family with a rod of iron and his seven sons had felt the brunt of his harshness but, his work done, he had nothing to prove and could show his grandchildren a better side.

When I saw him, I usually had him to myself and my early visits would often start the same way. "Hello, Grandfather." "Hello. You're Joe's boy, aren't you?" "Yes, Grandfather." "Ow's your mother?" "She's very well, thank you, Grandfather." "And your father?" "He's well too." And then we would talk. He was in his eighties by then and not very mobile but he still cut an imposing figure. He was hefty, full in the face and wore round-rimmed glasses that added to his character. He was clean-shaven and had the skin of a child. I picture him in a white collarless shirt and black waistcoat. And around his generous waist, his trousers were bound with a wide leather belt that fastened with a silver buckle; I sometimes wondered if that belt was the one he had used to beat his sons with. I wish I could remember the things he told me, but on the whole, I think they were not too significant or profound. We talked about sport and particularly about boxing. "Did you see the amateurs the other night? That heavyweight had him down easily, didn't he? Did your father see it?"

He made my Christmas once when I visited on Christmas morning. Several of my relations were there. I was fifteen. "Give him a drink," he told Aunt Nell in the assertive tone he used when addressing one of his children. "Want a lemonade, Joe Boy?" asked Aunt Nell. "Lemonade? Give him a rum and pep," he ordered, "Do you want a rum and pep, Joe Boy?" "Yes please, grandfather." I had never tasted rum before but the fact that he had acknowledged that I was old enough to drink it made me feel good.

He taught me to play cribbage and his mental agility impressed me as he computed the complex numerical possibilities that the game threw up. We would use matchsticks to mark our progress along the small rectangular board that he kept for the game. Learning from him and playing cards with him put me at once with a teacher and a kind of friend.

One story my grandfather told me has stayed in my mind. He was talking about his service in the army and recounted an incident when he was 'mopping up' after a battle in France. He was in a group of three. They were crossing the battlefield and his comrades decided that they should take it in turns to kill any wounded German they came across. His comrades had killed one each and now it was his turn. They found a young soldier in a shell crater, shivering and afraid. "I couldn't kill him, he was someone's son," he said. I was impressed with him for saying that; glad that because of my grandfather, one family had been spared the misery of losing a father or son.

UNCLE WILL

Uncle Will was the oldest of the brothers and named William after his father. He was hefty, loud and outrageous. In a family of piss takers, he was piss-taker-in-chief, but he could be funny too and good to be around when you weren't the target of his ridicule. He lived in Hoddesdon with his wife, Kitty Meacher, and Butch their big boxer dog. Kitty was small, plain and quietly spoken and she put up with a lot from Will. He made fun of her in company and she wasn't always able to find an adequate response. But despite her shyness, Kitty had things going for her too. Sometimes she did find a way to counter Will's arrogance and when she found the right words they would be delivered in a dry deadpan way that made him look foolish. It was to her advantage too that the Connollys liked her and tended to be on her side. Despite his arrogance towards her, Will knew that Kitty was the best thing that had ever happened to him and they seemed to have a good life.

Uncle Will was a soldier during the War; a sergeant, I think. If he was a sergeant, he would have been a good one because he had all the qualities needed for the job. He was tough and funny and always came out on top in a battle of words. I think he took part in the 1944 Normandy landings because my mum told me that she was in *The St Leonard's* one night when Will came in. He was in uniform and had come up from Kent on a twenty-four-hour pass. "I can't say much, but you wouldn't believe all the stuff they've got going on down there," he confided.

Will and Kitty lived in St Cuthbert's Road, Hoddesdon. It was a comfortable place; 'lived-in' but not shabby. Will had made a pond in the garden and stocked it with fish that just about survived Butch's occasional leaps into the water. I liked going to Will's not least because Kitty was a good cook and knew how to 'put on a spread.' With no children and both having jobs, Will and Kitty were better off than most of the Connollys and in 1954 they bought a new car. It was a grey Austin A40 and fresh from the factory. I had never been in a new car before; if people like us had a car at all, it would be black, small and at least twenty years old.

When we were on holiday near Whitstable, Will and Kitty drove down to visit us in their new Austin and I had the chance to look it over. It was lovely; something to be desired with its rounded lines and smart interior of cream upholstery. That evening we went to Tankerton for a fish supper, six of us packed into the four-seater. "We're doin' sixty," said Will as we sped along the road towards Whitstable. Sixty was real speed. George Mitchell who had brought us down from Poplar in his Vauxhall had managed forty-seven on a downhill section of the A20 and that was as fast as we got. For the drive back from Tankerton Will sat me on his lap: "Go on, you steer, I'll do the pedals," he said.

Will worked as a bus driver and I imagine life must have been difficult for his passengers, particularly those on the top deck when he took a bend at speed. He got his brother Peter a job as a bus driver too. After a year or so, they became coach drivers for the same company. Peter was the second youngest of my father's brothers and I liked him. He was quite unlike Will: quiet, considerate, unfunny and better-looking. When I was eight, he offered to take me and my mum on a day out to Clacton in his coach; no money changed hands just a nod and a Connolly wink. He gave us seats at the front just across the aisle from him and it felt special having my uncle as the driver.

It was sunny when we got to Clacton, the perfect day for being by the sea. Peter parked in the coach park and saw the passengers off. "Back here at four o'clock," he repeated as they each tackled the three steps down onto the ground. When the last of them got off, a large maroon-coloured coach pulled alongside us. Peter looked across to see if he could recognise the driver. "Bilmey, it's Will," he said, and it was. Uncle Will in a coach driver's coat and badge, grinning and waving at us as his passengers got off. "Come on, come over 'ere and 'ave a look at this one, it's better than his," he called, inviting me onto his coach. To have two uncles driving coaches and two coaches to myself felt really good. "Fancy a drink?" Will said to Peter as they stood chatting together between the two charabancs. "No, I'm going to get me 'ed down for a bit," Peter replied. "What time yer going back?" asked Will. "Early, four o'clock," Peter replied. "I might see yer later on but if not, I'll see you then," said Will.

At four the passengers were filing back on. Will was standing by the door of our coach chatting to Peter. He moved to go and then turned back. "Tell yer what, I'll race yer," said Will. "Fancy a race?" In more rationally-minded families such an invitation would have been instantly rejected. In fact, in more rationally-minded families, the question would never have been asked in the first place. "All right then," said Peter without hesitation. Then Will drove off with a wave of his hand and Peter followed, cautiously at first because the race wouldn't begin until we were on the arterial road. When it did get going it was thrilling. I was on Peter's side and wanted him to win. Peter was keeping up well, always seeking out the merest chink of overtaking space. Will kept out in front and closed Peter down so that he couldn't get by. Then, on a section of dual-carriageway, Peter got his opportunity. Going flat out, he edged past Uncle Will with me waving at him and Will pulling faces at me as we passed. We were the winners.

AUNT NAN

I never knew Aunt Nan very well though I met her a few times and I certainly knew about her. Nan was short for Mary Ann, a name given to Connolly women over several generations. My grandfather's sister was Mary Ann and her mother was Mary Ann too. Nan lived in Hoddesdon not far from Will. I don't know how Hoddesdon came to be so popular with the Connollys but Peter lived there too. Nan, the second of dad's siblings, was a formidable woman with a strong personality and an impressive physical presence. She was 'buxom' and attractive with a thick mane of dark hair backcombed into a stack that swept away from the forehead in a style that the

Connolly women all seemed to favour. Nan and her husband Charlie Bradford had five children the first of which was older than Danny, Grandma Connolly's youngest child, so Babs, my eldest cousin, had a baby uncle.

When Charlie Bradford died, Nan acquired an admirer; Edzie, a Polish ex-serviceman. Admirer? Lover? In 1954, if a widowed lady were to have had either so soon after her husband's death, it would have been quite scandalous and questions would have been asked about how well the two had known each other before the husband died. The scandal broke in June 1954 when Nan started to receive bullets in letters through the post. Grandma Connolly had died the month before and Nan had moved to Poplar to live with my grandfather in Zetland Street. It must have been a terrible ordeal for her and her family to get death threats but huge pinches of salt are needed when reading the press reports. The front page of *The Daily Mirror* for June 22 1954 led with the headline:

'BULLET IN THE POST BRINGS A DEATH THREAT TO FAMILY'

Below it a report read:

A letter threatening to kill a mother and her five children started a gunman hunt raging across half of England last night. *In the envelope addressed to widow Mary Ann Bradford, 51, was a bullet wrapped in paper.* ***The letter said: "This is a present for you and I have another for each of your family. I will let you have them as soon as possible."*** *The letter unsigned and posted in Manchester,* *was delivered to Mrs Bradford's former home in Hurford Street, Hoddesdon, Herts. Mrs Bradford's daughter, Mrs Babs Wilson, 23, took it to the county police. The police told Scotland Yard and last night –*

- *More than 27,000 police in London, Manchester and the Home Counties were on the alert for an armed man.*
- *Detectives sat in a Manchester boarding house waiting for a man. And*
- *Three policemen patrolled around a house in Zetland-street Poplar, London, where Mrs Bradford now lives with her father.*

All police looking for the wanted man were warned by Scotland Yard: "He has a pistol and ammunition."

Superintendent Leonard Elwell, Hertfordshire CID chief said: "I have not the slightest doubt from the wording of the letter, that the writer possessed the means to carry out the threats."

Mrs Bradford, pale and trembling, poured herself a cup of tea last night and said: "I can't understand it. There has been no trouble in our family. I can't think of anyone who could do such a thing. I don't even know anyone in Manchester."

Mr Bradford, dark and attractive, was formerly a cook at a Hoddesdon hotel but left soon after Whitsun. Her husband died about two years ago. Mrs Bradford has three daughters and two sons. The youngest of her children is twelve.

The story says so much about the Connollys and has given us a few laughs over the years. Taken at face value it is, of course, of great concern; a terrifying ordeal for a woman and her family to experience and the anonymous sender must have been crazed to have made such a threat. But if the police had probed a bit deeper, they may have found that there was a bit more to the story than the one they had been given. My explanation may be only conjecture because it is how the story was told to me, but I think that this is probably what happened:

Aunt Nan had a Polish lover called Edzie. Something went wrong with their relationship and she told him she didn't want to see him anymore. Edzie got angry. Fearing his wrath, Nan moved to Poplar so that he couldn't find her. Edzie, now passionately enraged, sends threatening letters to where he thinks Nan is still living, but Nan isn't there. Her daughter Babs collects her mother's post and opens the letter. Seeing the bullet, she has no option but to go to the police. In strait-laced England, Nan cannot admit to knowing the man; to do so would mean opening up their relationship to scrutiny and possible scandal. So, we are left with the unlikely story of a widowed lady, living with her elderly father, getting a bullet sent to her with death threats, completely out out of the blue from someone she doesn't know. As if that wasn't Connolly enough, we have the prospect of 27,000 police being alerted across the country and the wonderfully ironic comment about there being "no trouble in our family" from a lady whose family could start a fight over a boiled egg.

The newspaper reports ran for several days and, when the penny dropped that Nan was my aunt, some of my classmates at school took a peculiar interest in my welfare. It hadn't occurred to me that when the potential assassin said: *"This is a present for you and I have another for each of your family,"* 'family' could include me. The thought hadn't escaped Ronnie Kitts though. On our way into school, he said: "'Av yer seen the paper today? He's genna kill all of yer now!"

AUNT NELL

Aunt Nell was the third child of the family. Unlike Nan, she was neither buxom nor attractive, and she didn't have Nan's thick black hair. She was shorter than Nan and her face would never have been described as beautiful or pretty. Instead, she wore an expression of perpetual tiredness and often complained of headaches. She was straightforward to the point of bluntness and she didn't suffer weakness in others. She was a good, plain-speaking woman and she held her own in the Connolly family.

Nell lived downstairs in 28 Spey Street with her husband, Steve Burleson. My Uncle Pat lived upstairs with his family and when they moved, Grandad Connolly took their flat. Uncle Steve had the look of a man of his times and he resembled the comedian, George Formby. Like George too he was slow to cotton on to things, and he struggled in the company of the Connolly brothers. Nell was the brains and it was she who had to be dealt with if the banter turned against Steve.

In the summer of 1963, our family suffered a terrible tragedy when my cousin Tommy was killed in a traffic accident. On the afternoon of June the eighteenth, I went to visit my grandfather to see how he was taking the news. It was to be the day my grandfather died. Here is an account of that visit from *Journeys from Innocence*, my memoir of being a teenager.

'It was a warm sunny day and, as I crossed the debris that gave me a short cut into Spey Street, I could see that his bedroom windows were raised to let in the air; the net curtains were billowing out as the draught from inside pushed against them. I knocked and Aunt Nell opened the door. She looked anxious. "Come in, Joey. He'll be pleased to see you. He's not been well today." I followed her along the passage and stepped down into the small living room at the back of the house. I knew that I would have to eat something for, whenever I went, I would always be offered food and drink; it was part of the ritual of visiting Aunt Nell. "You hungry?" she asked in an almost accusatory way. "Not really, Aunt Nell." "What d'yer mean not really? You're either hungry or you're not. Have a bit of cake and I'll make you a cup of tea." That was Aunt Nell. She could be direct in her manner but she had a heart of gold and her mission in life was to feed any member of the family that came to the house.

I sipped the strong dark tea, ate my cake and we talked of Tommy. What was there to say? It was dreadful. Nothing that talking would put right and nothing we could change. "How's Uncle Tom and Aunt Aggie?" I asked. "He's coming round later; you might see him for yourself," said Aunt Nell. We fell silent and then she told me about Grandad. "He's not been well. I don't know what it is, it's probably all this, but he's been like it a couple of days now. I've got him up but he's only in his pyjamas. We'll go up and see him in a minute." I finished the cake and we went upstairs. Grandad was sitting in a chair by the window. It was airy and light in the room and the front of the house was getting the best of the afternoon sunshine. "You've got a visitor," said Aunt Nell as we entered. Grandad looked towards me and I greeted him. "Hello, Grandfather, I hear you're not very well." "Do what?" he replied, struggling to catch what I'd said. "You're not very well." "Sit over there, I'm all right," he replied. But he wasn't all right. His sharpness had gone and he was not breathing well. Then, quite unexpectedly, he became ill. I find it hard to describe precisely what happened but it must have been a mild fit or seizure. In the East End we called it 'having a turn.'

In the few seconds that followed, I feared he was going to die. I was scared and I felt ill at ease at witnessing the intimacy of so private a moment. Aunt Nell dealt with it well. She didn't panic and she gave me direction. "We need to get him into bed," she said. It was just Aunt Nell and me and I was the one with the physical strength. Together we lifted him and tried to move him across the room and onto the bed. It wasn't easy. He was heavy, his legs were not supporting his weight very well and he was in distress; wet at the mouth and gasping. He lost his teeth and his pyjama jacket gaped open. Suddenly this strong, invincible man was vulnerable and weak. We managed to get him to bed but the process wasn't a pleasant one. For me, seventeen years old, so protected from the harsher side of life, so used to adults dealing with the difficult things, it was a moment when my life took a big step forward into adulthood.'

Aunt Nell went on to have a good old age. After Steve died, she lived on her own in a flat off the East India Dock Road. She had friends, she dressed well and she kept her home looking good. She kept her Catholic faith too and attended mass at *St Mary and Joseph's* where she felt the benefit of being part of something bigger. Towards the end of her life, she was supported by a charity for the care of the elderly in Poplar. She was never poor and stayed independent to the end. And she repaid the kindness she had been shown by leaving part of her estate to the charity that had supported her so well.

UNCLE TOM

Tom was a bit taller than his brothers, thin with dark hair and the black button eyes of his mother. He lived in Rowlett Street off St Leonard's Road with his wife Aggie and their children Rita and Tommy. It wasn't a happy home. Tom was an unpleasant man; cocky and dismissive. He gave Aggie a difficult time and was hard on Tommy. It was an unpleasant feature of the father-son relationships in the Connolly family that the sons should be given a hard time by their fathers. Tom bullied Tommy, Uncle Jack bullied John, Pats bullied Patsy and Danny bullied David. I got the golden ticket with my dad and I was never treated in the contemptuous way that my cousins were by their fathers.

Tom worked for the Lusty Lloyd Loom furniture company in Bromley-by-Bow. He gained promotion and got himself noticed. He'd had a good war too, being the only one of his brothers to avoid conscription. When my son Joe asked my dad about his brothers' wartime service, he went through each of them in turn but never mentioned Tom. Joe was writing a family history for a homework project and wanted the full picture. "What about your brother Tom, though, grandad? What did he do?" Obviously embarrassed, he paused for a while then said, "Just put 'reserved occupation.'"

In the mid-1950s Tom was offered a job in The Gold Coast, the West African country now known as Ghana. It was a well paid position in a timber exporting company and he jumped at it. Leaving their teenage children behind, he and Aggie left for a life better than anything they could have hoped for in England. Tom was born for the colonial lifestyle; it pandered to his self-importance and raised his self-esteem. He left England an unremarkable middle manager, rapidly embraced the arrogance and privilege that went with British colonialism and returned a cocky expat full of affectation and boastful of his privileged lifestyle. His accent changed too, from aitch-dropping cockney to aitch-dropping posh and Aunt Aggie was now known as 'Agnes.' He referred to African servants as 'boys' and used the term 'Bwana.' And with all that came the rest of the colonial baggage: the assumed superiority of the British, the ludicrous rules and conventions, the unwarranted respect for 'betters,' and manners that mattered more than morals. When he came home on leave, he would tour the family, showing off his latest car and bragging about his servants. He was the wealthiest of my uncles and the only one that didn't give me a shilling or two when he visited. This vignette sums him up perfectly. He was telling us about a visit to his old firm, *Lusty's*: "I thought I'd drop into Lusty's for a spot of lunch with management. I was crossing the yard when I saw someone I thought I recognised. I pointed 'im out and asked who it was. 'That's Bill Golding,' said the MD. I couldn't believe it. 'E was still working in the yard. 'Oh no, it can't be the Golding I knew,' I said, 'I thought ee'd be at least executive class by now.'" Tom had grown up with Bill Golding and worked with him for years. He knew perfectly well who he was.

My cousin Tommy was four years older than me and when his parents left him to go to Africa he came to rely on my father for support. This is what I wrote about him in *Journeys from Innocence*:

'Tommy was a shy, nervous boy and a decent boy too. When he called at our house, as he did quite often, I would watch him closely,

admiring his modern clothes, his shoes and his hairstyle and hoping that, one day, I might be able to look like that too. Tommy came to our house because, with no father around of his own, he knew that my dad would always look after him and give him good advice when he needed it. Tommy's untimely death was so awful and brought sadness to our lives. He was in his early twenties when he died and had two young sons. He came off his motor scooter and a car following behind ran over him. The driver drove off and Tommy was left in the road to die.'

And this is what I wrote about seeing Uncle Tom on the night my grandfather died:

'Later that evening I went back to Aunt Nell's to see how grandad was. Several of the family were there; Uncle Jack, Uncle Steve and a few more. Sitting at the table in the chair I had occupied that afternoon was Uncle Tom. I'd not seen him for some time but he hadn't changed much. He was dressed smartly in a dark suit and crisp white shirt and he was wearing a black tie. With all the vanity I had come to expect of him, I saw that his hair was jet black, tinted with hair dye that left him with an unnatural look that seemed faintly ridiculous. His demeanour was brusque, almost upbeat, but giving nothing away of what was going on inside. I offered my condolences and told him how we all felt about Tommy. He spoke of Tommy with bravado, calling him "the little sod" with an intended affection that somehow misfired. It was impossible to gauge his feelings, but it was impossible too not to feel sympathy for a man who was enduring the hardest cut of all; the loss of a child.'

UNCLE JACK

My father was named Joseph John after his uncle, my Great Uncle Joe. As was the custom in the East End, I was given the name of my father. Pam and I called our son Joseph John and he called his son Joseph John too, so we have an unbroken line of Joe Connollys going back into the nineteenth century. Great Uncle Joe joined the Northumberland Fusiliers in 1914. He was wounded at the last battle of the Somme, taken prisoner of war and died in August 1918 from stomach wounds. He was twenty-three. My Uncle Jack was named after another of my grandfather's brothers, but one who led a longer and more prosperous life than Joe. I have photographs of the two. Joe's picture shows a young soldier, full-faced with smiling Irish eyes. Jack is rakishly handsome; his good looks set off to advantage by his London Fire Brigade uniform and silver helmet. Of the two, Joe has a little of me about him and Jack clearly resembles my dad.

In 1974 I visited my dad's cousin, Ernie Williams, to learn about Joe; Ernie was the keeper of the family history. According to him, on the day that Joe enlisted, he had problems with his feet and walked to the Stratford recruitment office in slippers. His last home leave was in December 1917. Ernie said that as he was opening the door to go, his sister Nan told him that she was looking forward to his next leave. "You won't see me again," Joe replied and she never did.

Ernie told me that Joe's brother Jack was still alive and living in Desert Hot Springs, California. He said that Jack had been a fireman in the London fire service but went to live in America in 1948. This puzzled me. It seemed so unlikely that a Poplar fireman should suddenly emigrate to America at that time; and not to the Eastern states either, but to a remote desert location in the West. "Why did he go?" I asked. Ernie gave a knowing smile and said: "Well...let's just say there was a bank robbery around that time too."

Ernie gave me Great-Uncle Jack's address so I wrote to him and asked about Joe. I got a full and heartfelt reply written in perfect copperplate handwriting on airmail stationery with not a bit of space wasted. He was genuinely pleased to have had a letter from one of his kinsmen and thanked me for getting in touch. I wrote back thanking him and got another letter as full and enthusiastic as the first. There wasn't much about Joe in either of Jack's letters but it is a great regret to me that I have lost them. Jack was over eighty when we were in touch and had at least one daughter, but despite my efforts to track down the American Connollys I have never managed to.

My Uncle Jack had none of the looks of his namesake. He was bald and far from handsome, although he may have been in his day. He lived at 63 Bracken House in Bow with Helen and their children, Dorothy and John. Jack could be tricky and difficult and the family had to gauge his mood before talking back to him. Helen was a New Zealander and met Jack when he was in the Merchant Navy on ships that went between England and New Zealand. It must have been hard for Helen to leave home for a life thousands of miles away in an East End flat with a man who could be difficult. Helen struck me as a good person but not a happy one. My cousin Dorothy was quiet and intelligent. She had the look of a Connolly and resembled Aunt Kit to some extent. She found life difficult at home and eventually left to live in America. In time Jack's family fragmented. Dorothy never returned and, when Helen went back to New Zealand to see her family taking John with her, Jack was left on his own for months.

Jack and my dad served on the same ship during the War and saw active service together in the Atlantic, the Mediterranean and North Africa. Their ship was a minesweeper, *HMS Burke*, and Jack was the ship's cook. When he received his posting to the *Burke*, he asked if my dad could join him and his request was granted. Before the war, Jack worked as chef on two ships: the *Rangatiki* and the *Rangitata*. He took care of the Captain on *HMS Burke* but he looked after himself and his brother too. "We got to eat everything the old man did and more," said my dad.

I liked Dorothy and John and I liked going to their flat. Doreen and I went there on Sunday afternoons to watch television. The journey there was a scary one: Sprattsies steps, Violet Road and Yeo Street were always deserted on Sunday afternoons. No one lived in Yeo Street. It was a creepy place; even the name was creepy. Most of it was taken up by an electricity station with huge wooden cooling towers that dripped water. Fifty yards down, it took a sharp turn to the right. That was the scariest bit of all because we could never tell what was around the corner. Our reward for tackling those empty streets was tea, cake and chocolate bars. After that we would sit around the small television set and watch *Muffin the Mule* and *Billy Bunter's Schooldays*.

Uncle Jack would often call on us in St Leonard's Road. Sometimes he came when my dad wasn't there but my mum never minded; she had an antipathy towards some of his family but had no problem with Jack. Doreen says Jack was her favourite uncle and that he kept an eye on us when my dad was in the Navy awaiting his 'demob.' "Do you remember the lovely cakes he used to bake for us?" she asked me once.

I didn't. My view of him was different to hers. I didn't dislike him but I didn't like the way he treated his family. He also frightened me one day when he did something that I cannot understand even after all these years.

Jack dropped in late one morning when my dad was on the early shift. He sat chatting for a while, finished his cup of tea and then made to go. Turning to me he said: "Would you like to come with me to meet yer dad from work?" I was relaxed around Jack and I liked the idea of surprising my dad, so I said yes. My dad's gas works was at Bromley-by-Bow and Jack's plan was to take us as far as the Sun Flour Mill at Limehouse Cut from where we could see him coming along on his bike. The Sun Flour Mill was a huge flour-making factory just off Brunswick Road. In 1965 an explosion occurred there and much of it was destroyed. A YouTube video about the incident shows exactly where I stood with Uncle Jack while we waited. About 40 seconds into it, the wall he stood me on comes into view; the bridge that can be seen in the background is the one my dad crossed on his way home. This link gives access to the video:

https://www.youtube.com/watch?v=WjyBCQoA8xw

It didn't take long to reach the Sun Flour Mill. Jack had his bike and he cycled there with me on the crossbar. We pulled off Brunswick Road, stopped by the canal and leant against the canal wall. The mill building was behind us and before us was a road that led down to loading areas where barges were emptied and filled. The wall above the canal was just a bit higher than a table top and capped with rounded stone.

We were early. "He won't be long," said Jack. I leant against the wall, looking up and down. There was plenty to see; a semi-industrial landscape of factory buildings, bridges and heavily-polluted water. Jack stood beside me casting the occasional glance in the direction of the gasworks. "I'll lift you up so you can see better," he said. "No thanks Uncle Jack, I can see okay," I replied. "No, let me lift yer up, you'll see better," he persisted. The low wall and the canal water below made me feel uneasy, but as long as I was on the ground and behind the wall, I was fine. "Come on, up yer get," said Jack. But I didn't want to be lifted up and I knew there was no advantage in being higher. Jack took me under the arms, lifted me up onto the wall and stood me there. I felt unsafe and frightened. Then he took his hands away and I was left balancing on my own with a drop before me down to the dirty water of the canal below. I was terrified. "I wanna get down," I protested. "I've got yer, you're all right," said Jack. Then he gripped my ankles and held them tight. "It's all right, I've got yer ankles," he said. I was panicking and scared. I couldn't move my legs; my body was unsupported and I feared I would fall forward into the canal and crash my head on the way down. "Let me go, please Uncle Jack, let me go!" But Jack held on. "Put me down, put me down!" What I sensed in Jack in those moments was a strange determination, a determined kind of cruelty the like of which I had never encountered in my dad. Eventually he complied and soon my father came along and I was safe. It had been a terrifying experience. Child abuse takes many forms.

My cousin John must have experienced similar episodes to that, along with a fair amount of humiliation and some beatings. Arthur Edwards, our family friend, was John's best mate. They went to school together and Arthur saw the family at close hand. He said that Jack was fastidious in the home; everything had to be wiped and put away clean and when he prepared food, he chopped up vegetables neatly like the chef he was. "He treated Helen like a servant," said Arthur. "She did what he told her to do and didn't seem to have much about her." He witnessed Jack's undermining of John too, "And John was a lovely, lovely boy," he said.

John was three years older than me and he treated me well. When he was sixteen, he would visit us on Saturdays and talk to me about music. He had a broad musical taste for his age and he loved live music. He'd tell me about his visits to the 100 Club in Oxford Street and the jazz he heard there. He was comfortable with 'Trad' and 'Modern' Jazz and he liked rock music too. When he came, he brought records with him and we would listen to them together. He'd tell me about the various musicians and the things to listen for. He trusted me with his records and would leave some behind for me to play.

I was thirteen and popular music belonged to my parents' generation. They sang the songs of their youth or those they'd heard from singers on television. I knew about rock and roll but I wasn't old enough to appreciate it; it belonged to teenagers and I was just starting out. The cause of rock wasn't helped by the fact that its most famous exponent, Bill Hayley, wasn't a rock singer at all but a chubby middle-aged country singer. One morning I sat on the floor reading the labels on the records John had left me: Stephane Grappelli and Django Reinhardt, Fats Domino and some rock singles. I took a huge '78' from its sleeve and held it carefully. *Hound Dog* by Elvis Presley. I turned it over and read the label on the other side; *Treat Me Nice*, it said. I lined up the hole in the record with the button in the middle of the turntable, placed the record down, turned the 'RPM' to 78 and pressed 'play.' The arm rose abruptly, swept across to line up with the first grooves on the disc then slowly dropped. A crackle, a hiss...and suddenly my life changed... really changed; and for the better. I had never heard anything as exciting as this. Elvis's jerky exaggeration, his attitude, the range of his voice, the excitement in his expression, the halting pauses and, most of all, the sexiness of the lyrics: "*Scratch my back and run your pretty fingers through my hair.*" That was the moment my life changed and I owe it to my good cousin John. I hope he had a good life.

AUNT KIT

Not long after my parents married, my mum put down a marker to show my dad that she was not going to be subservient to his young man's ways. It was a Saturday and she had made him a meat pudding for his lunch. My mum's meat puddings were just perfect and, of all the things she made, it was the dinner he liked most. He must have thought he had it made when he got married: a young wife to look after him and a nice little home to come back to after he'd been to the pub. That afternoon he told her that he was going for "a couple of pints" with his brothers and wouldn't be long and she told him that the dinner would be ready at half past two. The vegetables boiled, the pudding was cooked, she'd plated the dinner and he wasn't home. She waited. She ate her dinner. She put his over a saucepan of hot water to keep it warm. Three o'clock, four o'clock, five and then he came in. By all accounts she didn't make a fuss. She'd laid the table for him and he sat down. "Where's me dinner?" he asked in expectation; he was after all the man of the house, the young working-class Jack the lad, so he was entitled to have his dinner brought to him. My mum complied with his request and fetched the luke warm pudding. "Here it is," she said and tipped it over his head.

My mum was given a difficult time by some of my father's family and, although she could be nervous and lacking in confidence at times, she had a steely side that served her well and contributed to the success of her marriage. She put her foot down over mixing with some of the Connollys and was selective in who she would see. Of all of them it was Aunt Kit she disliked the most because Kit had mocked her and given her a bad time for not being a Catholic when she became engaged to my dad. Kit had a bad reputation too.

Aunt Kit was attractive, ambitious and clever; a remarkable woman in many ways. At eighteen she decided to become a fan dancer and went to the Windmill Theatre in Soho to audition before the impresario Vivian Van Damm. The Windmill was known for titillating revues in which naked women sat motionless whilst scantily-clad dancers gyrated around them. Nudity was allowed on stage only if the performer kept perfectly still and having fan dancers was a good way of attracting the customers.

"A naked dancing girl's body was concealed by fans held by herself and four female attendants. At the end of the act the girl would stand stock still, and her attendants would remove the concealing fans to

reveal her nudity. The girl would then hold the pose for about ten seconds before the close of the performance." (Wikipedia citing.)

Van Damm gave Kit's fan dance the 'thumbs down' so she never fulfilled her dream, but I imagine she went down fighting and the famous impresario would have heard a few colourful words before she flounced off back to Poplar flourishing her fans as she went.

Kit got a job at the Far Famed Cake Company. The Far Famed made cakes and biscuits in a factory just over the Chrisp Street steps from us. She lived with her husband Joe Snasdale on the Isle of Dogs with their children Kathleen and Peter. After quick promotions she was made manageress and put in charge of the workforce. No doubt she was up to the job, but she had a reputation for flirting with the bosses and that caused some resentment. Most of the workforce were women and Kit was unpopular with them. She was accused of getting the job by sleeping with the bosses in a kind of cake factory version of the Hollywood casting couch. It didn't help that she was tough and uncompromising with the workers either. Tom Brown, the managing director, became infatuated with her and they started an affair that lasted until Tom died. He moved into the Snasdale home and, inexplicably, Joe Snasdale went along with it. How it worked, I do not know, but Joe didn't move out, he just moved bedrooms. My cousin David stayed with them sometimes and he told me that Joe brought Kit and Tom their breakfast in bed.

Kit was canny and kept hold of her brothers. She encouraged them away from their homes and tolerated their affairs. But things went badly wrong when my cousin Tommy complained that Tom Brown had been rough with him when he went to visit Kit. With his dad in Africa, Tommy took his complaint to one of his uncles, my dad most likely, and word got round the family about Tom Brown's bullying of Tommy. The Connolly brothers could argue and fight with one another, but they did not tolerate threats from outside the family. Seeking to avenge Tommy's treatment, a group of them, including my dad, went to Kit's house to confront Tom Brown. The brothers called for him to come out and, when he did, there were threats and a bit of pushing and shoving on the doorstep. Kit joined in, the police were called and Kit threatened her brothers with legal action. The story made the *East London Advertiser* with a full account based on an interview she gave them. "It was gang warfare," she said. "They were rough. At one point I feared I would lose my dentures." Aunt Rose, never a fan of Kit, was outraged by her remark. "Lose me dentitures!" said Rose, "Lose me dentitures. Dentitures! Who'd she think she is? She means *false teeth!*"

The use of physical violence to resolve disputes was something the Connollys had inherited from childhood and the fracas over Tom Brown's treatment of Tommy was not the only time that Kit fell out with her brothers. She and Pats had a row once that ended with him slapping her across the face. When she told Tom Brown what had happened, he took two tough men with him and went to deal with Pats. My cousin Janice remembers seeing her dad being held over the kitchen sink and severely beaten.

Kit's ruthlessness was never more in evidence than when she sacked her sister Nell. Aunt Nell had a job at the Far Famed working in the canteen. It wasn't easy being Kit's sister because sometimes she took abuse from the other women for the way

Kit treated them. Aunt Rose worked at the Far Famed too; she and Nell went back a long way and they got on well. Maybe Nell's tenure at the Far Famed was doomed to failure from the start because she and Kit were bound to clash. Nell was straightforward and blunt and Kit was devious and wily. Kit was Nell's boss but Nell was Kit's older sister: manageress and employee, older sister and younger, it was bound to fail and Kit made no concessions to family either. The end came when she gave Nell an instruction in a rude and bossy way. Nell was angry; Kit's status meant nothing to her. "Who d'yer think *you're* talkin to?" she asked. "I'm talking to you," Kit replied, "And you can do what I'm telling you or get your cards." "Do it yer'self," said Nell and so Kit sacked her. "If you sack 'er, you can sack me too," chipped in Aunt Rose in an unconsidered moment of solidarity that found her and Nell back on the job market in minutes.

In 1967 Kit gave my cousin David a job at the factory to help him earn some money during the summer holidays. David was a typical teenager of his times; he played football, liked the Beatles and had long hair. As his hair grew longer, Kit began to complain. She insisted he wore a hairnet and kept on to him about getting a haircut. Poor David was in a dilemma and didn't know what to do; long hair or no cash? Eventually Kit decided for him: "You're sacked," she said and with that she had sacked her nephew as well as her sister.

My parents were in Italy when my grandad died so I was asked to represent him at the funeral. The fact that Doreen was older than me, was highly capable, a successful professional and the apple of her father's eye counted for nothing. In the old-fashioned lore of the Connollys, I was the son so I would represent my father. I took my place in line alongside his brothers and sisters as we waited to leave for the cemetery. In the quiet of the funeral car, I became aware of Aunt Kit. She had the reputation of a '*femme fatale*' and I hardly knew her, but she was kind to me and spoke gently as we made our way there. I met her for the last time a few years later in the saloon bar of *The St Leonard's*. I was nineteen and she was in her fifties, but she looked good. There was something attractive about her still and she certainly knew how to engage a young man. It was a nice encounter and I am glad that I was able to meet her as an adult and not as the little boy who was her nephew. When my mum and dad celebrated their golden wedding, we invited several of the Connollys to the party. Years had passed and my mum no longer had a problem with Kit, so she was invited too. She didn't come to the celebration but wrote a note apologising for her absence. It was articulate, formal and written in beautiful handwriting.

UNCLE PATS

There was a silliness about the Connolly brothers; trickiness and piss taking were hallmarks of their behaviour. I was four when I first felt what it was like to be their victim. We were on a trolley bus going to Stratford and Uncle Pats was sitting in front of me. Above us was an advertising card for Idris Lemon Squash. It showed a wrinkled lemon shedding tears under a caption that read 'Who made the lemon squash?' Below the furrowed head, another caption read: 'IDRIS. The Quality Soft Drink.' Uncle Pats thought it funny to compare the crying lemon's face to mine and kept reciting the caption to me. "Who made the lemon squash? *You did!*" It was an early initiation into the Connolly banter and I felt bad.

Uncle Pats lived in the flat above Aunt Nell's at 28 Spey Street with Nellie his wife and their children Pat and Janice. He was thick-set and bald; closer to his brother Will in appearance than to my dad or Uncle Tom, who were both dark and slim. Nellie was short and fair-skinned with striking red hair that earned her the name 'Ginger Nell.' To distinguish her from the other Connolly Nells she was also known by her family name of Whitnell. Aunt Nellie Whitnell was lively, straightforward and good to be around. Uncle Pats could be alright too, but he often drank too much and when he drank, he became argumentative. Nell and the children didn't always have it easy with Pats, and my cousin Pat experienced the harsh treatment from him that some of my other male cousins got from their fathers. I liked Aunt Nellie Whitnell a lot and I liked Janice and Pat. I liked Uncle Pats too but I think I knew him at his best and Janice and Pat may have a different story to tell.

When I was young our families got along well and we saw a fair bit of Pats and Nellie. They sometimes went to the pub on Saturday nights with my mum and dad, and when Rose, Charlie and Uncle Henry went with them, they would come back with a crate of bottled beer to keep the party going. Pats and Nellie came to the dances at Bromley gasworks too and when they did, I had someone to play with in Janice. In 1954 Pats bought a radiogram and we had some good times in their flat singing along to *Shake, Rattle and Roll, This Ole House* and other upbeat songs of the day. Pats played the music loud and it must have been difficult for Aunt Nell and Uncle Steve downstairs. In fact, sharing the house must have been difficult for both sides because Aunt Nell wasn't shy when it came to laying down the law.

We called cousin Pat 'Patsy.' He was three years older than me and about three years younger than Doreen. He went to Susan Lawrence too and having Doreen and Pat go through the school before me meant that I was often compared to them both. Doreen was at Alton Street and left when Susan Lawrence opened, but we had the same teachers and they thought highly of her for being capable, accomplished, good at music and sociable. Pat was popular with our teachers too and for much the same reasons. He was no musician but he was a fine sportsman and a good actor too. He excelled at cricket as a boy and played to a high standard for years. When I joined the junior school, Pat had just left, but his reputation was well established. Older boys would say, "You Patsy Conlie's cousin?" "You good at cricket?"

When the cricket season arrived, Mr Clark took us into the playground for net practice. I loved playing cricket but only with my mates in the street; chalked-up wickets on a wall and a tennis ball to whack. "Joe Connolly is Patrick Connolly's cousin," said Mr Clark to appreciative murmurings from the boys in the playground. "Colin Hogarth, you go into bat and Joe can bowl." Colin lived near me in Cobden Street and I'd played cricket with him a few times. He was an excellent batsman. "One ball each and then we'll rotate," said Mr Clark. The rest of the boys looked on in anticipation; would 'Hogie' smash me for six? I was dreading the prospect of bowling and hating the attention I was getting. "Bowl!" called Mr Clark, lowering his right hand like a test match umpire. I walked a few paces back, turned, then ran towards Colin. I swung my arm over, released the ball and it flew at him, smashing his middle stump so hard that it sprang back towards the ground. It was a complete fluke. Cheers and clapping. "Now Colin, you bowl to Joe," said Mr Clark. I was dreading this even more; we were playing with a real cricket ball. I watched as Colin turned to make his run. The ball came to me at speed and all I could think of was how to protect myself. I raised the bat with the flat of the blade at a slight angle. The ball struck it powerfully and flew away fast and hard. "Good shot, Joe!" said Mr Clark. The boys cheered; Susan Lawrence had got another Patsy Conlie. Except that I knew they hadn't.

Pat was clever and after taking the Eleven-plus exams, he got a place at George Green's in the East India Dock Road. There his cricket went from strength to strength and his acting flourished too. In 1956 I saw him in the school performance of *A Midsummer Night's Dream* and he played some very good comedy, hamming up the antics of *Pyramus* and *Thisbe* communicating through the wall.

Pat was a straightforward boy; a good boy. He just got on with things, always on his bike doing errands for his family or the neighbours. I felt easy around him; there was nothing bullying or boastful about Pat despite the difference in our ages. When I was ten, he and his friend took David Barnett and me swimming at Poplar Baths. The two of them jumped from the top diving board over and over again. It seemed so high to me but I longed to have a go. "I'll take you up if you like," said Pat. The four of us climbed the ladder to the top and I stood there looking down. "You don't have to jump if you don't want to," said Pat. It did seem a long way down but the prospect of jumping was tantalising. I hesitated, walked carefully to the edge and then stepped back. I walked to the edge again, considered jumping and stepped back again; I couldn't do it. "That's all right," said Pat. "Nothing wrong with not jumping." Lesser boys would have made fun of me for chickening out.

Between them, my cousins Pat, John and Tommy gave me some idea of what it would be like to have an older brother. Each of them brought something different to my life: Tommy with his shyness and good clothes, John with his taste in music and Pat with his common sense and decency. Janice brought something different too; she gave me an impression of what it would be like to have a younger sister. I spent a lot of time with her when I was young. Our families socialised and my mum looked after her while Aunt Nellie was at work. Janice and I were a little alike in looks and might have passed for brother and sister, but we were different in temperament. She was more confident than me and might dig her heels in if she didn't want to do something. If she didn't eat all of her dinner up, my mum would get anxious; what would Nellie Whitnell think if Janice came home hungry? Janice had an accident once that really worried my mum. We were playing in the recreation ground near Manorfield School and some boys were hogging the swings. Janice asked one of them if she could have a turn and when he got off, he heaved the swing at her and it came crashing down onto the back of her head. She bled heavily and I took her home to be cleaned and bandaged by my very worried mum. Janice still has the scars from the stitches she had.

I made up stories for Janice. They were always about Wee Wee our cat. She loved hearing them and I loved telling them to her. She had a fine imagination so she went along with the real-life situations that Wee Wee got herself into and never questioned their improbability. There were times when I couldn't comprehend Janice's naughtiness and I wanted to help her when she got into scrapes; but I loved her sense of independence and her determination. She was great fun and good to be around; the little sister I never had.

Doreen and I still see Janice and Pat and meeting them is enjoyable. Janice has turned into a version of her mum; straightforward, unfussy and a skilful and creative needleworker. Some of the work she produces is art of a very high standard. Fortunately for him and his family, Pat didn't turn into a version of his dad. Instead, he became a good husband and father. He achieved great things as a cricketer, ran his own business and lived well. The last I saw of Pats and Nellie was at my parents' golden wedding party. I have a memory of each of them from that evening. The first is of Pats. I was giving a speech in praise of my mum and dad and Pats heckled me; he just couldn't resist calling out. And I also remember having a lovely chat with Aunt Nellie Whitnell. Her passing remark to me was, "Your dad was the best of them all."

AUNT MABEL

Aunt Mabel was the youngest of my father's sisters and one that my mum liked; she chose her for a bridesmaid. We never saw much of Mabel over the years but it was always good when we did. She was a lovely person; open and well-meaning with a cheekiness that succeeded through personality rather than wit. She was given a hard time in the Connolly family and was often made fun of by her brothers for her looks and for being thin and a sissy. When the rise-taking began in that family, it was important to answer back but Mabel never quite had the knack of finding a good put-down.

Aunt Mabel was married to Johnny Kilgor and Johnny was like a male version of her. He was tall, thin and softly spoken. It must have been difficult for him to hold his own in Mabel's family because he seemed so different from her brothers. Being the type of man he was, he might have struggled with their cocky ways, even though he had been in the army and must have experienced that kind of thing before. It is never wise to speculate on a marriage from the outside, but Mabel and Johnnny's seemed like a good one. They had three daughters: my cousins Maureen, Christine and Pat. I remember them as girls in printed frocks with open-toed sandals and big bows of ribbon in their hair.

In 1958, Johnny got into trouble with the bookmakers. He owed them fifteen pounds, a considerable sum of money for people like us in those days. If he didn't pay, they would have come after him and he would have suffered physical assault. One Saturday, Mabel came to our house with Johnny to ask my dad for a loan. He gave them the fifteen pounds from his savings. This left very little for our family but he knew that it was the right thing to do. To his credit, Johnny paid back half a crown a week and met his obligations without fail. In recounting the dreadfulness of his experience with the bookies Johnny was full of praise for Mabel: "My May has been a brick throughout," he said. There was a benefit in all of this for me. Every time Johnny paid his half crown, my dad gave it to me to deposit at school as payment for my first visit abroad; a two week trip to Switzerland and Germany in 1959.

I saw May and John a few times towards the end of their lives and whenever I did, it was good. May was just lovely; a kind warm presence that brought me closer to my family with her lovely cockney voice and cheeky manner. I went to May's funeral and Johnny wept. A few days later, he died himself.

UNCLE PETER

Peter wasn't one of the cocky Connollys; he was quiet and more considerate. He married twice and had two families and all of his children were boys. Peter lived in Hoddesdon with Rose, his wife, and their sons John, Roger and Brian. Peter and Rose were ill-matched. She was hearty with a touch of the Women's Institute about her. He was from the East End and quite shy. I liked Peter and I didn't mind Rose, but something about her gave me reservations. She was organised and over-regimented. When Brian was christened, we stayed with her and Peter and I saw her operating at first-hand. She was potty-training Brian and went about it in a way that my mum thought ridiculous. She had a timetable for sitting Brian on the potty and, whatever she was doing and whether Brian was showing interest or not, she sat him on the poe and urged him to try. Once I saw her doing the chores with the pottied Brian under her arm and a brush in her other hand.

Rose and Peter were fond of Doreen and, although she was still a teenager, they asked her to be Brian's godmother. They were good to me too but I felt awkward with my cousins,

Roger and John, and much of the time I was with them they ignored me. When Rose's nephew arrived for the christening, Roger and John made a fuss of him. He, John and I were about the same age but I was never asked to join in. I was ten and self-conscious about my weight; they were slim and athletic. Their skin was brown and tanned; I was pale and went pink as soon as the sun shone. John and Roger weren't that bad to me, but they made me feel bad about myself. Not only did I think they were better than me physically, but they lived in a nice house with a front garden and I came from an old house in a rundown area.

The first time I stayed at Uncle Peter's I was about five and while I was there, I had my first proper bath. Peter took John, Roger and me up to the bathroom, ran a deep bath and we all got in, including Peter. It was such a lovely feeling to be sinking into hot water with more hot water on tap if the bath got cold. We lathered ourselves, floated boats, splashed around and stayed soaking long after Peter got out and the bath began to cool. That bath was one of the highpoints of my childhood and I enjoyed it so much. It was many years later before I was able to have a bath in my own home.

Peter left Rose and took up with another woman. Aunt Kit assisted him in the process. We never saw him for years despite the fact that he and my dad had been quite close. One day in August 1961, Doreen and I were in Chrisp Street looking for a present for our parents' silver wedding anniversary, when Peter came by with his new partner Val, and their baby. Val was pushing a 'high-rocker' pram and, when Peter recognised us, they stopped and Val let us see the baby. Peter and Val got married not long after that and had a second baby boy. Rose remarried too. I don't think Peter ever saw his first three sons again and we never knew what happened to them, but I heard that John signed to be a goalkeeper with Norwich City. Peter kept in touch with my dad and soon after we moved to the Hainault Estate, he and Val moved into a house two streets away. I saw him from time to time and my dad took Alice and Joe to see him sometimes too. In his later years, he seemed like a man who had found contentment. He had a good wife in Val and he saw out the rest of life pottering around the house and making a good job of his garden. It would be hard to find fault with Peter, but I will never understand how a man could cut his ties with his children in so complete a way as he did.

UNCLE DANNY

Danny had everything. He was good-looking, had a lovely wife, three great children, a nice house and one of the loveliest dogs I ever knew. But Danny had that aberrant gene that afflicted most of his brothers so he could be argumentative, stupid and envious of his son. Danny was the youngest of the Connollys and, being younger than Aunt Nan's oldest daughter, he was an uncle from the day he was born. He met Sarah, my Aunt Sally, in the late 1940s. She was small and attractive with a lovely smiling face and a personality to match. She was intelligent too and had plenty of common sense.

I spent more time with Danny and Sally than any of my other relations. They visited us in Poplar a few times and, when I was thirteen, Danny asked if I would like to stay with them for the weekend. I didn't need to think about it because

I liked him and Sally and I liked their children, David, Brenda and Sharon. Danny and Sally lived in Hainault, not far from Hainault Forest and the green open space of Chigwell Row. Poplar was my home but sometimes I felt the need to spend time in other, nicer places. I remember my first weekend visit: the smell of fresh washing, playing football with David and his friends, the playful antics of Major the dog, and the gathering of the family before bedtime on Saturday night. When the 'aberrant gene' wasn't in play, Danny was a good father and the family were happy around him.

I continued visiting Danny and his family on and off until I was nineteen. I was at art school the last time I went and I took them down a painting I did of Marilyn Monroe; it was my homage to Pop Art. Over the years I visited, I experienced Danny's family at first hand and saw it decline until the point when he eventually left. I saw him become increasingly difficult. I watched as Sally tried to manage him with tact. I witnessed his bullying of David, his illogicality and his increasing dislocation from reality. Brenda and Sharon will have their own stories to tell of their father's behaviour towards them, but I saw Danny's treatment of David at first hand and it was not good. David was three years younger than me and we got on well. It didn't take much for us to be friends because we both liked the Beatles, enjoyed kicking a football and supported West Ham. David was a nice boy and he didn't deserve the treatment he got from his father. All three of my cousins were nice. Brenda was blonde and funny, Sharon was small, dark and pretty too.

Danny's bullying of David seemed to begin when David entered adolescence. It doesn't take a psychologist to work out that some mothers resent the fact that their daughter is now more desirable than she is, or that a father might begrudge his son's new-found strength. Danny was like that with David. He nagged him for not getting on with chores, he found fault with the way he sat in his chair and he rounded on him when he tried to defend himself. I was often there when these things happened, a witness to Danny's behaviour. At times I found it difficult not to interfere and made tactful interventions on David's behalf, but I had to be careful. Danny would listen to me but I could only push my luck so far. I wasn't a member of that family and saying too much might make things worse.

I was there when Danny's bullying of David reached a particular low and David could do nothing right. Danny nagged him about the length of his hair but David answered back and, enraged by this, Danny told him to get into the garden where he would fight him man-to-man. In my opinion, only a particularly weak sort of man would say that to his son. I came into conflict with my father at times, but I never had to put up with anything like that. Most of the disputes I had with him were about my hair. As a boy, I had a 'short back and sides' like him, but when I was thirteen, I got a spikey 'crew cut' which was more fashionable. This met with his approval as did the 'college boy' that came next, but a 'college boy' took longer, so it cost more: it involved cutting the hair in layers then washing and blow-drying it into shape. After that, it was given a generous spray of hair lacquer to keep it in place. My dad liked the look, but he didn't approve of me paying six and six to get it done. "You're paying all that for a haircut. Lou does mine for one and nine," he said. I think he also felt that it was effeminate for boys to have their hair blow-dried and lacquered. As the sixties moved on, I grew my hair longer and by the seventies it was nearly down to my shoulders.

Danny couldn't stand the fact that David had collar-length hair. To him it was a symbol of defiance. In anger and frustration, he called on his brother Will, Sergeant-Major Connolly, to sort David out. David told me that Will had threatened to beat him up if he didn't comply.

Eventually Danny left. He just walked out on the family and left them to fend for themselves. David told me once that he stole meat from a butcher because the family had no food. Despite the hardships they faced when Danny left, the family survived and Sally sorted out her life. She met Ernie, a decent easy-going man with whom she found contentment. Danny met someone too and remarried. Helen, his wife, had received a good inheritance and was wealthy. Danny and she lived for a while in Poplar where Helen owned a drinks business in Aberfeldy Street. Then they moved to Devon where Helen bought a farmhouse and some land. Doreen visited them and thought Helen a pleasant, accomplished woman. "Too good for him," she said.

I lost touch with Danny's family. Brenda and David went to live in Bermuda and Sharon got married and moved further into Essex. Time passed. I was married with children but I never forgot Sally and my cousins and I always wanted to make contact with them again so I rang Aunt Sally. She was so pleased when I called and asked me down and after more than twenty years, I found myself on the doorstep of 421 New North Road again. Sally had aged well. She still had her smile, her warm demeanour and her pleasant easy-going way. It is difficult with the passing of time to place events in the right sequence but I think that Sally died not long after I saw her. I was sad when I heard of her death because she was someone I liked and respected.

* * *

Danny never lost contact with my dad. They often rang each other and did so until my dad died. When Helen died, Danny inherited her considerable estate and became a wealthy man. He was approaching eighty then and the money was of little use to him. By contrast, David was struggling financially and needed money. He wrote to his father seeking a reconciliation and Danny invited him down. The visit didn't go too badly, but I don't think David got any money. Instead, Danny courted the attention of my cousin Rita and promised to leave all of his money to her. When Rita died prematurely, he turned his attention to Doreen telling her that he wanted her to be his sole beneficiary, but she declined. By rights, the money belonged to Danny's children and this was his opportunity to make amends for the way he had neglected them over the years.

Doreen, Pat Connolly and I contrived to reunite Danny with his children in the hope of getting him to include them in his will. Doreen invited him to her house to meet David on neutral ground. They both accepted and Danny arrived early that morning having driven up from Devon. The day turned out to be a strange affair. David came about midday with his son and a friend. They stayed a short while then went across to the pub where they spent most of the afternoon. Everyone was polite when they returned but nothing much happened. Danny ate nothing and drank nothing all day; he was eighty and faced a long drive home. Eventually, Doreen, Pat and I left him and David together in the hope that they would lay the foundations for a more profound family reconciliation, but nothing came of the day. David left and, although we pleaded with him to stay, he refused and drove through the night to Devon getting lost on the way.

Eventually, Danny latched on to a third niece, Aunt Mabel's daughter Pat. She spent time in Devon, started paying him visits and befriended him. It didn't take long for Danny to tell her what he had told Rita and Doreen; that he would leave everything to her in his will. This time he'd found a niece that complied and Danny died leaving everything to her and nothing to his children. Feeling the injustice, Doreen, Pat and I tried to persuade our cousin to share the money with Danny's children. I drafted a series of letters to her and Danny's solicitor. Here is a part of one that went out in Sharon's name:

Our father walked out on us when we were young without making any kind of provision. In the months before he left, his behaviour towards us became particularly difficult and we went through a terrible time. After he went, our mother had very little money but he never saw fit to help her in providing for us. You can imagine that we felt very rejected by him and we have had to live with that rejection for most of our lives. Now we feel rejection again not only for ourselves, but also for our sons, his grandsons, one of whom he met in recent years and the other of whom he knew. Clearly our father had a desire to reward you but we feel that reward for any help and support you may have given him needs to be weighed against what he did to us, the effect it had on our lives and the resulting moral duty he had towards us.

We do not wish to obtain all of our father's estate but we do feel that, for you to take everything, and we, his children and grandchildren to have nothing, is very unfair.

Pat ignored all of the letters and Danny's children received nothing from her. When she died the family money that should have been theirs was lost to them for ever.

THE FACTS OF LIFE

When my mum knew that I was about to be born, she asked Doreen to fetch my nan. When Nanny Powell heard I was on the way, she told Uncle Henry to get the midwife. Henry got on his bike and pedalled as fast as he could to St Frideswide's Mission House in Lodore Street where the Anglican order of the Sisters of the Divine was located. The nuns and nurses at St Frideswide's delivered many of the babies in Poplar and the television series *Call the Midwife* is based on them. There is a subtle social message in the title of that programme, because no one would have been told to *call* the midwife. No one had a telephone so, like Uncle Henry, they would have been told to *get* the midwife.

Had I have been born twelve days later, I would have been the oldest in my class. As it was, I was the youngest and some of my classmates were almost a year older than me. Although I coped well academically, it meant that I was still innocent about sex when some of them were becoming more worldly. The midwives at St Frideswide's are an example of my innocence. I saw them passing by on their bikes nearly every day, but I didn't know what they got up to. I knew they had something to do with babies but had no idea what, until Johnny Purton put me out of my ignorance one day when he said: "They deliver babies 'a course. They 'ave 'em in them baskets on the front of their bikes and they take 'em round the 'ouses and give 'em out."

Sex was a commodity sold in newspapers and films in the 1950s. It was never spoken of overtly but alluded to with innuendo and guarded references. Media sex was about women. If an actress or film star made the news, the story would inevitably refer to her body shape: *"Marilyn Monroe, 36-24-34, flew into London last night..."* There were lots of cleavage photographs in the papers and pictures of film stars in clinging sweaters with their waists bound tightly by wide belts.

When it came to teaching children about sex in the 1950s, there was a social divide. Middle-class children learned about 'The birds and the bees,' a term so tactfully obscure that it might just as well have been called 'The bikes and the cars.' More down-to-earth middle-class parents would have told their sons and daughters 'The facts of life' but children like me were told nothing. No one at Susan Lawrence had been told the facts of life, none of the boys had anyway. It would have been different for girls perhaps, but I doubt it. My late wife Pam broke my heart once when she told me how she experienced her first 'period' when she was away from home on school camp and didn't know what was happening to her. I never wanted my father to tell me anything about sex; the very thought of that would have had me cringing with embarrassment. I can't imagine Mr Purton telling Johnny or Mr McAvennie telling Billy about it either. We didn't want to hear anything about sex from our parents but we needed to know.

Today, schools have 'Relationships and Sex' education as part of the curriculum; the government has even issued statutory guidance on how it should be taught. We got nothing at primary school and sex education at the Roan was limited to a study of the asexual reproductive processes of the amoeba and a showing of the film *To Janet a Son*. I am not sure how parents should tackle the question of what to tell their children about sex. It shouldn't be assumed that a child would want a parent to talk to them about such personal issues. Pam and I took the view that we would answer any question honestly if our children asked, but we would not foist the subject on them. I don't know if we were right to do that or not.

I don't think it mattered much that I wasn't taught about the mechanics of sex, but it mattered a great deal that I was never taught about women's bodies, the changes they undergo and the difficulties they can face with the monthly cycle. Pam experienced dreadful changes in her mood every month when we were first married and I thought that her sudden transformation from loving wife to one who criticised everything I did, was all about me when in fact it was just about physiological changes in her. I needed to understand that but I didn't.

Women were always clad when I was a boy; we never saw what was under the clothes. We never went to art galleries or saw pictures of nudes in paintings. I knew that women got big when they were having babies and I knew that some young women were really nice to look at, but nothing more than that. There were two nudist magazines that I sometimes got a glimpse of in school: *Spick* and *Span*. I think Ronnie Kitts brought copies of them in a couple of times. These little publications were produced for male titillation and showed pictures of naked women. Johnny Watton and I found a copy hidden under a brick on the Cobden Street debris once. I can't remember if it was *Spick* or *Span* but it didn't matter as they were much the same. What did matter was that we had a copy to ourselves and we could look at it as much as we liked without anyone knowing. It was disappointing though, because the photographs had been doctored to eliminate the details. Whereas the women were portrayed naked from the waist up, from the waist down their bodies were smoothed over and they looked like polished stone. Johnny and I were not going to abandon our treasure though and we replaced it under the brick for later reference.

I saw my first naked woman when I was ten and my parents took me to see a variety show at the *Queens Theatre* in Poplar High Street. It was towards the end of variety performance in Britain; television was keeping people at home and variety theatre was suffering. To boost audience numbers, the variety impresarios showed naked women in 'tableaux vivants' like the ones Aunt Kit aspired to appear in at the *Windmill*. It was a terrific show at the *Queens*, with great comedy, a rousing rendition of *Jerusalem, Jerusalem, lift up your hearts and sing* and a very tasteful tableau in which a huge newspaper at the back of the stage, cleverly painted, had a photograph of a naked woman on the front page, except that it was an actual woman and not a photograph. To meet the requirements of the Lord Chamberlain, the performer kept perfectly still. The display had enough artistic quality to pass it off as tasteful rather than smutty but we all knew what it was about.

In my last year at Susan Lawrence some of the older children in my class talked openly about sex and used terms they'd picked up from their older brothers and sisters. I heard accounts of exploits in air raid shelters, but I think it was mostly bragging. There were rude songs and jokes too and most of them were funny. Ann Field, a homely, quietly-spoken girl brought a rude doll into school once. It was a kilted Scotsman and when his tummy was pressed his kilt flew up and three little balloons inflated to give a passable impression of what could be expected to be seen under a kilt. The little balloons were stretched so thin when they were inflated, that they would have inevitably burst before long; once that happened, the flying kilt would have revealed a more sorrowful sight.

In the summer before I left Susan Lawrence, the older boys in my class devised a bizarre ritual that the rest of us were obliged to participate in. On Friday afternoons the girls were given needlework lessons and the boys had 'quiet reading' in the library under the supervision of Mr Howell, the Headmaster. At the beginning of the lesson, we would pick a book and then sit down to read it. The chairs were arranged in a square so we faced one another. Once we were settled, Mr Howell would leave us to get on with his work. His office was nearby so it was easy for him to keep an ear and look in from time to time. We knew when he was coming because his chair made a noise when he stood up. The bizarre ritual involved opening our books, taking out our willies and playing with them. We chose the books for privacy rather than literary merit so the bigger ones went first. Once we were ready, Colin Hogarth or Jackie Painter would instruct us to start: "Wankers' Club be...*GIN*." The majority of us were shy participants but no one wanted to be a prude and the older boys couldn't see what we were up to behind our books anyway. Most of us just sat there with our willies out not knowing what to do and it is no irony that the book I usually chose was *Doctor Dolittle*.

About that time, I got a girlfriend. Having a girlfriend meant nothing really, but if a girl agreed to be your girlfriend it gave you a bit of status. Mine was a very nice girl called Ann Radley. Ann lived in Overstone House on the Lansbury Estate. I called on her there once and took her a Mars Bar as a present. The process of getting a girlfriend involved saying, "Will you be my girlfriend?" That heartfelt profession of affection over, the girl would either say "yes" or "no." If she said "yes" then you could pass little slips of paper to her with the words "I love you" on. If you were lucky, you would get one back with the same message or, better still, a *Love Heart* sweet bearing the same inscription.

There is a darker side to sex that some children have to endure. I was fortunate never to have been molested or assaulted as a child though twice as a teenager I had to fend off unwanted groping from older men. Other children were not so fortunate. Terry Martin, a boy from Ullin Street, told me that the lodger in his house touched him intimately and he didn't know what to do about it. He was two years younger than me, about eight I think, and the situation was complicated because his parents liked the lodger and trusted him to look after Terry when they were out. "Tell your dad! You must tell your dad," I told him. In my first year at Roan one of the boys in my class bragged about sexual acts he performed on a man who gave him a lift to school. At the age of eleven, this unpleasant boy was already corrupt and corrupting.

Fortunately, these were the only cases of paedophilia I ever heard of, though it would have been happening to lots of children. It was quite common for children to be followed by men, though, and we all feared strangers. Doreen had a long walk home along Railway Street when she went to Sunbeams and she was frightened every time. Not long before she died, Margaret Wardell told her that she was followed all the way from Chrisp Street by a man once. It was no innocent encounter: when she stopped, he stopped, when she crossed the road, he crossed over too. She ran the last part of the way home and he quickened his pace to keep up. "Nanny Powell's door was open so I ran inside," said Margaret. "When I told her what happened, she grabbed a knife from the kitchen drawer and chased him up the street."

We were innocents as children. I never heard the words 'penis' or 'vagina' until I was at Roan. In my first year there, Dix Valentine and I once tried to work out what the word 'homosexual' meant. Dix cleverly concluded that as 'homicide' is murder and 'sexual' is about sex, 'homosexual' must mean murder with a sexual motive. I never heard of homosexuality until I went to Roan and I never knew a man in Poplar whose sexuality was in question. Sometimes a man might be called a 'mummy's boy' or a 'Nancy boy' but nothing more explicit than that. I imagine that homosexuality was never considered possible in male-dominated working-class Poplar, although of course there must have been plenty of gay men around. Actual Nancy boys sometimes visited our local pubs. They came from out of the area and went around from one pub to another. Visits by Nancy boys were well-received by the regulars and I can't recall hearing of any hostility.

My dad and Uncle Charlie would imitate Nancy boys after they'd seen them in the pub and from their renditions it seems that they were very camp and effeminate. I saw two Nancy boys once when I was about eight. Two men walked past me and my friends as we were playing in Cobden Street. They had just left *The Cobden,* the pub on the corner. They wore grey double-breasted suits and their hair was wavy and long; long at the sides, swept back off the forehead and curling up at the back of the neck. Their swaying gait and general demeanour were quite different to those of other men.

IN SPITE OF ALL THE DANGER

The Quarry Men were schoolboys who formed a skiffle group in Liverpool in the 1950s. One of the first songs they recorded was called *In Spite of All the Danger* and it was sung by a young John Lennon and an even younger Paul McCartney. I have borrowed their title because I see now that I faced lots of dangers as a boy and yet managed to survive them. The greatest danger was illness. In the year I was born, over sixty-five children in every thousand died before they were five; in 2020 the figure was 0.4. Scratch below the surface and there would be a significant class difference in that 1945 figure.

I was ill more often than my children ever were. Diarrhoea and sickness were frequent and more serious diseases like diphtheria were common too. The people in St Leonard's Road kept themselves clean, but standards of hygiene were poor. Food was handled without concern for cross-contamination; chicken was put in the butcher's window next to sausages and steak. People came from the toilet and continued their day without washing their hands. Fishmongers struggled to keep flies off their fish, fresh foods were wrapped in newspaper and in the corner shop where we stopped to buy a penny drink on the way home from school, the glass was refilled for the next boy or girl without being washed properly. No one in the street had a refrigerator so food went off quickly. Sometimes meat and fish were already bad when they left the shop. Eggs were often rotten; the smell was obvious as soon as they were cracked open. We never washed fruit and vegetables and the fat in the chip pan stayed on the cooker hob for days.

Everyone smoked in our unventilated houses and the air outside was polluted from coal fires and factories. Fogs happened every winter and London fogs were severe and dangerous. A foggy morning would turn into a foggy day and, as fires were lit and factories started up, the fog grew denser unless there was a wind to take it away. Clothes were covered with smuts from the air and washing had to be done again. When we blew our noses, the handkerchief would be black with smuts. In 1952 the fog was worse than anyone could remember. One night we waited anxiously for my dad to come home from work, peering through the window into the dense fog outside in the hope of seeing his bike. When he did get through, he arrived like a hero bearing a flaming torch. He had carried it all the way from the gasworks. A bus driver in Brunswick Road was completely lost and he called to my dad to ask where he was. With his torch to light the way, he led the driver all the way to the Blackwall Tunnel.

In 1956 the Eden government took drastic action to clean up the air in our country. It was one of the most important pieces of legislation ever to be enacted and it saved thousands of lives. When local councils or City mayors attempt milder versions of the same thing today, they are pilloried by politically correct libertarians, climate change deniers, backward-facing newspapers and cranks. Eden would have struggled with that. Housing conditions contributed to our health problems too. The roof above my parents' bedroom leaked whenever it rained and my room and theirs had damp on the walls on which fungus grew. Poor hygiene, filthy air and insanitary housing; it is no wonder that we got ill.

* * *

There were other dangers I faced too, most of them of my own making. Playing on the railway was one. The line on the far side of our debris was always busy with 'locos'; goods trains going in and out of the docks, some chugging along slowly, others fast and empty. Sometimes a loco would go by backwards and occasionally two came joined together with nothing to pull. Seeing them was a pleasure and we always hoped that the next one would be puffing clouds of white steam and not just pumping smoke. The railway wall was about eight feet high. Climbing it was difficult but it wasn't too bad when there were three of us to help each other up. We went onto the railway only occasionally and when we did, it wasn't to play or cause damage, but to make knives from six-inch nails. There were big nails on the debris if you looked for them and if not, the older boys might give us one they'd taken from home. With the nails in our pockets, we would scale the wall, place one on the line and wait for the next train to crush it flat. Trespassing on the railway was a serious thing, so as soon as the nail was in place, we would climb back over the wall as quickly as we could. Once the train disappeared up the track, we'd retrieve the flattened nails, bind the ends with string for the handle and the job was done. Sometimes the thrill of playing on the lines was so great that we did linger there: jumping on the sleepers or balancing on the rails, frightened of getting caught and frightened of being hit by a train but willing ourselves to stay there until we heard another one coming.

There were two pedestrian bridges over the railway: 'Chris Street' steps and 'Sprattsies' steps. The first linked our neighbourhood to Chrisp Street market and the other we called Sprattsies steps because it was next to the Spratts' dog biscuit factory. Chris Street steps were wide with tubular metal handrails on either side. The first flight led up from the pavement in Railway Street to a second set up to the bridge. The planked wooden walkway over the railway was contained within high metal walls that ran the length of the bridge on either side. The tops of the walls were fairly wide, just under a half a metre, perhaps. At the Chrisp Street end, it was possible to climb on the stair rail and heave yourself up onto the end of the bridge wall. Curved spikes, embedded in concrete, were in place to deter anyone from climbing but, in spite of them, Johnny Watton and I managed to get up onto the end of the wall quite easily.

One Saturday we climbed up and stood together on the plinth that held the lamp on the Chrisp Street side. From there I looked along the top of the wall and wondered how far I could get if I started walking. The urge to cross the bridge was hard to resist and we set out together towards the other side, me first and Johnny following. There was nothing to hold on to up there and a sheer drop to the railway twenty feet below, but the width of the wall made it easy and I kept on walking, feeling no fear. As we neared the steps on our way back, I saw a policeman with an Alsatian dog coming up them. He had almost reached the top when I recognised him. It was John McDonald, a young PC who lived in Brunswick Road. John and his dog were often seen around; we knew him and we liked him. He was young, from Poplar and a good neighbourhood policeman.

John must have been alarmed by what he saw. Facing him were two ten-year-old boys in a very dangerous situation. If he startled us, we might fall. If we felt threatened, we might panic and try to get away. As it happened, he dealt with us perfectly. "Come on boys, let me help you down," he said in a calm and unthreatening way. We walked cautiously towards him, Johnny first then me. "Kneel down and turn towards me," said John. He held out his arms and Johnny and I were brought down safely. There was no recrimination, no telling off. He just pointed out the danger we had been in and got us to agree that what we'd done was stupid and wrong. When he left, John, Johnny and I were all on the same side.

* * *

I was never in trouble with the police; none of us were. We were boys who were naughty rather than bad. I never stole, though I did pay in rupees once when I bought Billy Mac and me a choc ice each in Woolworths. The young assistant accepted the coins without question; the young assistant was Doreen and she has always denied that the deal ever took place.

Johnny Watton and I had a close escape from the police when we were almost caught smoking on the bomb site. It was a Sunday evening in winter, about seven o'clock and dark. "Do ya fancy getting some fags?" asked Johnny. It didn't take long for me to agree; I had never smoked before and I wanted to try. "How much yer got?" he asked. "How much are they?"

I replied. "One and six for ten," said Johnny. "I've only got fourpence," I said. "I've only got a tanner but we can get a packet of five *Anchor* for ninepence," said Johnny.

There was an off-licence at *The Foresters*; a kind of small narrow bar with its own entrance that sold alcohol, sweets and tobacco to take away. It was a separate part of the pub where children were allowed to buy things. Doreen sometimes went there to get Nanny Powell a jug of mild and bitter. The 'offie' had its own special smell; like a pub without the smoke; corky from the barrels and with a whiff of stale beer. I never liked going there because it could take ages to get served.

I pushed the door and it opened with a loud 'ping.' There was no one waiting to be served and no one serving. Johnny took the money from his pocket and began tapping gently on the counter to attract attention. After a few minutes a young barmaid appeared. "Five *Anchor Tipped* please," said Johnny. "Ninepence, please," said the barmaid. She took the money, pressed the keys of the till and the coin drawer sprang open. She clattered the money into the tray; three penny coins into one part and a 'sixpenny bit' into another. "Thank you," she said, handing the thin cardboard packet to Johnny. "Can we have a book of matches too please?" I asked. "We don't sell the books but I can give you one if you like." She went into the pub and came back with a small folded book of matches. We were ten years old and it was obvious that we were buying cigarettes for ourselves but there was never any challenge.

We took our cigarettes onto the debris and lit a fire a little way back from the Butler's back fence. When it got going, Johnny opened the packet of Anchor and took out two of the thin little cigarettes. He gave me one and put the other in his mouth. After a few tries I got one of the matches to light and held the flame to the tip of Johnny's fag. He did the same for me and now we were smokers. I don't remember what that cigarette tasted like; holding a cigarette and looking grown up mattered more than the taste. The fire lit up our faces and we turned our backs to the houses in case someone saw what we were up to. The firelight dazzled our eyes and prevented us from seeing into the darkness of the debris, so we didn't notice the two policemen on bikes when they pulled up in Woodin Street. "Oi! Come here!" one of them shouted. We screened our eyes and saw two hefty constables on bikes. "Run!" shouted Johnny but I was already off by then. We fled towards the gap next to Aunt Mary's and the policemen set off after us on their bikes, taking different directions around the block in a clever pincer movement to catch us in St Leonard's Road.

I got through the gap with no idea of where to go next; the policemen would arrive in seconds. Johnny sprinted off into Zetland Street and I ran along the airies to the Strecker's where Danny Strecker had left his motorbike parked against the wall. I crouched beneath the tarpaulin cover and peeped out through a rope hole, hardly daring to breathe. At once the two big Raleigh bikes appeared from different directions. They stopped, circled a couple of times then went off in the direction of St Michael's church. I didn't move for ages. When I got home, I knew I was safe; no one could accuse me of anything now; the policemen never saw my face. It was a feeling of such relief.

* * *

What are the elements of danger for a child? Perhaps there are two. One is being in danger and the other is doing dangerous things. The first is about bad things happening that are out of our control but the second is about choice: doing something for the thrill of sensation or the chance of getting caught, putting yourself at risk to see how much you can take, seeing how far you can go without getting hurt. Johnny and I were in danger when we walked across the railway bridge but we had chosen to do it even though we knew it would be dangerous. Life on the debris was dangerous too; there was so much that could cause us harm. But we chose to make it more dangerous in so many ways.

Fires were a perpetual danger. We loved having fires but they frequently caught us out. We burnt our hands, got smoke in our eyes and singed our hair; we breathed in fumes and went home reeking of woodsmoke. The bonfires we made for November the fifth were enormous and collecting the wood for them was a danger in itself. Fireworks were dangerous too and we were reckless with them. Boys held lighted bangers in their hands until they started fizzing, then threw them at one another. Rockets, launched from milk bottles, sometimes toppled over and went skidding along the ground into the legs of those nearby. I went to sort out a Catherine wheel once because it didn't spin. It exploded in my face and hit me hard against the teeth. We put potatoes into bonfires and burnt our hands getting them out. Then we burnt our mouths from eating them too hot.

There was plenty of asbestos on the debris; shattered remnants from bombed-out houses. We called it 'asterbaster' and handling it was dangerous, though we didn't know it at the time. Burning it was worse. Billy Mac was good at finding asbestos; "Let's get some asterbaster and build a fire," he would say. When he'd got enough, he would give us some each. If the pieces were too big, we would smash them against stones to break them up. The best thing about asbestos was that when it grew hot, it exploded with a bang sending white flakes into the air that fell down on us like snow.

* * *

Having wars was one of the biggest dangers we faced on the debris. Wars were stone fights that we had with children from other streets. Our enemy was usually Jackie Painter and his pals from Woodin Street. Wars were territorial: we had our debris and Jackie had his. Stone fights were usually pre-arranged. Someone would ask if we wanted one and if there were enough of us, we would say "yes." When war was agreed we'd collect stones for the fight: the smallest were just pebbles but the largest could be the size of house bricks. The war started when the other side appeared and began throwing. We'd throw back and so it would go on. But there was more to wars than that. There was targeting and timing too and we were canny about who to aim at. The most important thing was to know how to avoid stones as they came at you. You kept an eye, judged where the stone would land and leap to one side at the last moment. I loved stone fights, they were exciting: the delight of releasing the stone, the beauty of the trajectory, the effect it had on the other side. I don't think there was much malice in our wars. We didn't want to harm anyone, we just wanted to defeat them. But wars were dangerous nevertheless.

Mary Stock was hit in the face once and the wound was just a fraction below her left eye.

Other gangs caused bigger problems than Jackie's did. John Rodway and Brian Commons had gangs to avoid. John was a tough boy who lived in St Leonard's Avenue, big for his age and strong. Brian was smaller and, in his way, more unpleasant. Whereas our wars with Jackie ended in a mutual withdrawal, wars with John Rodway's gang could get you taken prisoner and beaten. When I was five, I was a victim of Rodway's gang. My friends had knocked for me to come out with them but I had to wait. They said they would see me on the debris and went off to play. It was a Saturday morning. I was wearing a short-sleeved shirt, short trousers with braces and Wellington boots. I looked for the boys on our debris but they weren't there, so I crossed Cobden Street onto the Railway Street debris but still couldn't find them. Then, quite unexpectedly, some boys appeared from out of a bomb shelter. It was John Rodway and three of his mates. I turned and ran for home. "Get 'im," shouted Rodway and he started chasing me. He was big and fast and soon gained on me. I kept ahead of him as I crossed Cobden Street onto our debris, but he was right behind me. "Why hadn't he grabbed me?" I wondered, but John had better sport to enjoy. He had collected some small stones and was lobbing them into the backs of my Wellingtons from behind so as to fill them up. Like a stag at bay, I headed through the gap between the houses in St Leonard's Road and onto safe ground. Rodway gave up and I lived to fight another war.

* * *

Going 'over the Dissie' was a dangerous thing to do. The Dissie was a disinfectant distribution centre in Bow. Every summer, we would make the journey over Sprattsies steps to the depot in Violet Road. Although it was a wholesale centre, the Dissie also sold bleach straight from the vat to take away. Bought like this, the disinfectant was cheaper than buying it in shops. On 'Dissie day' we'd meet in the morning with bottles and flasks and load them onto carts and old prams. There would be about eight of us and five or six carts. It was a hazardous thing for children to do. There was the risk that a bottle might break, and stoppers and bungs sometimes leaked bleach onto our skin. The biggest risk was carrying the carts and containers up and down the steps as the loads wobbled and tipped their way towards us.

* * *

Crossing roads was a much greater risk than crossing Sprattsies steps with flagons of bleach. In 1954 there were 219,380 deaths or injuries from traffic accidents in Britain and, although the population has grown by sixteen million since then and there are three times as many vehicles, the death rate on our roads has halved. Were it not for Johnny Purton, the 1954 statistic would have been smaller by one.

One June evening, Johnny knocked to ask if I wanted to go with him and Uncle Jack to a pub in Aberfeldy Street to drop off some racing pigeons for collection. It was a Monday so the birds would have been travelling a long way to be released; somewhere in France perhaps. Jack never said much and didn't have many friends but he seemed to be at ease in the presence of other pigeon fanciers. Johnny was his pupil; Jack taught him a lot. Even at eight he had a good knowledge of pigeons and could talk about them with authority: "That's a pied cock and that's a checkered hen," he'd say. "This one's just a young'un." He handled pigeons with confidence too, holding them firmly in his hands allowing only their heads to stay free.

I sat waiting on Johnny's airie and Jack came out wrestling an old pram through the front door with some difficulty. With not even a grunt of acknowledgement in my direction, he lowered it onto the pavement and went back inside. A few minutes later he emerged again with a basket of pigeons. He put the basket onto the pram, strapped it in place and covered it with a cloth. Then we set off with Jack in front and Johnny and me behind. Seeing Jack and the pram was a comical sight. It looked like he was pushing a baby draped in cloth; take off the cloth and you'd get a big surprise. It was like something from *Alice in Wonderland*.

We crossed Teviot Street by St Michael's church and carried on down to Brunswick Road. As usual, it was busy with traffic and we waited for the lights to change. But Jack was impatient. He was set on getting his pram to the other side as quickly as he could, so he left Johnny and me behind and took his chances with the road. Johnny ran after him and was soon on the other side. I followed, but half way across I saw cars coming and turned back. At that moment Johnny called to me. "Look at this," he said, pointing to something on the ground. Curious to see what he'd found, I hesitated, turned and was hit by a motor bike.

I've no memory of the impact of the collision but it must have been quite a strong one. Witnesses told me that I was thrown in the air and landed several feet away. That was certainly true because the next thing I remember was lying by the kerb on the other side of Dewberry Street surrounded by people. A lady was looking down at me. "You'll be all right, don't worry, son," she said. "We've called an ambulance." "I wanna go 'ome," I said, "I'm all right, I ain't hurt." "They'll just want to have a look at you. You'll need to let the doctors see you," said the lady. "I want my mum. I only live round there, let me go 'ome." "You've 'it yer 'ed, son," said a man, "They'll 'av to 'av a look at yer." In a few minutes the ambulance arrived. I was able to get into it without much help and I didn't have to lie down when I was inside either. Once I had settled, I put my hand to the back of my head and felt an enormous bump. That's when I knew it could be bad. Head injuries were serious. I might have damaged my brain. I could hear the bell of the ambulance as we went along; a high-pitched ringing to move traffic out of the way. So this was an emergency and things were obviously serious. Through the darkened windows I saw familiar streets and buildings passing by; the fire station, the library, the back of Spey Street and Uncle Pat's house.

But how would I know if I had damaged my brain? The thought nagged at me as we hurried on our way to St Andrew's Hospital. Then I had the good idea of setting myself a test. I would say some of my times tables, starting with a hard one like nine. If I could do it, I would be all right. I went through the table quickly; 'nine nines are eighty-one, 'ten nines are ninety, 'eleven nines are ninety-nine,' 'twelve nines are a hundred-and-eight.' It was all still there; I wasn't going to lose my mind.

The ambulance sped past the Sun Flour Mill, turned into Devas Street and pulled up at the hospital. I don't know how long it took to be seen by a doctor but I think it wasn't long. I was undressed, put into a hospital robe and examined. As I lay on the bed, I noticed how dirty I was. The nurses had taken off my plimsoles and socks and my feet were black with dirt. We didn't have the money to keep replacing shoes and my plimsoles were full of holes and worn. Because the plimsoles had holes, my socks had holes too and because of that, the dirt from the street had made my feet filthy. "Can I see my mum and dad?" I asked when the nurse put me into my robe. I had never been alone without them like this before. The doctor examined me, decided I had to be admitted and I was taken up to the children's ward. There I was bathed, given a fresh nightshirt and put to bed. Everything was so clean and light. The bedclothes were sharp and white like *Cartridge paper*. A nurse tucked me in so tightly that I couldn't free my arms. I had been captured and was now a little prisoner. It was early evening.

"There's someone to see you," said a nurse and my dad was there. My heart swelled at the sight of him; I felt so happy and safe. "Hello Dad." "What you bin up to, boy?" "Got run over, Dad." He couldn't stay long. He was at work and he'd been allowed out for just a little while. I wanted so much for him to stay and I wanted my mum too, but hospital rules were strict and I wouldn't see either of them until visiting time on Wednesday. When he kissed me goodbye, I smelt the familiar factory smell of him; soap on his skin and onions on his breath.

The ward was long and wide. Generations of children had lain along its walls since St Andrews opened as the Poplar and Stepney Sick Asylum in 1868. It was clean and light with a long table in the centre and a kitchen and bathrooms at the end. Iron bedsteads gave it an old-fashioned look like wards in pictures I have seen of wounded soldiers recovering in World War One.

I spent a restless night. I managed some sleep but was woken twice by nurses who came to check on me. The ward was dark, save for a shaft of dim yellow light from above the nurses' station. I fell in and out of sleep and was woken not long after five by the sound of a vacuum cleaner. Porridge and eggs. Toast. Weak grey tea. Doctors came; nurses took my temperature. I wasn't allowed to get up. "I'll bring you a bottle," said a nurse. I had a water jug and wasn't thirsty but the bottle she brought was not for me to drink from. "Use this and we've a pan if you need to do something else," she said. Another long day followed and another tedious night. Another early awakening and more checking up. "You can get up tomorrow," I was told.

I was eight and had put on some weight. I was a chubby boy now and didn't like it. When they bathed me on the third morning, the nurses considered me alongside a boy who was chubby like me. "Well, and who should we start with?" asked one. "It's six of one and half-a-dozen of the other." I didn't mind her saying that, she was just being jolly; but I was self-conscious and hated being overweight. The next time a doctor came, he brought others with him. He pulled up my pyjama top and showed them my back. "You are going to be all right, but you have been a very lucky young man." Turning to the others he said: "Look at his back; a perfect imprint of the bike's handlebars and lamp." "His fat saved him," one of the nurses joked. They laughed and I cringed.

Children came and went as the days passed and I got to know some of them. To my surprise, one was John Rodway, but hospital had tamed him; he wasn't a problem now and showed a better side. The most interesting of my fellow patients was a girl called Elaine. She was the first truly posh person I ever met. She was stout, chatty and plain and spoke with a lovely disarming lisp. She liked talking about the Queen and quizzed us all about our encounters with her. "Have you theen the Queen?" she asked when it was my turn. "The day after the Coronation," I boasted, knowing that Elaine could never match that. "Have you?" I asked. "Only a glimpth," she replied. 'Glimpth!' No one I knew would ever have said 'glimpse' let alone lisping it like Elaine and in such a posh voice too. Over the next few days, I contrived to get her to say it again. "Did you see the Queen close-up when she went by?" I asked. "No, I only caught a glimpth," replied Elaine to my great satisfaction.

At six o'clock on Wednesday the visitors' bell sounded and there were my mum and dad with bags full of supplies and smiling. They loaded my locker with chocolate and apples and handed me a pile of comics. "Old Brum came over this morning," said my dad. "He's sent you in six new-laid eggs. They're for you and no one else so I've written yer name on 'em." Old Brum and Jeannie had nothing. The eggs they got from their chickens were so important to them. And even now, when I think of that...when I think of that...

* * *

I knew my parents were married because we had a picture of their wedding and they kept the decoration from the top of their wedding cake in a glass cabinet at home. In the wedding picture my dad is wearing a stylish single-breasted suit and holding an impressive Homburg hat. He looks more than a little drunk too. My mum is surrounded by bridesmaids and looking stern. The picture was taken in someone's backyard; probably Nanny Powell's.

Why do I mention this? Well, on my fourth morning in hospital, two Irish nurses came to ask us where we intended to worship on Sunday morning. "Catholic or Church of England?" they enquired. We told them our denominations and they wrote them down. When I said "Church of England," they seemed surprised. "Church of England? Are you sure you're not a Catholic?" "No, I was Christened Church of England and I go to St Michael's church." "But with a name like Connolly surely you must be a Catholic," the nurse persisted. "Well, me dad's a Catholic but me mum's Church of England," I said. "Where did they get married?" she asked. "Poplar Church, up the main road," I replied. She turned to her colleague. "Poor child," she said with sadness in her voice, "His mother and father are not married." I was shocked by this and sought to correct her. "They *are* marrid, I've seen a photo," I said. "Not in the eyes of God they're not," she replied.

That was Catholicism in 1954 and those Irish nurses were brought up not to question the teachings of the church. Because of that, an eight-year-old boy, in hospital and away from home, was told that his mother and father were not married when he knew that they were. That incident must not misrepresent my feelings for those Irish nurses; they were kind to me and as much the victims of religious dogma as I was. Most of the nurses I saw were from Ireland, but there were a few black Caribbean ones too. One of them, nurse White, stays in my mind because she was so nice and the first black person I'd ever met. There were English nurses too but not many. They were like the girls who went to Doreen's school; tidy and nicely spoken. The ward sisters were all English; they were 'frosty' and they had authority. Sisters were in charge of the nurses and nurses did as they were told. With no other adults on the ward, nurses did everything.

St Andrew's had been designed for a model of healthcare that kept people in beds and accommodated them in numbers. It was old, institutional and large. On the way to the ward, the trolley porter told me that the corridor we were passing down was a quarter of a mile long and, apparently, he was right. The age of the building didn't matter on the wards because they were clean and well-kept, but beyond them parts of the hospital were bleak and depressing.

On my fourth day I was taken outside to sit in the fresh air. A nurse led three of us to the end of the ward and out onto a metal landing by a fire escape. The landing was rusting and grubby. From it, I could see down to Brunswick Road and beyond to my dad's gasworks. It was a dispiriting experience. The view offered a tantalising glimpse of freedom but I was a captive in pyjamas, watching life go on but not being able to take part in it.

On Sunday, we ate our lunch together at the long table. At two o'clock, the bell went and the ward filled with visitors. I had been in hospital for nearly a week and had only seen my mum and dad once. No one else in the family had been allowed in to see me. This time everyone came: Doreen, Aunt Rose, Uncle Henry and Uncle Charlie, taking turns to sit by the bed, but only two at a time as that was the rule. "What did they giv yer for yer dinner, Joey?" asked Aunt Rose. I told her we had lamb. "It was lovely but the mint sauce was narf watery, Aunt Rose." The ward sister came to talk to my parents before they left. "A doctor will take a look at him in the morning and if he is all right, he can go home," she said. I was examined the next day and seven days after I'd been hit by the bike, I was home.

The shock of my accident must have been awful for my family, and for my mum in particular, because she was such a worrier. I can imagine what it would have been like for her with my dad being at work and not knowing how badly injured I was. The news of my accident quickly got around; neighbours, aunts, uncles, friends and schoolmates soon knew what had happened. Ronnie Kitts came over on his bike to ask how I was and reported back to my teacher and classmates when he got back to school. "I ain't seen nuffink like it. There was lots of people runnin' in and out of eachuvverss 'ouses with bottles of brandy in their 'ands."

It is an ill wind that blows nobody any good and my accident turned out well for Doreen. The motorbike rider was a studious sixth-former at George Green's. When he found out where I lived, he came to ask how I was. Once reassured, he came back again with a box of chocolates for Doreen and an offer to take her to a show in London. He never brought me anything and he never came to see me. When I came home, I asked Johnny Purton what it was he had called me back to see on the night I was knocked down. "A butterfly," he said. "A big blue 'un.'"

* * *

In telling these stories, a picture emerges of a robust boy: one who enjoyed taking a chance, a street urchin, a bit of a rascal, naughty but never bad. But that is misleading. I was never really brave. The dangers I chose to face were ones that offered me thrills and excitement. I engaged in them unthinkingly. Bravery is about more than that; it is about facing danger in a considered way because it is the right thing to do. If I was ever brave, then maybe it was when I rode Billy Mac's bike all the way home from Sidcup with only one brake and a nervous Billy to look out for. What the stories do not show is a cautious boy; one who often thought others were better or stronger than him, one who sometimes shied away from things he didn't want to face, one who cared too much about what others might think of him. "Joe's a worrier," Miss Woods once told my mum, and she was right. I wasn't always such a good boy either. Egged on by others I did things of which I am not proud; awful things like being cruel to the man in the sweetshop and taking 'knock down ginger' much too far. I was all of these things and I was a kind and thoughtful boy too. We are complex.

LOUSY BUT LOYAL

I saw a photograph once of a street party somewhere in the East End. The party was to celebrate the Silver Jubilee of King George the Fifth. In it, the houses are hung with flags and bunting; people are looking happy and above them a banner reads: *Lousy but Loyal*. When I first saw that picture, it delighted me with its cheerful portrayal of a community of people like mine and I loved the cockney wit of the caption too. Now I am not so sure.

I imagine that the people in the picture would have enjoyed proclaiming themselves 'lousy but loyal'; they would have seen the irony and got the joke. They would have laughed at themselves. But the hard message in the picture is really about knowing one's place; it is about inferiority and deference. The proclaimed loyalty may have been for the King, but the King came with a package of rules, titles, customs, manners and ranks that guaranteed privilege for the few at the expense of everyone else.

If you want to know about the people those East Enders were pledging their loyalty to, then read the diaries of Duff Cooper or, worse, those of Henry 'Chips' Channon. Laid bare in those accounts is a society of idleness and greed where wealthy people obsess about jewellery, country houses and dining out. Channon, an American 'outsider,' is desperate to be included in upper-class society and fawns over aristocrats and royalty. When I read his diaries, my thoughts about the *Lousy but Loyal* picture changed, because now I understood what Channon and his like would have made of it. They would have felt justified in their superiority by seeing the 'lower classes' admit to poverty and deference. They would have held them in contempt. They would have laughed *at* them and not *with* them.

When I was four, I was taken to see King George the Sixth and his Queen as they drove along Burdett Road on a tour of the East End. I saw them again three years later when George planted a tree in the grounds of my school. His death in February 1952 had a tremendous impact. We had seen pictures of him waving farewell to his daughter at London Airport as she left for Africa; a sick man in an overcoat watching and waving as the plane took to the sky. But although his frailty was there for all to see in those pictures, his death was unexpected and took the nation by surprise.

George had been a reluctant monarch. He was shy and had difficulty pronouncing his words. His brother dealt him a bad blow by abdicating and two years after George was crowned king, the country was at war. But he became a symbol of strength during the war and complemented Churchill's bullish audacity with his constancy and quiet reassurance. Unsurprisingly then, when I was young, the monarchy was popular because it was in good hands. George's death was big news. Headlines like *'A Nation Mourns'* were not hyperbole but a true reflection on how millions of people were feeling. His funeral took place on the 15th of February 1952. It was a school day; cold and overcast. We were asked to wear something black to mark our respect. I wore a black tie like all men did at funerals. The ceremony was broadcast on radio and we listened to it in the classroom. "When the two minutes' silence is declared, you must stay as still as statues," said our teacher. I was leaning into a cupboard when the gun sounded for silence and, as I froze, my black tie continued swinging from side to side and I felt I had let someone down.

George's wife Elizabeth became unpopular in the years after he died. Maybe the country was so taken by her daughter that the tubby middle-aged Elizabeth could not compete. But we liked her at our school because she visited us a couple of times after George died. She was patronne of The London Flower Lovers League and took her role seriously, or so it seemed. We were all members of the League. Being a flower lover involved growing daffodil bulbs in pots. Elizabeth came to see the daffodils when they were in bloom and we were given certificates if they were considered good enough. The Flower Lovers League was a fine idea because children across London, many without gardens, were able to grow and appreciate flowers of their own.

The Coronation of Elizabeth the Second was a massive affair. It held the attention of the nation for months and was followed with interest throughout the world. Like hundreds of streets across the country, St Leonard's Road planned a street party for the day. Mrs Skeets from Billy Mac's buildings set up a committee and my dad and a few others were on it with her. They met around the table in our kitchen and I was impressed by how capable they were. Mrs Skeets chaired the meetings with the lightest of touches and had a knack of getting people to act rather than talk. Companies were asked to give their products: crisps from *Meredith and Drew*, chocolate bars from *Rowntree*, paper hats, flags, badges and balloons from other firms. Every child was given a coronation mug and a pen and pencil set too. People decorated their houses with flags and posters and George Butler built a stage on his airie.

My dad bought a television so that we could watch the coronation broadcast. It was a Ferguson with a twelve-inch screen and, at eighty-four pounds, the most expensive thing we had ever owned. Coronation day was wet. The rain never stopped falling but the parade in London went ahead. My mum put chairs in front of the television and invited Nell Smith and Mrs Stock to watch the day's events with Nanny Powell and us. The parade was long and impressive with thousands of marching troops, world leaders in carriages, cavalry and marching bands. It was the swansong of the British Empire and, in its way, a final celebration of victory in World War Two. When the crown was lowered onto Elizabeth's head Mrs Stock said, "Gawd bless 'er," and Nanny Powell toasted the newly-crowned queen with a glass of stout: "Gawd bless yer, Liz."

The street party was called off because of the rain. There were to be races, a fancy-dress competition, a beauty contest and a tea party, but it was too wet to go ahead with them. Instead, the 'guvnor' of *The Foresters* opened his pub and we wandered around in fancy-dress costumes most of which had previously seen service as bed sheets in houses up and down the street. We had our street party the following Saturday. Tables were laid end-to-end and covered with cloths and food. The sun shone and it was a great little party.

Elizabeth chose to visit the East End the day after her Coronation. It was a canny decision on her part, I think; a clever way of bonding with her poorer subjects. I saw her close-up that day as she drove slowly past Poplar Town Hall but I had to wear an eye patch because I had developed a painful stye on my left eye. I told the story of how I saw the Queen in a poem I wrote for my grandchildren. It's an accurate account of that day and here are the last few verses:

"As we waited on the kerbside for the new queen to come by,
I quite forgot my eye patch and the nasty little stye.
"She's running late," a policeman said to someone in the crowd.
"She's nearly here," another called, (his voice a bit too loud.)

"She's up the road!" a man yelled out, "She's getting pretty near."
With that the crowd towards the church
Gave one enormous cheer.
Then motorcycle policemen came, not really very far,
Riding in formation followed by a big black car.

And then the best thing happened, the best that it could be,
Because the Queen looked up and gave a special wave to me!
I knew the wave was meant for me for I had caught her eye,
A little boy who wore a patch because he had a stye."

SIR LUCY LAWRENCE

When Manorfield school opened along the road in Wyvis Street, someone asked Aunt Rose if I was going to leave Susan Lawrence and go there instead. "No, they're genna keep him there," she said. "That Sir Lucy Lawrence is a very good school." Aunt Rose was right; Susan Lawrence was a very good school. It nurtured my imagination and helped me to solve problems, think creatively and show leadership to others. I left Susan Lawrence a capable mathematician, a confident writer and a working-class ten-year-old who could appreciate classical music, poetry and the works of Shakespeare.

"What is the city but the people?" Shakespeare asks in *Coriolanus*. In the context of education, we might paraphrase that and say: "What is a school but the teachers?" Schools exist for the children, but it is teachers who can change their lives. I was given a good start at Alton Street by Mrs Byford and brought on at Susan Lawrence by teachers who were patient, capable and sympathetic. My first teacher there was Miss Woods. She was short and tubby with a pleasant voice and an engaging smile. I thrived under her guidance particularly in aspects of literacy. Miss Woods read to us a lot and encouraged us to read. She chose stories with odd, funny characters that engaged us with their antics. She developed our handwriting too. I progressed through the Marion Richardson writing books and began to form cursive letters from repeating patterns.

Mrs Henry was my first teacher in junior school. She was stocky, middle-aged and always in control. She sat at her desk much of the time and never ventured far, but she knew us so well and she knew how to move us forward in our learning. Mrs Henry was thorough and persistent. Her emphasis was on standards and she expected the best. She taught us to take responsibility; if we made a mess, we had to clear it up. She was harsh on wrong-doing and praising of success. She gave us routines to help things run smoothly and she had lots of monitors. There were milk monitors, ink monitors, monitors to sharpen pencils and monitors to give out the awful cod liver oil capsules that were meant to keep us healthy. At the end of every day, we had a routine to send us calmly on our way: "Stand…put your chairs on your desks…hands together and eyes closed." Then a short prayer and "Amen." "Goodbye children." "Goodbye, Mrs Henry." "Don't run!" On Fridays it was different. Before we went home, she would announce her 'workers of the week' and four or five of us would be given a threepenny piece or sixpence as a reward for working hard or doing a good deed.

Mrs Henry had no family of her own but it was obvious that she liked children and she cared about us. Her husband was the same. Mr Henry came in to play the piano from time to time or help with PE and games. He was a nice man; short, bespectacled and with a face that was quick to smile. Every weekend during our last term in Mrs Henry's class, she took groups of us to her house in Blackheath for Sunday tea. It was a big class so it was a big commitment, but the Henrys did it because they were good people who liked children.

* * *

Mr Thake taught me for the next two years. Alan Thake: funny, imaginative, clever, caring, tough when he had to be, and so much more. When we went swimming, he was in the pool with us. When we did country dancing, he took a partner and skipped around the hall. He pulled our legs and made us laugh. He told us stories and held us captive with his style. In a world where men could be detached or dull, here was a different sort of man; someone with imagination and wit. I thrived under Alan Thake and I know that I owe him so much. In my last year of infant school, I was taught by Miss Williams, a lovely young Welsh teacher. She was lively and animated with bubbly hair and busy arms that protruded from the smock she wore to keep her dresses clean. I really liked her; everyone did. Her presence didn't go unnoticed by Mr Thake either and one day we were told: "From now on Miss Williams is to be known as Mrs Thake."

The Thakes lived at 54 Kenilworth Gardens in Brentwood. I know that because Mr Thake brought in copies of the *Daily Express* from home to cover the tables when we did painting. Each copy had 54 Kenilworth Gardens pencilled on the top for the paper boy to see. Mr Thake was a Labour man politically, so his choice of the *Daily Express* might seem odd, but the *Express* was a good read in those days and Alan Thake was intelligent enough to make his own mind up about politics. I think that he may have been active in politics too but, if he was, he never showed us any bias. My first headmaster, Mr Mills, was a Communist, but I never knew that until I was told it by an ex-pupil about ten years ago. He never gave a hint of his political persuasions and I imagine that, like other British Communists, his allegiances may have changed after the Russians invaded Hungary in 1956.

The classrooms at Susan Lawrence were light and airy. Enclosed bridges led across to them from the upstairs corridor. They faced south towards the river and the strong afternoon sun that flooded in was filtered by huge Venetian blinds that gathered dust along their slats. Save for the blackboards behind the teacher's desk and the inkwells in ours, our classroom looked much like classrooms do today. The walls were light, the furniture was modern and the floor was laid with synthetic tiles. High on the wall at the back of the class was a clock with attractive black numerals on a white face. A red second hand moved jerkily around the dial. It was a thing perfect in its simplicity.

Wherever we were in school, our surroundings were pleasant and modern. The scale of the building was right, the layout was interesting; it was a good place to be. The walk to the Juniors' hall took us through the best part of the building up a broad open staircase like no staircase I'd seen. The hall was the heart of the school. It was where we danced, prayed, listened to music, acted, sang and exercised. We assembled there every morning, led in class by class to the sound of classical music. We would sit cross-legged and listen until the piece was over, then a teacher would talk about what we'd just heard: Handle's *Music for the Royal Fireworks* or a piece from Tchaikovsky's *Nutcracker Suite* or *Mars, the Bringer of War* from Holst's *The Planets*.

On Tuesdays we were taken to the hall for *Music and Movement,* a radio programme for schools. "Find a space all to yourself and *breeeeathe*." "Now stretch and stretch, with your arms to the sky." "Now you are a leaf tumbling softly to the ground." "Now be a twig, brittle and stiff." We did our best, but the posh voice and the silly things we were asked to do made us glad when it was all over. It was much better when we made our own music. Percussion with its wonderful drums, maracas, triangles, castanets and tambourines. Then the lispy sound of recorders as the class played *Clair de Lune* in unison. All that and the pleasure of playing a xylophone too. We sang, not always well but heartily: folk songs and traditional airs, songs from Scotland and military ballads.

'O soldier, soldier, won't you marry me
With your musket fife and drum?
O no sweet maid I cannot marry you
For I have no coat to put on…'

We had PE in the hall or in the playground if the weather was right. I loved the apparatus we used: plastic hoops in primary colours, bean bags in red blue and green and big wooden skittles in those colours too.

The most uplifting music I ever heard at school were the tunes we had for Country Dancing. The music was joyous and the titles were romantic: *Haste to the Wedding, Dashing White Sergeant, The Eightsome Reel,* and *Strip the Willow.* Try listening to *The Eightsome Reel* without wanting to dance. Country dancing was the best thing we ever did at school. Everyone enjoyed it, boys as much as girls and our teachers joined in. Each Christmas, Poplar Borough Council held a country dance party for primary schools. The Civic Theatre would be full of local children from Poplar and Stepney. We all knew the same dances and performed some of them together in our hundreds. My dance partner was Pamela Lyons. Pam was a very nice girl but taller than me and heavier. One afternoon when we were rehearsing for the dance party, I felt her hands slipping away as we twirled around. Charged with centrifugal energy, Pamela flew away at speed and hit one of the big hall windows with a bang. Had the window not have been made of reinforced glass, Pam would have had a terrible accident and had the window been open, we may not have had Pam at all.

Things changed when Mr Thake went into hospital and Mr Silva took his place. Silva was a difficult and unpleasant man. He was tall and dark with a menacing look and we feared him. He would sit with his feet on the desk or prowl around the room waiting to jump on someone for making a mistake. He shouted a lot and was free with his hands; shouting and smacking were his preferred methods of control. However, his bullying rebounded on him because the gutsier children sometimes hit back.

Eventually, Silva left and an Australian teacher took his place. He was a better replacement in every way. We soon got to like him and even the toughest in the class responded to him well. He had an easy way with us and told us his name. Teachers never told us their names but he was informal like that. We put his casualness down to the fact that he was Australian. He took a group camping one weekend and here an element of concern arises because some of the boys said they saw him naked in the tent. Nothing else happened, but he stayed that way and didn't cover up. We thought it odd that he was seen naked but we didn't think of it as sinister. As an adult I see it differently now. I cannot say if his nudity had a sexual motive or not and I have not named the man, but I know for sure that teachers should never appear naked in front of their pupils.

* * *

Mr Thake left in 1955 for promotion and Mr Clark replaced him. Philip Clark was everything a teacher should be and a good, decent man too. He came into teaching after serving in the RAF; a young idealist who knew what his mission was and did all he could to achieve it. He didn't have Alan Thake's animated flair, but his humour was just as good and his teaching equally as effective. It was my last year at Susan Lawrence and I was now in a 'top class.' Teaching a top class came with the responsibility of preparing children for the Eleven-plus examination. There were two top classes at Susan Lawrence: ours and Mr Enervor's. When the Eleven-plus results were announced, it became clear that the classes had been streamed because none of Mr Enervor's children were given a grammar school place and eleven of Mr Clark's were.

There was no 'cramming' for the Eleven-plus. As the exam grew nearer, we were given past papers to try, but the curriculum remained broad and interesting. Mr Clarke had a love of drama and by the end of the Easter term, our skills had become quite sophisticated. He taught us how to improvise, how to move in a confined space and how to speak quietly on stage and still be heard. He read to us from Shakespeare and skilfully decoded the language. He cast Janice Watkins and me as Macbeth and his wife once, and we improvised the murder of Duncan in front of the class. We were confident in doing that because we knew what the issues were and were capable of acting them out.

Mr Clark was like an anti-hero in a 1950s British film; the kind of film that dealt with down-to-earth issues and ordinariness. He was short and fair with a moustache that he probably started growing when he was in the RAF. He had a wife and two daughters and he lived at Loughton in Essex. Although he had children of his own, he thought it right to give time to us when he could have been with his family. One Saturday he took a group of us to Epping Forest. It was raining heavily when we arrived and it poured for the rest of the morning. We sheltered under the trees for a while but it was hopeless and we just had to get out of the weather. What was he to do? He was a teacher with a dozen drenched children, miles from their homes and with no other adult to help him. "I know somewhere we can go," he said, and led us out of the forest and into a leafy avenue of respectable-looking houses. He stopped at one and we waited by the gate as he knocked on the door. It opened. He had a word on the doorstep and we were invited in.

The house belonged to a friend of his. Although he turned up out of the blue with his collection of young East Enders, his friend was quite unfazed. She welcomed us, showed us through to a big scullery and we took off our things. There was a mangle in the corner, the type with wooden rollers. "You can use that if you like. It will get the worst of the water out." So, we did, and summer rain oozed from our soggy coats and socks. After that, things got better. We ate our lunches, dried out and the rain stopped. For the rest of the day, we had the forest to ourselves and it was perfect; another world.

On Wednesdays Mr Clark took the boys to the cinder pitch in Glaucus Street for football. I remember a pass I made once, a diagonal ball that cut through the middle of the field and set up an attack. "Bold pass there!" shouted Mr Clark and I felt terrific. I do not know if he was a footballer himself but he knew how to get us to play, and under his guidance, Susan Lawrence won the East London Schools' Cup. Our best players were selected to play for East London and some went on to play for West Ham. David Barnett and I were on milk duty once, piercing the foil bottle tops and putting drinking straws through them for when the class came back from break. Looking down into the Juniors' playground, I saw a little boy with long red hair. He was being chased everywhere by a group of others but they could never catch him, he was so fast and free. "Who's that?" I asked. "That's Harry Redknapp," David replied. Harry went on to become a fast, exciting winger for West Ham and I saw him play many times.

When Phillip Clark was eighty, Doreen and Valerie Vint, another ex-pupil, decided to take him to lunch. Harry Redknapp was now the manager of West Ham and Doreen thought it would be nice if he could sign a birthday card to Phillip for them to give him at the meal. When she rang Harry's office, Harry cut into the call. "Oo's that? What d'ya want? Phil Clark? When's 'is birthday? All right, bring 'im along to…" and he gave them a time and named a restaurant in Barkingside. I can only imagine how Phillip Clark must have felt when Harry walked in. The story is a tribute to them both. Harry's birthday gift to Phil was his time. He was the manager of a premier league football club but he stayed at the lunch for over two hours. In fact, Harry gave more than just time because he picked up the bill too. When Mr Enervor was in hospital dying of cancer, Patsy Holland, another West Ham star, sat by his bed; a good Poplar boy like Harry and another who didn't forget his teacher.

* * *

The Eleven-plus came with anxiety. I worried about taking the exams and then I worried about the outcome. We were used to doing tests but these were different: printed question papers; total silence, watched by teachers; those you turned to for help were now outsiders looking in. I wasn't over-confident but I knew I had a good chance. I was good at English and fine with maths too. My biggest uncertainty about Eleven-plus exams wasn't the maths but the verbal reasoning aspect of the English test. *'Peas are to a pod as bricks are to a...'* The answers could come from general knowledge and getting them right could be easy but some questions were open-ended and required logic. Maths could involve logic too. Here's a maths question from a 1950s paper, maybe it was the one I took.

'A train leaves London at 11.30 a.m. and arrives at Bristol at 1.30 p.m., after stopping from 12.10 p.m. to 12.20 p.m. at Reading, which is 36 miles from London. It travelled both parts of the journey at the same rate. Find the distance from London to Bristol.'

The day the results came out, Raymond Holmes and I were at Cardinal Griffin School helping to set things up for a play we were performing there that evening. Like me, Ray was in the running for a grammar school place, but we didn't know when we would hear. We got back to school just before the bell went for home and on the way to our classroom we were stopped by Mr Howell. "Come 'ere, boys," he said in his rich Welsh baritone. He looked serious; we thought we had done something wrong. "I have got the results of your Eleven-plus exams." Now I was really concerned; his tone and demeanour made me fear the worst. Then he paused, jabbed a finger at each of us and said: "Grammar, grammar."

Now my time at Susan Lawrence was over. It had taken me in at five with whatever abilities nature had given me and nurtured them to make a boy who thought that almost anything was possible. At a low point in my life and facing my final assessment at Bath Academy, I reached back to Susan Lawrence in the hope of finding something that could help me; reassurance perhaps? I found the children instead and feared for their futures. I was nineteen when I wrote this:

THE AIR YOU BREATHE

The air you breathe my children,
Settles on the classroom blinds in layers;
The man who made them didn't think of that.

Your teacher is a politician
And he's teaching you today
And the lady with the needle
Says her words a different way.

The clock is black and white and red
And stands aloft above your head
With plans for you, my children

Whilst far below, a second is an hour
But only for a day or two,
And eating taters with your knife
Will rapidly dissolve
In mounting moments to a life.

The yellow hoops and those of blue
And tambourines that bang the tune
And silence in the testing room
Are all for you, my children.
The silent tests will never end
And milk-toothed mouths that call you friend
Will hum injustice in a trend
Too late to ever make amend.
I wish you well, my children.

THE LADY WITH THE NEEDLE

Nothing much frightened me at Susan Lawrence save, perhaps, for the threat of having 'the needle.' We were given lots of medical care at school and the emphasis was on prevention. We had milk to strengthen our bones and cod liver oil capsules because they were thought to have health benefits. There were regular dental checks and eye tests and we were weighed and measured. Once a term, the school nurse came to check our ears and hair and in the quiet of the medical room, she would take a steel comb and pass it carefully across our scalps in search of head lice.

In schools across the country, the school nurse was always known as 'Nitty Nora the Flea Explorer,' and ours was no exception. Although she was a significant adult, she was not like a teacher because she wore a uniform and she 'did things' to you. Our nurse spoke in a quiet Scottish voice and was the only person at school to call me Joseph and not Joe. If Nora came to give injections, word got round quickly because everyone feared 'having the needle.' When a monitor came with a list of names, the class would freeze: "The following people please go down to the medical room now..." Some of us were vaccinated more than others because of their particular vulnerabilities, but everyone got the needle in the end because the government decided to act decisively when a Poliomyelitis pandemic hit the country in the 1950s. The immunisation programme was so successful that the disease was virtually eradicated. There are no 'Nitty Noras' anymore and less preventative medicine is provided in schools. The level of health monitoring we received doesn't seem to happen now and that must be a lost opportunity.

A GAME OF CRICKET

By 1956, the Lansbury Estate had realised the aims of its creators and was now a settled and contented community. The cornerstones upon which it was based - neighbourhood schools, local churches, a marketplace and a care home for the elderly - had produced a good quality of life for those who lived there. I saw that process unfolding in my school as teachers, children and parents grew closer together to build a contented community of our own. Much of the success was down to my first headmaster, George Mills.

George was a man confident in his own authority; a down-to-earth Englishman. He was an ordinary man, a bespectacled man who wore brown: brown suits, brown waistcoats, brown ties, brown shoes and brown socks. He spoke plain English in a plain English way. He was a man of common sense and not given to frivolity. He was sometimes described as "a dry old stick" and he certainly was that, but under his leadership the school became a place of learning where children's lives were enriched by so much more than just the basic curriculum. George wasn't much liked and he wasn't even likeable, but he had what it takes to lead. It was he who introduced country dancing to Poplar schools. Under his leadership the arts became an integral part of our school lives. He established a parent-teacher association and it flourished. There were dances, talks and sports events. The PTA dances were good: music playing from loudspeakers, teachers dancing with parents, and Mr Hunt shouting, "Play *Sugar Bush* again!" whenever a record ended.

There were quieter evenings too. Sometimes speakers were invited to give talks on subjects like child behaviour or reading. I cringed once when my dad asked a psychologist, "Why is it that every time I ask my son to do something, he always says 'wait?'" He said it for amusement and it got a laugh, but I think that the psychologist was looking for something more profound.

One summer's evening in 1956, the Lansbury project reached perfection. It was the night of the parents and teachers cricket match. The lower playground was full with parents and children lining the pitch. There were cheers and claps as Mr Howell and Mr Enervor, bats in hand and 'padded up,' walked out to take their places at the wicket. It was a tight match and I think the parents won, but what mattered wasn't the result, it was what the match represented. It showed us that we were part of something good; that we were together. Boys played for the teachers, dads showed their children a sporting side they hadn't seen, mums bowled or took a few turns at the crease and people stood together and cheered. After a while, David Barnett and I went up to our classroom to get a better view. As I looked down, I saw my dad go out to bat; I saw him hit a few respectable shots and I was so happy. The evening was warm and perfect, everything around me was modern and good, people were mixing together who'd never met before. That moment, when I saw my dad playing cricket, that was the moment when the Lansbury project achieved perfection.

AN INTERVIEW

When Doreen left Alton Street, she was offered a place at a central school. 'Centrals' were established after the war to provide a more technical, vocational form of secondary education. There were two good ones locally, but her teacher, Terry Russell, said there was a better one in Greenwich and she should try for that. Education was important to my mum and dad and they rated Terry's opinion, so the following September, Doreen started at Greenwich Park School for Girls. It was a brave decision to send her there because it was a long way from home and it involved a complicated journey: a bus to the Isle of Dogs, a walk through the Thames foot tunnel and another walk to the school near Greenwich Park. Doreen did well at her new school and after a year, she was given a place at Roan Girls, a grammar school nearby.

Like Doreen, I had options when it was my time to move schools. There were several grammars in the wider area and three local ones of which, Coopers Company was reckoned to be the best. Doreen was now deputy head girl at Roan and she said there was a Roan boys' school with an excellent reputation and I should try for that. We could apply for three so I made Roan my first choice with Coopers second and George Green's third. My application went in and I waited to hear if I would be offered an interview. I waited and waited; we all waited. Ronnie Kitts was the first to hear; he got invited to interview at Coopers. Then, a few days later, Pamela Lyons was offered one at Coborn in Bow Road. Raymond Holmes was next; his first choice was George Green's just around the corner from where he lived. A few more anxious days passed for me until an envelope arrived inviting me to 'attend The Roan School, Maze Hill, Blackheath S.E.3 for interview.'

The Roan was impressive in so many ways, not least its location being beside Greenwich Park and just along from Blackheath. The building was impressive too: handsome and symmetrical with a double-porticoed entrance, doric columns, a fine clock set in a pale-green cube and an elegant columned bell tower crowning it at the top. Above the door was the John Roan crest, the same crest that Doreen wore on her blazer pocket.

My father took me to the interview. He held my hand as we walked up Maze Hill to the school, knowing, I am sure, that he must soon let go, that I would have to make my own way from then on. Any apprehension I felt left me when I entered the building; it wasn't that I felt a sudden surge of confidence, but because a process took over and I had no choice. We were met by a prefect in the entrance hall and taken to wait in a gallery that overlooked the school hall. A few minutes later another prefect arrived and led me to a pokey little room that served as a book store. Inside, two prefects with notebooks were sitting at a scratched wooden table. They put me at my ease and one of them asked me about my tastes in reading. "Tell us about a book you have read; something you liked," he said. I knew I was on safe ground because I had read lots of books and wouldn't have to struggle for a reply. "*Kidnapped* by Robert Louis Stevenson is one I liked and *Children of the New Forest* by Captain Marriott is another." "What did you particularly enjoy about *Kidnapped*?" I was fine now; we were talking about books and I knew what I liked.

After that, the other boy took over. "I am going to give you something to read for us," he said, handing me an open copy of *Treasure Island*. "Start at the first paragraph and read down to the bottom of the page." It was quite a long piece with plenty of opportunities for slipping up but I didn't falter or stumble over the words. When I had finished reading, they thanked me and asked me to wait outside. A few minutes later one of them handed me a piece of tightly-folded paper. "Give this to the Headmaster," he said. Once he had gone back inside, I unfolded the paper to see what was written. They had given me two grades and, looking at them, I reckoned I had done all right.

Dad was waiting outside the Head's office when I got back. "How did yer get on?" he asked, but before I could answer, the door opened and we were shown inside by the school secretary, a heavy-set man in his fifties with a face fixed into an unnatural smile. The office was spacious and light; it spoke of quality but not of money and, like the façade of the building, it too was impressive. Mr Gilbert was seated behind a large desk. He looked just like I imagined the headmaster of a 1950s grammar should look: tall, silver-haired and dignified in his pale-grey suit and black academic gown. He welcomed us, asked for the piece of folded paper, scanned it quickly and put it to one side. Then the interview began.

The Head's questions didn't stretch me much, but he was canny and it was clear that he knew exactly what he was looking for. Occasionally my confidence left me and I felt like a boy in a place he didn't belong, but 'Gus' Gilbert steered me back with some open questions and the interview was straightforward from then on. Eventually he gave me some maths calculations to do and turned to my father. He said a few things to him about the school and his expectations and after that it was over. In dealing with us, he had struck just the right balance between rigour and informality.

Two weeks went by and then another envelope arrived. A fatter one this time. It contained a letter offering me a place at the school and a list of things to buy: school blazer, school badge, school tie, two grey shirts, two pairs of school socks, a school cap, a metal cap badge, an enamel house button, football kit in house colours, football boots, PE shorts, rubber shoes for PE, a fountain pen, pencils, maths equipment, a satchel or briefcase and an outdoor coat. The cost was enormous for my family. As everything came together, my things were laid out in the front room ready for my first day. In quieter moments, I would go in there and try on my blazer or breathe in the delicious smell of my new leather satchel.

DAVID BARNETT

David Barnett was a friend from home and a friend at school. We were good mates but I never spent as much time with him as I did with the other boys because he lived around the corner in Chadbourn Street and that made a difference. When I was ten, he asked me to go to a play centre with him at Marner School. Marner was opposite St Andrew's Hospital and a fair walk from home, but the play centre offered us a good reward for doing the journey. There was so much for us to do there but David and I usually ended up playing football. It was football that made us friends, that and David's easy manner and quirky sense of humour. The Barnetts were a nice family. All of them were friendly and we knew them quite well. Doreen was at Alton Street with Douggie, one of David's brothers, and she became friends with his sister Thelma too.

When he left Susan Lawrence David went to St Pauls Way in Bow, but we continued being friends. In the evenings and at weekends we would go to a patch of worn-out grass down by Manorfield School and he would hit shots at me from a distance. David was a good footballer and I was a fair goalkeeper so our kick-abouts were entertaining. He supported Charlton Athletic and I went with him to see them play a few times. Eventually our friendship lapsed but I often got news of him. Doreen was in touch with Thelma and she kept us up-to-date with the Barnett family. David worked as a school keeper in Stepney so he hadn't moved far from Poplar.

In 2001 I was asked by the Head of Susan Lawrence to make a speech to ex-pupils at a reunion she was arranging to mark the school's fiftieth anniversary. I accepted a little reluctantly and went along. The hall was full when I arrived but there was no one I recognised because most of the guests were from later years than mine. In the speech I spoke about the walk from Alton Street when the school opened, mentioned a few teachers by name, gave a couple of anecdotes and then it was over. I had work the next day and a long drive home, so I didn't stay long. As I made to leave, a man in a fashionable jacket stopped me. "Hello, Joe, I'm David Barnett," he said. David and I talked easily as if no time had passed since we'd last met. We reminisced, caught up on our lives and had a laugh. I said, "Why don't we go on a walk around the school and have a look at it?" "I'd love that," said David, so we did. We went to every part of it from the upstairs hall to the dining room. As we went around, I was struck by how good it still was; how well it worked as a building and what a pleasant place it was to be. Eventually, we went into the classroom, our classroom, Mr Thake's classroom, and we looked through the window just as we had on the night I saw my dad hit two decent shots at cricket; the night when the Lansbury project achieved perfection.

"GIV US A TOON"

Keith Carter was a skinny boy with lank dark hair and features not unlike those of the family in Van Gogh's *Potato Eaters*. Keith was straightforward and easy to get along with and he and I were friends. Out of the blue one day he told me that he had a gramophone I could have. We had nothing to play records on at home and I was pleased to say, "Yes." He didn't want any money for it; all I had to do was take it away. Keith lived in a block of flats in Ricardo Street opposite the school and the following Saturday I went there to pick it up. When I arrived, the gramophone was standing in Keith's hall with a cloth over it. He uncovered it and I was surprised by its size. It was no portable gramophone, more a piece of furniture, a cabinet on legs with a hinged lid. It stood nearly four feet high and I had expected something smaller. "Do you want to hear it?" Keith asked and I nodded. From a drawer at the bottom of the cabinet he took out a large 'seventy-eight' record; it was Eve Boswell singing *Pickin a Chicken*. He wound the mechanism, put the record in place and set it to play. *Pickin a Chicken* started up with surprising volume and a very agreeable tone. "I'll give you a few records to start you off," said Keith.

It was a long walk from Ricardo Street to St Leonard's Road and I dreaded lugging the big old gramophone all the way home, even with Keith to help me. But it wasn't the physical challenge that concerned me, it was the potential the journey had for causing me dreadful embarrassment. I just didn't want to be seen with a gramophone in the street. Keith had a pram to put the player on and the plan was to put it across the top and wheel it home. We got it down the stairs easily enough and

I waited on the pavement while he went back for the pram, but such was my inhibition that all I kept thinking was, "Please don't let anyone see me..."

The journey was bumpy and difficult. The cover kept falling off and there were too many kerbs. The smaller ones were all right, but at the steeper ones we had to take the gramophone off the pram in case it fell into the road. Inevitably, we had to cross Chrisp Street steps; twenty-four up and twenty-four down. It was a hot afternoon and my hands were sweaty. We stopped at the bottom, stood the cabinet upright and tilted it forward to get a grip. Then, with me at the front and Keith at the back, we started up the stairs. It was hard work. My hands were wet with sweat and I started to lose my grip. "We'll have to put it down or I'll drop it," I said. We stood it down, changed ends, rested, and had a think. We were becoming a Poplar version of Laurel and Hardy on the steps with a piano in their film *The Music Box*.

We got to the top and were setting up the pram for crossing the bridge when I saw someone coming the other way. It was a middle-aged man and he had obviously had too much to drink. "Please let's just get past him," I thought, "Don't let him stop to talk to us." But that was never going to happen. The man swayed gently towards us, stopped, looked at the gramophone and said, "What yer got there then?" It was, of course, obvious what we'd got. "It's a gramophone," said Keith. "A gramophone? Genna giv us a toon?" We stood there unmoving. "Go on, giv us a toon," he persisted. "Let's 'av a bit of a knees-up, cum on, ain't ya got no records?" He wasn't going away. It was just what I'd feared. I was dreading that someone might come along. "We've got a couple," said Keith.

"Got any Winifred Atwell?" Keith opened the cabinet and took out the big black shiny disc on which Winifred Atwell's brilliant version of *The Poor People of Paris* was etched. He wound up the gramophone and the record played. The drunk was happy and for a few minutes we stood there, an unlikely trio, listening to Winifred playing on a railway bridge. What does this say about me as a boy? A few weeks before, I had been balancing on top of the wall of the same bridge, high above the railway and oblivious to the danger, but the embarrassment of being seen with a gramophone was something I had feared so much more.

PLAYS

Stage fright was not a fear I experienced at school and we put on lots of plays. Having the name Joseph meant I was usually cast as Mary's husband at Christmas and I became used to leading an imaginary donkey around the hall with a girl called Mary as the school sang *O Little Town of Bethlehem.* In coronation year, Susan Lawrence put on a pageant to celebrate the life and times of the first Queen Elizabeth. Our class told the story through the lives of ordinary people and I played *Neddler the Pedlar,* a trader who went from town-to-town selling things from a tray. The part of Neddler came with a really good costume that was basically a jester's suit with bells. I loved wearing it and when I brought it home to be washed, I put it on a lot and jingled my way around the house.

The following year I played King Richard the Second in a re-enactment of the Peasants' Revolt of 1381. It was quite a story. England was in radical turmoil and violent rebellion had spread throughout the country. Wat Tyler, the leader of the Kentish rebels, demanded that the King should meet him and his followers at Greenwich. We had spent time learning about the issues and I had a fair understanding of why the downtrodden peasants were so angry. The moral right was with them, but Richard had our sympathies. He was only fourteen and he must have had some courage to ride out to meet the rebels face-to-face. He placated them with concessions but later went back on his word, so he wasn't such a benevolent monarch after all. Anyway, I loved playing the King. I had a crown and a cloak and people to attend on me. I entered from the back of the hall and walked slowly through the audience to a regal fanfare. The play was good drama but not such good history; Richard was the hero when he should have come out of it with his reputation tarnished. Some of that must have been due to my glorified portrayal.

I was a king in a comedy once and had to condemn a man to death. When the prisoner collapsed in dread at being told he was to have his head chopped off, the king's next line, "Never mind, it won't take long," was meant to get a laugh. But I misunderstood and thought it was meant sympathetically, so I delivered it with all the sorrow and compassion I could muster. The audience roared; it was the biggest laugh of the play but I didn't know why. I learned something from that; if you want to get a laugh from a double-entendre, play the ambiguous line with apparent sincerity. A double-entendre is much funnier when the rude meaning is delivered that way… may I take down your particulars?

GOING ON HOLIDAY?

Whenever my mum was asked if we were going on holiday, she would say, "No, we're going out for days this year." She said it in a way that implied that not having a holiday was a considered preference; as if a few days out were of equal value to two weeks by the sea. Most people in St Leonard's Road went out for days, but not by choice. We could never have afforded a holiday in those years after the war and neither could our neighbours, but in 1954 that changed and my dad started looking at holiday advertisements in *'Daltons Weekly.'* After a few weeks of searching, one caught his attention:

Four-berth caravan on private land, five minutes from the sea. Bus services to Whitstable and Canterbury stop nearby.

We booked it for August so now when mum was asked if we were going on holiday, she could say "Yes, we're having two weeks near Whitstable." The caravan we chose was at *Victoria House*, Pean Hill on the road to Canterbury. We didn't have a car so my dad paid George Mitchell to take us there. It was early when George arrived and pouring with rain. He tied our cases onto the luggage rack of his old Vauxhall and my mum, Doreen and I squashed into the back while my dad took the passenger seat. It was a long drive to Whitstable, made longer by wet roads and bad traffic. The road through Rochester was drenched with rain and blocked with traffic, but by the time we arrived, the roads had emptied and the rain had stopped.

Victoria House and the land around it were owned by Violet and Egbert Bowden. They were good people, straightforward and practical. Egbert's name caused us a few smiles in private but we never let on. The Bowdens had two daughters, a little older than Doreen. They were both nice and they made a fuss of me. They joined in our games and, on my birthday, they bought me a present. Violet took care of the holidaymakers so it was she who showed us the caravan. It was cream and green, rounded at both ends and quite small. Three steps led up to the door which could open separately at top and bottom like the doors of a stable. Inside it smelt of butane gas, cleaning powder and things that had spent a winter stored away; to me it was the smell of holiday.

I was smitten by the caravan and by how it all worked: seats that turned into beds, a table that folded away, a kitchen that had everything but took up hardly any space at all and windows that looked out onto lovely countryside. The land around was pleasant and open. It was a large plot, almost a small meadow, surrounded by trees, with a view across a wide Kentish valley to higher land and two distant houses, one with a blue-slated roof, the other with a roof of red tile. Beyond the trees, a narrow lane ran for a mile down to Seasalter, a seaside village with a beach of shingle and shell.

The two weeks we spent at the caravan were the happiest of my childhood: fish suppers and knickerbocker glories, card games at night and hours and hours in the sea. Not far along the road to Canterbury was a Walls ice cream depot that sold blocks of ice cream from big freezers. Next to it was a hedged field with a cherry tree hung with ripe fruit that we picked and ate with our ices. We visited Canterbury and I saw the relics of the Black

Prince in the Cathedral there. We had bus rides to Whitstable and paddled rafts in the sea at Tankerton. "I like Tankerton," my mum would say, "it's select." I was bought a beachball from Woolworth's. It had panels of different colours and I would press my nose into it to take in its delicious smell of powdered rubber. On the first Saturday we saw the Whitstable Carnival with floats, bands and a carnival queen seated on her throne on the back of a lorry, trying her best to look like Elizabeth the Second. The annual carnival gave the people of Whitstable a chance to dress up once a year and be a little silly in public. With its modest flamboyance and self-conscious eccentricity, the carnival epitomised the England of 1954.

One lovely evening we went for a walk along a nearby lane. As the trees gave way to open farmland my dad left the road and went into a field of ripened wheat. He picked two heads of seed and brought them back. "They make flour out of these," he said, "taste it." I refused. "Jesus said you can only eat 'em when you're in a field and then only if your 'ungry," I told him. I'd learned that at The Five Ways. On our way back, we stopped by a stile and looked down into a field where tents were pitched in rows. It was a summer camp for teenagers and they were enjoying themselves hitting tennis balls and playing rounders. A girl in green slacks looked up and pointed at us. "Look everyone, up by the gate," she called, "we've got an audience." Her voice was loud and imperious. It should not have mattered to me but it did. She was mocking us. She had pricked the bubble of that lovely evening and diminished me and my family in just ten words. That's the effect that posh people so often had on me then; they made me feel second-rate.

Sometimes it rained in the night and the sound of raindrops falling heavily on the roof made me feel smugly contented as I nestled deeper into the bedclothes. In the morning, with the door open, the smell of wet grass would waft in and my lungs would fill with new air. It was so different to Poplar; even the air tasted good. One rainy afternoon I lay on the bed with my dad and listened to his tales of life in the Royal Navy. His stories captivated me: how he dived into the sea from the top of the ship's funnel, how he and Jack got the best of food because Jack was the ship's cook, how the sea tossed violently in storms, and always mentioning 'Gib', Gibraltar, where he was based for over three years.

Among his stories was an account of how he and his pals broke up a fight across the Mediterranean in Oran. "We went up some steps to a park, sat on a bench and had a smoke. There was no grass, the ground was dry..." He went on to tell me of how two groups of Arabs arrived and started shouting and pushing one another. Some took out knives and brandished them ready for a fight. The sailors watched them for a while but when things turned nastier, they went in after them. The men fled and peace returned to the park. Sitting on a bench nearby was a woman with two children. As my dad and Uncle Jack were leaving, she came across and thanked them for what they had done. She was Jewish and had lived a frightening existence under the regimes of Nazi Germany and Vichy France. She was indebted to the British for the part they had played in liberating her country and because of that, and for their bravery in ending the fight, she invited dad and Jack for a meal with her family. From the account he gave, the meal was exotic and the food was plentiful. They were invited a second time and the hospitality was just as good. Once, when he saw Pam and me eating olives, he asked for one. "When did you get to like olives dad?" I asked. "I had 'em in Oran," he replied.

There were lazy times when we would lie together on the bed and my dad would sing. I think he fancied himself as a singer and he liked to 'do a turn' at a party. One of his numbers was *Wanderer* by the 1930s singer Al Bowlly

'Leave me alone, let me wander
Don't tie my hands, just let me roam
I'm like a bird, just vying for space
Give me grove and a sweet meadowplace
Gone is my craving for the orchard
Give me a beer and summer high
So please let me wander, the countryside to ponder
A roaming vagabond am I.'

When I was older the words amused me, especially when I heard my dad proclaiming himself to be 'a roaming vagabond.'

One song has lingered in my mind ever since that holiday in the caravan. It tells the story of Kevin Barry, an eighteen-year-old medical student who was hanged by the British Army for refusing to give the names of other Irish nationalists involved in the fight for Irish independence. It is a powerful and affecting song which, at times over the years, has been banned from public performance in Britain. My dad sang it to me in a gentle, sorrowful way. I understood the meaning of the words and I felt regret. I have many reasons to feel good about being British but the execution of a young medical student for refusing to divulge the names of his comrades is not one of them. What puzzles me is how my dad came to know the song and know it so well because it wasn't broadcast or performed in England. Perhaps a hundred years after the Connollys first came to London, they still identified with Ireland and its history.

* * *

I had my ninth birthday while we were away. My presents included a pair of binoculars and an orange vinyl football. The beachball I had was good but the vinyl ball was smaller and easier to hold onto in the sea. If I missed a catch when we were playing and the ball skimmed away, I would swim after it and use it as a float to get back in position. When our game was over and Doreen and my dad went back on the beach, I would stay in the sea on my own. Over a day, I would be in the water for hours. I loved the sea, but it nearly took my life.

When I was in the water by myself, I liked to sit on the ball and grip it with my legs to see how long I could hold it there for. When it flew out from under me, I would swim after it and get it back. Sometimes I would rest on my back, cuddling the ball with both arms and enjoying the rise and fall of the waves. I was doing this once when I realised that I had drifted out of my depth. I straightened my legs to check below me but I could feel no shingle or sand. I punched the ball towards the beach and swam after it reckoning that, with a few punches, I would be back in shallow water. I did this a few times before I realised that, instead of getting nearer to the shore, I was being taken out to sea by the ebbing tide. It was a terrifying realisation and

I felt suddenly alone and afraid. Again, I struggled to make my way back but I was drifting further out. All I could do was hold on to the ball and hope, but I was tiring and holding on was becoming difficult. I knew I should call for help but for a while, English inhibition made me reluctant to draw attention to myself.

Eventually I called to my dad but, although I could see my family on the beach, none of them could hear me. I was getting weaker but I knew that I had to keep my arms around the ball for, if I lost it, I would certainly drown. "Help! Help!" I cried, and "Help! Help!" again. I was desperate now and didn't know what to do. Then I heard someone calling. "We're coming, hold on." It was a man in a small dinghy who was out sailing with his children. They came alongside and soon they had pulled me into their boat and I was safe. A few minutes later I was queuing for ice cream on the grassy lawn at the top of the Tankerton cliff. How different things might have been; the fulcrum of our lives is no bigger than a pinhead.

That holiday in 1954 was the only one I had with my family. We went back to Whitstable the following year but this time Rod came too. After that we 'went out for days' every year until I was sixteen and then I went away with my friends. The family holidays we had with Pam are precious to Alice, Joe and me. They are 'in the bank', they are there forever, they cannot be taken away. We had lots of them and they were all good. That holiday in Whitstable is a treasured memory for me too: two weeks when I had my father all to myself; two weeks when he wasn't working shifts or doing overtime or being at work on Christmas day. Without that holiday I would never have heard his stories about the navy, or listened to his songs, or seen what a powerful swimmer he was. I would have missed the laughs we had with my mum, the ball games with Doreen and that special feeling of being together in the darkness of the night.

THE GASSIE

Bromley Gasworks was such a big part of my life. It fed me, entertained me and taught me what industry was really like. I never remember my dad working anywhere else until I had grown up and was working myself. The Bromley site was large and complex. It skirted the river Lee and ran from Plaistow to Bromley-by-Bow. It was a place that people went to only out of necessity. The air reeked of sulphur dioxide; it was noisy, trains ran across the centre, coal heaps stood high, lorries came and went, coke was bagged and sent away and smoke rose high from chimneys. It was hot, intimidating and dangerous, like some awful town encountered in a nightmare.

At the Plaistow end, oblivious to their location, stood a small run of workers' cottages with washing on the lines, curtains at the windows and carefully-tended gardens. Beyond them and dwarfing them with their scale, stood eight enormous gasholders like great un-budging soldiers asserting their authority. These were splendid structures. They were unique, they looked like nothing else. Within a frame of girders and columns, huge drums for containing gas rose and fell according to how full they were. Because they were erected by the Victorians, these gigantic pieces of industry had some classical elements chosen to evoke the past. The columns were Doric and Corinthian in style like those of ancient Greece, but made of iron rather than stone; the Victorians may have been romantics but they were practical too.

Across form the gasholders, the site spread haphazardly towards the canal. There were hot dangerous places where coal was burned and gas purified, locomotive sheds, buildings for managers and office workers and beyond them, the workers' lobby and canteen. Nothing matched. It was a place that had grown according to need; there was no cohesion or design. The process of making gas was dirty and dangerous; it took a constant supply of labour and raw materials. Supply had to be constant because demand never stopped. So, when something went wrong, workers were called from home and given no respite until the problem had been solved. Here is an extract from a letter my dad sent me when I was a student. It is dated the 27th of January, 1964.

'Sorry I haven't written before as I have been very busy at work, spending lots of time over the normal working hours, and believe me I've been very tired at the end of the day in fact I've been 7 – 3 for the last three weeks without a day off...'

When I was eight, he took me into work with him. I remember how uncertain I felt crossing the big open area with its sunken railway lines and lorries passing randomly across. As we walked, he pointed things out to me: the retort house, the purifier, the condenser, and as he did, I began to understand what was going on. He took me into the loco shed and I saw engines like the ones that passed along the railway at the back of our house. They were bigger close up: large, dirty and black. My dad lifted me up onto the footplate of one and I met the engine driver. He was on his own, getting the engine ready for a run to collect coal. "I'll take yer for a ride if yer like," he said.

Standing on the footplate was intimidating. It was like being in a black metal shell. Small jets of steam leaked out from pipework and much of the floor was taken up by coal. The driver heaved a shovelful into the firebox and the heat from inside was intense. The fire was moving frantically and the flames were almost white. I was excited but my excitement was coupled with fear. The driver adjusted the controls and the engine moved slowly out of the shed and into the open. "Let 'im blow the whistle," he said, raising his voice to be heard above the noise. My dad held me up and I pulled the cord. It was a sublime moment for me. 'Beep beep, beep beep,' it trilled. "That's enough or you'll 'av me in trouble," said the driver. We got as far as the retort house and stopped. A few more adjustments and we were reversing slowly back towards the train shed. It was such a good thing to do. Something to tell the boys at school. But it was hot, noisy and unpredictable; a telling introduction to industry.

Not long after my dad wrote the letter telling of his long hours, he had an accident that almost took his life. Something had gone wrong in the retort house and he was sent over to help sort it out. He was standing by the huge furnace when a blowback of flame hit him at force and filled his lungs with hot poisonous gases. He was wearing overalls but had no other protection: no goggles, no fire-proof clothing, or mask or hard hat. The blast threw him back and he was left unconscious. In the ambulance, the crew fought to keep him alive. His heart stopped for fifteen minutes but they persisted and brought him back to life.

In 1974 the Government passed the *Health and Safety at Work Act*. Had the legislation been in place when my father had his accident, he would have been better protected. He would have been given a mask to wear, fire-resistant overalls, goggles and a hard hat. Nowadays, the term *'Health and Safety'* is often derided. At best it becomes a lazy cliché for people who don't want to bother giving more detailed explanations when something potentially hazardous has occurred: "You can't do that its health and safety." At worst it is used sarcastically by backward-thinking people who wish to attack what they perceive to be intrusive liberal ideas. I have none of that and I always push back. The same people would have railed against legislation to stop children being sent up chimneys or complained about laws to protect miners underground. I was told once by a smug individual at a sports centre that I couldn't use a corridor to the pool because of "health and safety." I could see a ceiling tile had come away and was hanging loose. "That could be dangerous," I said. "And there's a health issue too?" "No health issue here," he said. "Oh, I thought you told me there was a health problem as well as a safety one." He looked at me quizzically. No one likes a smart arse but sometimes it's right to be one.

* * *

My dad loved the camaraderie of the lobby. It was a place that belonged to him and his mates. It is where they cooked, took their breaks, showered and had their lockers. There were pranks and laughs, nicknames and card games. He told me once how a line of them danced a version of Freddie and the Dreamers' *You Were Made for M*e in the showers, all of them in unison doing Freddie's hopping dance steps. He thought it was hilarious and it probably was. Over the years I got to know most of his workmates: 'Jock' Burnett, because he was a Scot; 'Dinya' because he said things like: 'You went down there yesterday, Joe, dinya?'; 'Mummy's Boy', a bit of a milky character; 'Dikko', Charlie Dixie; 'Blakie' Johnny Blake; 'Hauntsie', Ted Haunts.

There was a hierarchy of respect given to my father's friends. Johnny Blake was his best mate. He was much younger than dad and dad helped him out when things went wrong in his life. He often visited us and we all liked Johnny. Jock Burnett was older and much-respected as was Tom Clark. Tom had no nickname and I always called him 'Mr Clark.' Tom and Jock's wives were held in high regard too. Jock's wife was called 'Nessie.' Then there was Ted Haunts, a tall, heavily-set man with staring eyes. Apparently, Ted was terrified of beetroot and the sight of it would make him panic. Hauntsie was quite a comedian too. One evening at a gasworks dance, he approached our table and said to the women, 'Do any of you ladies want a pee?' They reacted with shock and outrage until, to much laughter, he opened his palm to reveal one small garden pea.

Things were bought and sold in the lobby and some of them defied explanation. My dad often brought home delicious Percy Ingle sponges. They came in cake boxes with Percy Ingle graphics on the side. How he got them I cannot imagine. Maybe there was a corner of the lobby with a small cake-making facility where some of the chaps baked the sponges whilst others printed up the boxes for distribution. When Bromley gasworks was nationalised in 1949, it became part of the North Thames Gas Board. Not long after, the company started distributing towels for the workers to use for showering. Each one had NTGB stencilled on it. They were meant for use at work and not to be taken home but, of course, they were. My dad gave me one for showering at school. It was a very nice towel but I felt embarrassed at having to dry myself on one with NTGB printed on it. "If anyone asks you what it stands for just say 'not to go back,'" he said. That is funny to me in so many ways, all of them affectionate.

* * *

I felt a sense of society at Bromley. It was more than just the place where my dad worked. I knew his mates and they treated me well. I saw them with their families at the social club dances and I went to some of their houses. There were children's parties at Christmas. The food was good and the presents were generous. We were well looked after and given a good time. Gassie children's parties were better than pub ones or the ones at St Michael's church; they were more in touch with who we were and what we liked. The last one I went to was in 1958. I was 13 and just ready to move on. They played *Stupid Cupid* by Connie Francis, a light-hearted song and full of vitality. A group of us danced in the middle of the canteen floor. It was the first time I ever danced with girls.

Gassie dances were held in the works canteen and they were good. Tables and chairs were set out around the dance floor and there was a stage at the far end where the band played. At the opposite end by the door, a few tables were left for shift workers to have their food; it was a working factory after all, and the work never stopped, so there were always a few night workers in overalls having a meal break as women in dance frocks and men in suits danced a Foxtrot or Quickstep nearby.

The canteen wasn't well lit; there were no decorations to enhance it and the only concession to dancing was a sprinkling of French chalk on the floor to stop dancers from slipping over. How unromantic it seems, a drab utilitarian canteen in a gasworks trying to become a ballroom. But it wasn't unromantic or drab; it was exciting, colourful and alive. The reedy vibration of the saxophone, the thump of the drums, the crash of the symbols, the soft huskiness of the clarinet and the tuneful piano coaxed the dancers onto the floor and drove the evening forward. A waltz to *Where is Your Heart?* A *Foxtrot*. Then a fast one; *Shake, Rattle and Roll.* Another fast one and another until someone said, "I'll 'av to sit this one out, I'm all out of breath."

And then the interval: beer bottles accumulating on the tables, trays of sandwiches handed around; David Whitfield singing *Cara Mia* on the loud speakers while the band have a break; people up and about going from table to table to chat with those they hadn't seen for a while. And for children, the chance to slip away and explore the games rooms behind the stage with their huge snooker tables fit for professionals and dartboards with scores chalked up from the last matches. Then into the lobby to have a wee and see where my dad and his mates met and cooked and showered. I got locked in a toilet cubicle in the lobby once and couldn't get out. I shouted but there was no one around. In desperation I climbed the door and dropped to the other side leaving it bolted. It stayed that way until the following day when some of the men on the early shift became concerned for the occupant who had been inside for some time and wasn't answering their calls. Medical staff were alerted and the door was forced open. I told my dad it was me, but I doubt if he would have admitted it to his mates in the lobby.

The band resumes. Glasses of gin and orange and bottles of beer have had their effect. More and more get up to dance. The band drives them on. The band is good and knows what to do. The last half hour is the best; the communal dances. The Valeta, the Gay Gordons, a Conga and then the Hokey Cokey where everyone joins in; great rings of people putting their left legs in and shaking them all about, holding hands, moving back then rushing forward again until they almost meet in the middle. And then *Knees Up Mother Brown* the cockney anthem, the best dance of all. "Play it again!" someone shouts to the band and they do but faster this time. And after that the last waltz and then it's all over; lingering farewells, cold air from outside and just a few night workers left in the drab canteen. "What is the city but the people?" "What is a ballroom but the people?"

In the 1960s liquid gas from Algeria replaced coal gas and Bromley became a gas storage facility. Fewer workers were needed and in 1969 my dad took voluntary redundancy. We had moved away from Poplar by then and the journey to work would have been long and expensive for him so leaving Bromley made sense. He had given twenty-six years of his working life to the industry and once it had nearly killed him. The damage to his lungs from breathing foul air caught up with him eventually and at the end of his life he needed oxygen to breathe. He didn't get much redundancy pay but the company gave him a present in recognition of his 'long and valued service.' It was a cheap barometer. I don't know what he thought of this token of appreciation but he put it on the wall in our new home on the Hainault estate. The arrow on it always pointed to 'Clearing windy and cool' and never altered whatever the atmospheric conditions outside. According to the Bromley gasworks barometer, the weather was always going to be 'clearing windy and cool.'

THE PEOPLE WHO CAME

Ours was an open house. People were always dropping in. Those who knew it and experienced its welcome still talk about it with fondness. To Doreen's college friend Mavis, it was a home. To Betty Smith, an Irish barmaid who spent Christmas with us once, it was a place in the family she never had. Jean des Touches, from France would say, "You see, it is just a little house, but to me it is a *palas!*...a *palas!*" Food played a big part in the welcome we gave. My mum always managed to find an extra plate and fed whoever happened to be there. She was a wonderful cook and rarely got it wrong. But for all that, when I was at Roan, I was ashamed of my home and never wanted anyone to see it. All of the other boys had bathrooms and lived in nice places, or so it seemed to me, but I lived in a house that was listed for slum clearance. I was in a geography lesson once when the teacher said, "What sort of a man would let his family live in a house with a leaking roof?" I thought of my father and the plastic sheets he had fixed above our beds to stop the rain from coming in.

To be ashamed of one's home is a terrible thing; it is inhibiting and it prevents you from leading a fuller life. One day my schoolmates came over on their bikes to see me. I saw them arrive from the bedroom window and told my dad to say I wasn't home. What would they have thought of my house? I couldn't bear to think of them seeing inside. But that was all about me, not them. They were just friends who hadn't a thought for anything other than what I meant to them; I could have been living in a very nice house or a house due for demolition, it would have made no difference to how they thought of me.

All that changed when I met Terry Lawlor. Terry lived in a downstairs flat in Grenfell Street, Greenwich, a red-bricked row of terraced houses sandwiched between the gasworks and Tunnel Avenue. That part of Greenwich was like an island cut off from the rest of the borough. There were just a few houses, the traffic-ridden tunnel road and manufacturing buildings that went back to the river. On a bad day, the factories gave off a smell like overcooked gravy. Sometimes the pollution was so bad that the air had a bluish hue.

Like me, Terry came from a working-class family in a poorer part of London. Neither of us had homes that, in material terms, matched those of most of our schoolmates and although this shouldn't have mattered, in those days it did. Neither of our families had money to spare or took holidays or ate in restaurants. Our parents were not homeowners and the homes we lived in were old and without a bath or indoor toilet. And because of our education, even at eleven, we knew more about some things than our parents did. In meeting Terry I had found a boy at school who I knew I could invite home and, in time, he became part of my family.

As I grew older, I felt relaxed enough to have other boys from Roan, but only a few: Dave Bryan who lived near Terry in an upstairs flat in a house like ours; Jim Godfrey because he was a Communist, so I thought he would be unjudgemental; and Huw Croxford a lanky, easy-going boy who played the saxophone in pubs around Greenwich. Huw was orphaned and lived in Vanbrugh Castle, an RAF residential home for the sons of airmen who had died in service. Neither Terry nor any of the others made me feel inhibited or uncomfortable about my home, but I never invited anyone else from school.

Huw stayed once when I was away at college and his overnight presence led to an amusing misunderstanding. Doreen gave him her bed and took mine because hers was a much better room and Huw would be more comfortable there. Every morning on his way to work, Uncle Charlie would tap on Doreen's window to make sure she was awake. When she heard him knock, she would pull back the curtains and wave. When Charlie knocked the morning Huw stayed, the curtains moved and he found himself staring at Huw's long manly features. Charlie waved and moved swiftly off. Huw waved back. "Your neighbours are very friendly," he told my mum over breakfast. "One of them tapped on the window and waved." "Doreen 'ad a bloke in bed with 'er this morning," Charlie told Rose when he got home from work. "Good gawd 'amighty!" replied an astonished Rose.

* * *

When I was ten, my dad told us that the wife of Bill Fuller, one of his workmates, had recently had a baby and couldn't cope. There was no paternity leave and Bill may have lost his job if he took time off to look after her. Bill was a lovely chap and my dad was concerned for him and his family. He asked my mum if the baby might come home to live with us until his mother could cope again and she agreed at once. Mrs Fuller was having a severe breakdown and the baby stayed with us for months. Things were different in those days; nothing was official about the arrangement but circumstances like these were common when my parents were young; to them it was just what you did.

I saw my mum and dad in a new light when little Colin Fuller came to live with us. They were parents to an infant again and taking on all of the responsibilities that parenting entails. My mum was a natural. She knew intuitively what to do, when to feed, when to change, when to lay down, when to pick up. When the baby was windy, she held his back straight and gently patted it until a little burp popped up. When he cried, she held him close and stood rocking forwards and back, singing as she did and nestling his head into the crook of her neck. All these things I watched and learned from so that when our children were babies, I did the same with them and did so again with my grandchildren the second time around. We were sad when baby Colin went back to his mum but pleased that she was well again. Some years later at a gasworks dance, Bill Fuller came up to us with Colin, now a grown boy with black curly hair. "These are the people who looked after you when you were a baby," said Bill. Colin looked at us and gave a self-conscious smile. "Thank you," he said.

ROD

Rod was like no other man I have known. He was complicated, talented and a man of unique contradictions. He was a working man who liked opera, a socially-conservative *Guardian* reader, a trade union official, a zealous Catholic and a man whose passivity turned to difficult bouts of irrationality towards the end of his life. He came from Dublin and it was because of him that I came to know and love Ireland. Being Irish, social status meant nothing to him, but he often made clear his disdain for the English upper classes. He was a man's man; his workmates respected him even though he was so unlike them. At lunchtimes in the Bow Common gasworks, he would sit reading his *Guardian* while the other men read the *Mirror* or the *Sketch*. None of them seemed to mind the differences between themselves and him or even notice them.

Rod's full name was Roderick Joseph Clery. He was born to John and Margaret Clery in February 1923. He grew up by the sea in Sandymount and was taught by the Christian Brothers. He was intelligent. He had an analytical and at times, illogical mind. He was a capable mathematician. He appreciated music. He could draw up plans, take an engine to pieces, decorate a house and talk about politics. He spent years at sea and the sea never really left him. He built a dinghy from scratch when he was in his fifties and learned how to sail. Then he bought a bigger boat, one with a cabin and sailed it in the waters around Maldon in Essex. He studied navigation, bought an even bigger boat and planned to sail to France. He was unflinchingly Catholic and ever-prepared to condemn Communism and Free Masonry, the two 'great evils' which, according to Vatican teachings, were the enemies of the Faith.

Rod was the most hospitable and generous man I ever met. If you admired something of his, it was yours. If he had a sandwich he would offer you half. He enjoyed a drink but took greater pleasure in offering a drink to his guests. He made wine and beer with varying degrees of success and his failures were often due to his desire to drink his brew well before it was ready. The best beer he ever made was a near-perfect bitter, but I put its excellence down to the fact that he had forgotten he'd made it and we came upon it later by accident.

When I was seventeen, he taught me to drive. Before we started, he insisted I apply for a test cancellation (if someone cancelled their test it was offered to a name on the cancellation list at short notice.) Rod was a thorough teacher but a harsh one and I never really enjoyed my driving lessons. We went out every night and he drilled me until I was frustrated and angry inside. I would practise a manoeuvre until I thought I'd got it right but he would tell me to do it again. "You're not parallel to the kerb," or "Now do it again and hold it on the clutch for longer." But his rigorous instruction paid off. I got a cancellation and passed my test just three weeks after he started giving me lessons.

Rod was an optimist when it came to teaching me about repairing cars. He would explain patiently how the various components fitted together and what they did. I spent hours with him in the kerb outside our house while he pumped oil into an axle or sought inaccessible bolts to free up a part of the engine he wanted to remove. In time I came to know a lot about car repairs. I knew the names of various parts and had a fair knowledge of what they did. I could clean spark plugs, replace batteries and change tyres. Once I even replaced a set of brake pads by myself. But my motives were purely economic; I did it because I had to. I hated 'doing' cars. Rod never understood that and persisted in helping me whenever the need arose. One cold February night as I lay on my back in the gutter, holding the torch for him as he fiddled with a part of the suspension, I vowed that, as soon as I could afford it, I would never, ever, repair a car again.

Like all true eccentrics, Rod was naturally so; there were no contrived props or affectations to create an image. The house he and Doreen moved into in North Weald had a large garage at the rear but he never kept a car in it. Instead, he adapted it for work and pleasure. One half became a fully-functioning workshop, the other a fairly convincing version of a Spanish bar. The workshop end was crammed with tools, machinery and bits of motor car. The bar end had dispensing optics, a good supply of wines and spirits, castanets, a large sombrero, a wall-mounted guitar, a shelf for glasses and a mirror. It was possible to move effortlessly from repairing a clutch to swigging a beer and sometimes that's exactly what Rod did.

* * *

If contradiction, eccentricity and 'difficult bouts of irrationality' were part of Rod's make up, it was probably because he came from a family where those characteristics were noticeably present. John Clery, his father, was a singer in his spare time and performed at various venues around Dublin. He fought in the British army in the first World War and I got the sense of him being pro-British even during the struggle for Irish Independence. His wife, Margaret Clery, was a lovely person. She was small and gentle with a smiling face and a voice that could soften the heart with its humility. My dad used to say she was a saint and she did indeed seem saintly in many ways. She was a music teacher and taught piano in the front parlour of the family house in Sandymount. The walls around the old upright piano were hung with framed certificates she had been awarded for her music over the years.

Like Rod, John Clery was an eccentric too. He was self-absorbed and illogical. He looked and behaved like a character from a James Joyce novel; Stephen Dedalus might have passed the time of day with him on a walk along the strand at Sandymount. He liked to reminisce and his lack of self-awareness and verbosity could be hard to endure. Nothing was left out of a story; he gave every detail. His grandson Robert set me up with him once in Dublin. "You were in the First World War, grandad, weren't you?" he said. "Joe is very interested in the First World War so why don't you tell him all about it?" For the next hour-and-a-half, I was old John Clery's captive and he did tell me about it, every bit he could remember and he could remember a lot. Robert closed his eyes and fell asleep and I don't think I have ever quite forgiven him for that. Robert is the son of Rod's younger sister, Maureen. Maureen could be the subject of a book in herself and I am not going to tell her story here, but suffice it to say that she is feisty, courageous, over one hundred years old and still dancing.

Rod's sister Babs and brother Sean fared less well in their lives. When her marriage broke down, Babs became obsessively religious and proclaimed religion whenever she got the chance. She told me once that I would make a wonderful priest; it was an opinion I didn't share. Towards the end of her life, she became irrationally religious and went around Dublin wearing white and pale blue clothes to resemble the Blessed Virgin Mary. Like Rod, Sean was a talented engineer and had a good reputation for the work he did. But Sean was a loner. He never left home and before he reached old age, he had drunk himself to death.

* * *

Rod's flat in St Leonard's Road became a meeting place for all sorts of people. He turned the front bedroom into a sitting room and it was a good place to be. There I met local politicians, Catholic thinkers, Irish nurses, nuns, priests, the odd academic or two, Irish men and women trying to make their way in London and lots of Rod's relatives. Uncle Willy came once. He had emigrated to New York when he was young, did well and never married. He had plenty of money and owned an enormous Buick limousine. Willy was dull but we paid him great deference and tried not to mind too much when he started bragging. John Branagan was a regular visitor. John was a local councillor who eventually became Chairman of Education at the Inner London Education Authority. When I was thirteen, John and I watched a television interview together given by Clement Attlee. "This is historic," said John. "It is very rare to see an ex-prime minister speaking about his time in office." How times have changed.

Mrs Clery came several times. Once when she visited with her friend Mrs Kennedy, she declined the offer of a lift to mass and said it would be nice to walk to the church instead. When the two of them came back, they were full of praise for the priest and said they had enjoyed the mass very much. Unknowingly, they had taken holy communion at All Saints, an Anglican church in East India Dock Road. When they found out what they had done, they locked themselves in their bedroom and cried for hours. Rod eventually took them to see Father Ellis at the Catholic church in Canton Street. He told them that they had not committed a sin and that the Vicar of All Saints was a good friend of his.

Rod's genius with car engines was constrained by the fact that he didn't have a workshop. It wasn't possible to use the backyard for repairs either, because it meant taking everything through the flat downstairs. When the weather allowed, he carried out repairs in the street, but more complicated jobs had to be tackled inside and preferably on a bench. His solution was to take the engine up to his flat and repair it on the kitchen table. He'd assemble a lifting gang to help him: my dad, me, Uncle Henry or Uncle Charlie and we would hoist the engine out of its mounting and carry it up the thirteen stairs to the flat.

Rod was inventive too. He made things for his cars that no one else had in theirs: a lamp that swung out from under the dash board to read maps by, a draw-tray to keep documents in and housing for a portable radio. One of his best inventions was an intercom system that he set up between his house and ours. He bought two old telephone sets and two electric bells and fitted one by his bed and one by Doreen's in our house. It enabled him to give her an early morning call or have a chat before they went to sleep. Aunt Rose was very impressed by this and it prompted the best 'AuntRoseism' ever when she told a neighbour: "All 'e has to do is press a button and 'e can get 'er on the intercourse whenever he likes."

When Alice was born, we asked Doreen to be her godmother and this triggered an unpleasant reaction in Rod. He was angry at Doreen for agreeing to take on the role in a Protestant service and he refused to come to the Christening. He softened his position in the end but only came to our house for the reception when the christening was over. He had been very unkind to Pam and me and he never spoke to us for quite a time. A few months after the christening he was diagnosed with cancer and a little after that he died. I am no medical expert but I think that the cancer may have affected his brain; it wasn't like Rod to be so unkind to us. We made our peace before he died and I am grateful for that. He was an exceptional man.

OLD ROB

I always felt uneasy about Albert Robinson, 'Old Rob,' the man next door. Maybe it was his face that made me wary. He had the beady eyes of a mug-shot criminal and eyebrows that gave him a Satanic look. Rob and his wife Aileen lived in the flat below Rod's. We never socialised with them, but in those early years, they sometimes came to the Bromley gas work dances. Rob's Quickstep was a revelation and he and Aileen could perform the complicated Fishtail movements like professionals.

There was no side to Aileen; I found her straightforward and honest. But Rob was devious and the kind of man who would never let the truth get in the way of a good boast. He once told Doreen that he missed out on getting a place at her school because he spelt a word wrong. "I passed every bit of the scholarship but they turned me down for spelling 'Furrow' wrong: 'F-U-R-R-O-W.' See, I can spell it now." Leaving aside the unlikelihood of failing 'the scholarship' by misspelling just one word, there is the question of Rob's gender too; Doreen's was an all-girls school.

Rob's driving was a problem for all of society. Whatever vehicle he was in, he drove it as fast as he could and relied on heavy braking and the goodwill of others to survive. He bought a Bedford van in 1958 and adapted it for camping. One Easter, he asked my mum and dad if he and Aileen could take me camping for the weekend. Without asking me they agreed. I hated the idea and protested long and hard but it was no good; they thought that it was kind of them to ask me so I must go to Great Yarmouth with them. But I dreaded going; it was bad in so many ways. I liked Aileen but I feared Rob and didn't trust him. My heart sank when he told me that Aileen was to sleep in the van and I would share a tent with him. I feared sexual molestation or physical attack, maybe both at the same time. I was in fear of his driving too and Great Yarmouth was such a long way. The journey up there was terrible. Rob drove so fast that at every corner and bend I slid from side to side in the back like a loose parcel. Several times I held my breath as he got too close to the car in front or tried to overtake when to do so was madness. Aileen was my salvation, her presence would keep me from harm, but there was nothing she could do about Rob's driving.

The sleeping arrangements were a nightmare in every sense. I was never going to take my clothes off in front of Rob so I said I was cold and I kept them on. I prayed that he would do the same. I still cringe when I think of that dreadful night in the tent with him so close, fearing I'd be touched or murdered. Thankfully nothing happened but sharing a tent as a child with an adult you are terrified of is a horrible experience.

Of the two, it was Aileen who was more like us. She had a family and they were important to her. Rob had no family, or if he did, they never came; family meant nothing to him. Aileen's family were from Manchester and they sometimes came to stay. They were friendly people and easy to get along with. I liked their accent and enjoyed the stories they told of the banter between the United and City supporters. Her nephew visited from time to time. He was a likeable chap about Doreen's age and they went to a party together once, but eventually he stopped coming and the other relatives stopped coming too.

Aileen did her best to be Rob's wife but she put up with too much for too long. She had always made trips back to Manchester and, as time passed, her absences became longer. Once she was away for several weeks and her disappearance led to speculation. "I reckon Old Rob's dun 'er in," said Aunt Rose. When Aileen finally returned there was no explanation. She and Rob resumed their life together but, after ten years of marriage, she went home to Manchester one last time and never came back.

* * *

It didn't take long for Rob to go off the rails after Aileen left; without her he did what he liked. People came and went, many of them young and most of them female. Rod had made a good home for himself upstairs, but there was a constant uncertainty about who was living downstairs and sometimes we feared for his safety. He put locks on his doors to make them more secure but he still had to pass through Rob's kitchen to get to the toilet. One day an ambulance was called to Rob's flat and a young man was taken out on a stretcher. He looked pale and unconscious, like he was the victim of a drug overdose.

For a while, two young women moved in permanently. They were short, bouffant-haired and in their early twenties. Rob gave them the front room to have for themselves and they stayed there all day with the curtains drawn. Lorries began pulling up outside the house and men went inside. "Is this the place, mate?" a driver asked my dad once as he was getting into his car. I won't describe his response other than to say that it was robust and expressed in 'industrial language.' Not long after that, I saw a man jump over the back fence when I was in the garden. Uncle Charlie saw another do the same. "Old Rob's running a knockin' shop in there," he told my dad and he was right.

When I was older, Rod's flat became a retreat for me and I often had it to myself when he wasn't there. He never minded me using it, but I hated taking the few steps from the front door to the stairs or going through to use the toilet in case I met one of Rob's residents. It was the convention with shared houses for visitors to knock once for downstairs and twice for up. Rob's ladies didn't know that and would show their disappointment when they opened the door to me and realised that I was not one of their calling men. Rob explained their presence by lying. He lied a lot but he wasn't very good at it because his lies were often ridiculous. His big lie about the ladies was to say that they were all his nieces. "They're not 'is nieces," said Aunt Rose, "He's got a hireem in there." The idea of Rob having a harem caught on and from then on we called him 'Sheekie.'

A few years after Aileen left, Rob got a lady friend. She was younger than him, mid-forties perhaps, thin and slightly-built. She was neither pretty nor plain and her clothes had an old-fashioned look. Rob would bring her home in his van and they would hurry inside. Sometimes she would arrive on her own, walking from the direction of East India Dock Road. She was physically disabled and had a severe limp that caused her upper body to sway from side to side as she walked. If Rob wasn't home when she came, she would sit on the window sill and wait for him to return. From what I saw of them together, it was clear that she had a strong affection for him. It was clear too that the affection was only one-sided. I don't know how long their relationship lasted but eventually she stopped coming. For a while before that, she visited once or twice a week but the door was never opened to her. Rob was either out or pretending to be. One evening she waited in the rain for nearly an hour before giving up. I was sixteen and idealistic and I hated the way that Rob treated her. So, powerless to do anything about it, I did what any self-respecting teenage idealist would have done in the 1960s; I wrote a poem.

It seemed to be raining engine oil
And nobody noticed the cripple girl
Sitting outside, waiting for the snide
Who had shown her five minutes of life.

Fortunately, that is all that still exists of my poem. It is definitely of its time; *'raining engine oil'* indeed. There are elements of me that I recognise in those four lines though. I have always reacted to injustice and unfairness and sometimes that has got me into trouble. I have often sought to express my feelings through writing too. There is naivety in the poem, of course. It has the 'black or white', 'right or wrongness' of a teenager's take on things. I am pitying someone who may not be seeking pity. I am feeling sorry for someone because they are disabled when to set aside their disability would, perhaps, be better. But that said, it feels right to feel sorry for someone treated the way that this woman was treated by Rob.

Rob was a fantasist so his lies had him at the centre of the most unlikely action. "I've got to go; the Prime Minister wants me to fill up his fancy woman's swimming pool and I've left the water running." "Where does she live, Rob?" "North Hertfordshire," he replied. Lying was frequently his response when the rates were due to be paid. He and Rod paid equal amounts to the council and Doreen made sure that they were paid on time. "I've had a big bill, Dor; I'll pay yer in a week..." But Doreen stood her ground and always got the money. She had a great way with him; she took none of his nonsense and he liked her for that.

Eventually the men stopped coming, the 'nieces' left and things went quiet for a while. Then Rob started selling things. "Do you want any coffee tables, Dor?" he asked. "No, Rob." "They're nice: wooden legs and glass tops." Detergent powder, hand tools and men's underpants were available too. What Rob was up to became clear when the things he offered starting appearing on the *Police Five* television programme. Proof that he was a 'receiver' came when the programme presenter announced the theft of a lorry load of children's pandas from a warehouse in Dagenham. A few days later Rob waylaid Doreen: "'Ere Dor, want any pandas? Two pound each."

When our houses were due for demolition, the council gave Rob the tenancy of a flat in Three Colt Street, Limehouse. Doreen went to see him there a few times but then things moved on. We never saw him again but we could never forget him. Albert Robinson: a bad husband, a disreputable lover, a dreadful driver, a liar, a fantasist, a receiver of stolen goods and a brothel keeper...but the irony is that we could never really dislike him.

AUNT GLADYS

Aunt Gladys was one of those aunties who isn't really an auntie at all; she wasn't a relation. She lived in a ground floor flat in Radford House next to the McAvennie's. She was small and plain but she knew how to dress and made the most of herself. She wore rimless glasses that suited her and her make-up was never overdone, but two conspicuous moles on her face defied the concealment of her best cosmetics. Because she had a good job and no children, she was better off than most of us, and she had a good job because she was intelligent and articulate.

Gladys was married to Victor Middleton, a large, ponderous man who never had much to say. Theirs was a loveless marriage; at best, their relationship could be described as one of mutual tolerance. They rarely bickered in front of others, but there were frosty moments when Glad expressed her disapproval with silence or the raising of her eyes. No one ever said it, but it was clear to everyone that Gladys and Vic were stuck with one another and could find no way out. Gladys married Vic because she was young, vulnerable and had no home or family of her own. After their wedding, they lived with his parents so Vic became the boy who never left home. It might also be said that he was the boy who never grew up. When his parents died, life went on much the same for him. Gladys cooked, cleaned, did his washing, ironed his things and paid the bills; he never had to take responsibility. They lived like that for the rest of their lives: Vic childlike and dependent, Gladys acerbic and resentful, marooned together like strangers on an island.

Glad was gregarious and outgoing. She liked a party and needed plenty of company but Vic never wanted to socialise. She had physical needs too, but he was either unwilling or unable to meet them. They never went out together and they had very different interests. Vic made a life for himself outside of the marriage and Glad did too. For him it was his bike. He was keen on cycling and went riding at weekends. Cycling introduced him to others and he made a few new friends. Glad built her own social group and over time it became quite large. She called it her 'little gang.' All of the adults in my family were in the gang and Glad was 'gangster in chief.'

In more liberal times, Gladys and Vic would have ended their marriage by mutual consent. They would have divorced and moved on. But to be divorced in the 1950s was considered scandalous and working-class people rarely did it. So Glad and Vic stayed together in an atmosphere of tension; two individuals who just happened to share the same home. Vic was unable to give her the things she wanted; affection, physical love and social fulfilment and she resented him for that. She cared for him and showed him concern, but years of neglect had embittered her. She was never alone, but she was always lonely.

'Aunt Glad' was in my life from my early childhood. I remember her cutting sweet coupons from her ration book for Doreen and me or getting us free tickets for the pantomime. She worked for a coach company that specialised in seaside outings and West End shows. Her job was to manage the fleet of coaches so that they were efficiently deployed. Because of her position, she got us free coach trips to Clacton, Margate and other seaside places. But set against these kindnesses was a more embittered side of her character. She was mistress of the rhetorical put-down. 'Oh, *don't be like that!*' she'd say in a scornful way if someone didn't give her the answer she was looking for. The expression was nothing in itself, but the delivery combined mockery and disapproval. She just had a way with putting people down; her words were innocuous enough; it was the way she said them that carried the sting.

Glad could be generous; there were cards and birthday presents but I thought that sometimes she gave to get something in return. Reassurance? Recognition? Friendship maybe. When I was a student, she gave me money every time I went back to college. I'd rather she hadn't because I was always expected to go round and thank her in person. This meant an awkward half hour in her flat drinking tea and being polite. It was generous of her to give me it, but I thought the money was not really for me but for my mum and dad's friendship.

The 'little gang' became a social success. Glad arranged outings to big variety shows in London and blockbuster films like *Ben Hur* and *The Sound of Music.* Top of the list was *The Black and White Minstrel Show* which seemed to run in perpetuity at the *Victoria Palace.* As soon as one season ended, Gladys was booking everyone for the next. "Who's up for the *Black and White's*?" she'd ask. Once a year, she organised a weekend trip to Blackpool to see the lights. She loved these trips because it meant spending a whole weekend in company. By all accounts Blackpool weekends were lots of fun with silly hats, pranks in the hotel and singsongs on the coach. But there is a limit to the number of times one might wish to see Blackpool's illuminations or sit through an evening with the *'Black and Whites'* and eventually interest tailed off.

Gladys's neighbours, Nell and Fred Vint, were also gang members. Nell was a lovely person and unlike Gladys in so many ways. She was big, blonde and funny with a natural warmth that she never had to work at. She was fat and so was Fred. Nell would always refer to herself as being fat, but my mum would try to reassure her that she wasn't really fat at all. "You're not fat, Nell, you're just big-boned." 'Stout' and 'well-built' were other euphemisms my mum would use to avoid hurting Mrs Vint's feelings despite the fact that Mrs Vint didn't mind being called fat at all. "Nell, I *am* fat," she would say. Glad and Mrs Vint often dropped in to see us in the evenings. They would sit side-by-side on our precariously fragile chairs and stay chatting until about ten. When we had visitors, we turned the television off; it was a rule of the house that I resented at times. But when Nellie Vint came, I never minded because it was so nice to have her there.

The 'gangsters' were of a type: middle-aged working-class Poplar people. They came as couples: Min and Stan, Connie and George, Ethel and Len. But there were exceptions. Nell Perera a quietly-spoken single lady from Malta was one, and she was popular. Then there was Pete the pianist who went on the trips to Blackpool and to most of the shows; he played the piano at parties too. "Pete's got a lovely touch," Glad would say, oblivious to the potential her remark had for misinterpretation. Gladys was in charge of deploying drivers for the coach company and would choose the ones she liked best for the Blackpool trips. Mr Price who worked for the company often went too but, like Pete, his wife never came with him.

Across the porch from Gladys lived Joe Gaylor and his wife Flo. Joe was cheerful and lively; a small man, not quite five feet tall and always ready for a chat. Flo was taller than Joe and looked scary. She had a sunken mouth and wild wiry hair that would never lie flat. Life became very difficult for Joe when Flo started to lose her mind. She began to wander off and he would have to search the streets to find her. Often, she would go up to people she never knew and ask to go home with them. It must have been hard for Joe in the flat having to deal with Flo's behaviour and trying to prevent her from getting out. Gladys tolerated the Gaylors but it was a tolerance tinged with a degree of disdain. As Flo became more difficult, Gladys would go into the flat to help Joe out and when her visits became frequent, the rumours began. "Old Joe's got 'imself in there," said Uncle Charlie. The rumours that Gladys may have been having an affair with Joe arose because it was apparent from the way she was around men, that she was in need of them.

Vic often spent weekends with his friends in Southend and when he was away Gladys would invite the gang around for an impromptu party. Vic's absences worked for them both because he was spared the awkwardness of being around when Gladys's friends were there, and she had the flat to herself for the weekend. Mr Price and Pete came to Gladys's 'do's' but rarely on the same night. Whichever one of them was there would usually stay behind after everyone else had gone. If it was Mr Price, Glad would say he stayed late because he'd had too much to drink and was waiting for the alcohol to wear off before driving home. In Pete's case it was because he wanted to stay on to play the piano. These late-night dalliances led to more rumours, and the rumours became a dreadful reality in the early hours of one Sunday morning when Mr Price suffered a fatal heart attack and died on Gladys's bed.

Gladys was a victim. She was the victim of poverty and neglect as a child. She lived a loveless life and was the victim of a society that expected people to stay married even if the marriage was a bad one. She was outward-going and craved society, but to obtain it, she had to create a social life of her own. She was human with all the natural desires of a woman, but she endured years without having them fulfilled. These things made her bitter and difficult to like at times, but she was not a bad person, just someone unfortunate enough to live her adult life in 1950s England.

JEAN DES TOUCHES

Jean des Touches arrived in Poplar as a recently-ordained priest fresh from his seminary in Louvain. It was the practice in those days for young priests to experience parish life in another country and in 1967 it was Jean who came. He was given a room at the clergy house in Canton Street and expected to play a full part in parish life. My father felt sympathy for these young men: foreigners, away from home, living in a community of older priests and thrown in at the deep end with the parishioners. He would invite them home for a meal and introduce them to Doreen and me so that they could meet people nearer their own age. In 1966 it was Father François who had come. François was a short, rugged fellow of peasant stock from Nouvelle-Aquitaine. He soon got stuck into his parish work and quickly became popular. He was a priest from and of the people. He danced at the social club, enjoyed a drink and sometimes 'did a turn' on the guitar.

François never cared much about his appearance and often looked unkempt. His hair was untidy, his black cassock ended three inches from the ground and he was forever in a rush. Jean was less impulsive than him; quieter, more cautious and better-groomed. I never saw Jean in a cassock; he preferred a well-cut jacket over a clerical shirt with trousers that were always neatly pressed. He kept his hair tidy and well-cut. His nails were clipped and clean. He was handsome in an interesting way; his face was made slightly imperfect by a diagonal scar to the left of his chin. Rimless glasses and a French cigarette hanging at an angle from the corner of his mouth completed the look and gave an impression of educated sophistication.

Jean came from a family of French nobility; after 'des Touches' a string of other names followed, one of which was 'de Lentieres.' Having a name made up of a string of names is a mark of the old aristocracy in France. His parents, Monsieur and Madame des Touches, were old-school and conservative. They were from Clermont-Ferrand in the Auvergne. Monsieur des Touches had been a high-ranking army officer in the Second World War and had sided with the Pétain government. Vichy, the capital of Pétainist France, is not that far from Clermont and Monsieur des Touches had, in effect, taken the side of the Nazis.

Jean was one of six children, the second of three sons. His father insisted on directing them into the professions of his class. There was to be one son in the army, another in the clergy and one in a prestigious profession like medicine or law. His daughters were expected to marry well, have children and keep a good house. Jean's younger brother was a doctor and the older one an officer in the army. Two of his sisters 'married well' and had children. Only Elise, the youngest did not fulfil her father's ambitions. Elise was a troubled individual, erratic and given to bouts of depression.

Jean became a regular visitor to our house in Poplar. He and I got on well and we spent hours talking together. As I got to know him better, he began to share some of his deep concerns with me. Fundamentally he was having doubts about being a priest and felt he had been made to take holy orders by his father against his will. Although he was in his early thirties, he had never had a life of his own. He had gone into the army straight from school to do military service in Algeria and, when that was over, he joined the seminary. He didn't know what to do about his situation and was growing increasingly unhappy. He could not face his father with his concerns and he did not know how to tell the church about them either. I listened to him a lot and Doreen did too. I could understand his apprehension but I knew that he must follow his instincts and leave the priesthood and I told him so. For someone in Jean's position there could not have been a better place or time to be than London in 1967. It was a city freeing itself from social repression and the constraining rules of the past; a place where people were allowed, actually encouraged, to follow their own path.

With our help and support, Jean took his decision. He went first to see his mentor in the seminary in Belgium. Far from admonishing him, the mentor priest said that he should do what his conscience told him and if that meant leaving the church, it would not be a sin. Having taken that difficult first step, he now faced the much harder task of telling his parents. This proved to be an altogether more difficult encounter and it did not go well. He was met with a firm rebuttal from his father and told to return to the seminary at once and re-join the priesthood. When Jean insisted that he would never go back, he was virtually disowned.

For a while he continued living at the clergy house where the other priests had shown him understanding, but he could not stay there indefinitely. He needed money and time to sort himself out. Realising Jean's difficult position, my dad found him a job at Lusty's timber factory by the canal in Bromley-by-Bow. Jean was pleased to be getting this first taste of independence but we were very apprehensive about how it would go; a young French ex-priest in the tough, crude society of Poplar working men. Jean had worked in a timber yard in Bremen when he was a student, but it was a smaller, tamer world than the full-on factory life of *Lusty's*. We were anxious for him on his first day and my mum invited him to eat with us that evening.

Before I describe Jean's account of how it went at Lusty's, I should say a bit about how he sounded when he spoke English. His voice was strong and clear and his accent stereotypically French like a French accent played for comic effect in a badly-acted play. In both English and French, he expressed himself emphatically and with animation; there was lots of passion when Jean spoke. There were plenty of head gestures too and much stressing of key words. Sometimes he would raise his hands and hold them apart from his ears as if inviting his listeners to pay more attention. Most endearing of all were his spoken mistakes. When Doreen sent him a postcard from the Lake District he told us that she was "spending two weeks in the district lake."

Jean arrived straight from work the evening he started at Lusty's. He washed his hands and came to the table. The dinner was ready and my mum dished up. We couldn't tell from his demeanour if he had been ravaged by beasts at the factory or suffered mockery or ostracization. Eventually one of us asked the key question, "How did if go today?" Jean didn't hesitate and came straight back. *"Marvelllerse!! Marvellerse!!"* he said to our great relief. "Well, you see, I am there only a few minoots and a man he came to me and said, "'Ah ham Bill, this is Alf, we will 'elp you if you want to know anything.' They are very kind to me these men." I could sense the relief going round the table. "Then, you see, it is time for lunch but I have nothing because there is no café. Bill and Alf see me and they say 'We 'av samweech of cheese. You must take some of hours.' You see Bill and Alf are very good men, *very* good! When I was in Germaneee no one spoke to me like that. No, this Lustie is a very good place."

We relaxed and the conversation lapsed as we got stuck into our food. Jean was sitting on my right. No one was speaking; all that could be heard was the scraping of knives and forks on plates. Then, from out out of the blue, Jean landed a bombshell. "Pass the fucking salt," he said. And then: "Mrs Connolly, this is a fucking good meal." We froze. I leaned into him. "Jean, that is a very bad word, we never say that word in here." Jean seemed surprised. "But yes. Bill and Alf, they say it all of the time."

* * *

Jean got a job as an au pair to a wealthy Jewish architect and his family in Golders Green. When he arrived, he was told, "If there is a fire, the first thing you must do is save the Cézanne." I visited him there once and met the family. They were charming and polite to me and we managed some small talk before going up to Jean's room to sample the whisky he had bought. On the way up, he warned me to be careful of the paintings on the stairs. To my surprise they included a not-unimpressive Cézanne. I passed it with caution, making sure to leave plenty of room between it and my left shoulder.

One nice feature of this urbane and sophisticated family was that they ate chicken soup nearly every day. Jean said that the chicken pot was never emptied just added to with chicken bones and scraps from other meals. I found it strangely reassuring that these wealthy people, comfortably established in the upper levels of London society, should still adhere to the customs they had inherited from centuries of getting by against the odds in places far away.

Jean left that family to become a live-in carer to an ex-RAF officer in a flat at the Barbican in the City. The man's name was Mr Aitkin and he had suffered terrible injuries when the aircraft he was in was shot down. The traumatic incident had left him disabled and he was unable to walk or take care of himself. Mr Aitkin was a perfect gentleman; friendly and unassuming, generous and polite. He had a passion for music and was a regular attender at The Royal Opera House in Covent Garden. He was something of a fixture there and a space was always set aside for him in the aisle to the left of the stage. There he would sit in his wheelchair enjoying some of the greatest operatic performances it was possible to hear. Jean liked and admired Mr Aitkin and when I met him, I could see why. For his part, Mr Aitkin became very fond of Jean and it was hard for him when, after nearly two years, Jean decided to move on.

He went to Italy, to Trento, a small Tyrolean city in the North. Things went quiet for a while although we never lost touch. He became a teacher and not long after that he wrote to say that he had met an Italian woman and they were to be married. Her name was Tiziana Strippoli and she was a philosophy teacher. Her name captured my imagination; it was a very sexy name. I imagined a slender dark-skinned young woman with long black hair and lovely limbs. Jean was handsome after all, so he must have met someone beautiful.

The following summer he asked me over to stay and I met Tiziana for the first time but she was no Italian beauty. She was not characteristically Italian at all, but Celtic in appearance. She was in her late thirties, fair-skinned, freckled, hefty and ginger. She would not have looked out of place on a farm in County Mayo. Not that it should have mattered; it was his choice anyway, so I had no right to be disappointed by her appearance. What did matter though, was that Tiziana had a very peppery temperament and was hard to please. She didn't take to me at all and I got the sense that she was very possessive of Jean. She and Jean lived with her mother, a dignified old lady from Rome. Tiziana was harsh to her at times, cutting across her in conversation and showing displeasure when the old lady ventured an opinion she did not agree with.

Jean and Tiziana rented a flat in a Tyrolean house in La Faida de Piné, a village in the country not far from Trento. It was a lovely place and they spent most of their weekends there. I went to stay there for a few days and experienced the pleasant country lifestyle of the rural Trentini. We picked fungi in the forest, had them fried in butter, drank the local wine and enjoyed a glut of figs from the trees nearby. I sketched a lot and slept outside under the stars. Tiziana mellowed towards me, particularly when she saw the drawing I made of her; it wasn't meant to be flattering but it did show her at her best.

One afternoon we went for a walk in a national park. It was a remote, lovely place. Tiziana wore a white shirt with large navy shorts and red socks. The overall effect reminded me of a burly England footballer. She and Jean liked to sunbathe naked and Jean said we should find a suitable place to lie down. I had nothing against outdoor nakedness but if it was to be me who was naked, I wanted to be miles away from anyone else and certainly not anywhere near Tiziana and Jean. The search for a suitable spot caused an argument. Every time one of them found what they thought to be the ideal place, the other would find fault with it. It was very hot and their tetchiness erupted into a row. Tiziana was shouting and in her temper, she smashed her hiking stick hard against a rock several times. Jean responded in French with all the gestures and emphases his Frenchness could afford. Tiziana stormed off in the direction of the Dolomites with Jean hurrying after her. I went my own way, found a very secluded spot and lay naked in the shade for the best part of an hour.

* * *

By the late sixties I was engaged to be married and Jean and Tiziana had moved to Paris. I met my fiancée Christine when I started teaching in Bethnal Green. She was outward-going, intelligent and very attractive but, although we were together for four years, I was never sure about being married to her and it wasn't until I met Pam that I learned what it really meant to be in love with someone. Jean had got a job teaching French to overseas students at the *Alliance Française* in the Boulevard Raspail and Tiziana taught philosophy to older students at a lycée not far away.

In 1969 Jean found Christine and me a flat in Marly-le-Roi, a commune in the South-Western suburbs of Paris. It was cool and modern and it allowed us to live together as a couple. Soon we adopted the lifestyle of the young suburban French: commuting into the city every day, shopping locally and eating in bistros and cafes. In the evenings we would have dinner with Jean and Tiziana or they would take us to meet their friends. One evening we were special guests at a dinner given by Jacques and Marie-Claude, an affluent young couple who lived in a gated house in a leafy part of Marly. Jacques was a doctor who, at thirty-four, had made good progress in his profession. Marie-Claude worked in medicine too and was a pharmacist.

Jacques and Marie-Claude's home, its tastes and furnishings, expressed who they were and what they aspired to be. They had not been married long but had already acquired several pieces of antique furniture: some of it rustic, some of it sophisticated and all of it old. The walls were hung with pictures of rural landscapes and photographs of family members from *'la belle epoque'*. In the dining room, a large table was laid with crystal glass and silver cutlery on a fine linen tablecloth edged with lace. The meal was complex and interesting. There were several courses, one of which included a confection of pureed chestnuts that would have passed muster in a top Paris restaurant. The downside to the evening was that Jacques and Marie-Claude had a servant who waited on us at the table. I disliked having someone to wait on me and I felt uncomfortable. Christine and I were naturally inclined to hand the plates to her when they were to be taken, but Marie-Claude made it clear that no one was to help her and we had to comply.

A second dinner we went to was very different. Jean had a cousin in Paris who lived near the Canal Saint-Martin. She was about thirty, tall and attractive. Her name was *Françoise* and she lived on her own in the downstairs flat of a house that opened directly onto the street. We went there with Jean and Tiziana and two of their friends from Clermont. The room wasn't very large and we squashed around the table. Françoise sat next to me and when it came to clearing the first course, she asked me to help her take the things away. In the kitchen it became clear that she had taken a fancy to me: standing too close, exaggerating her interest in what I said and fixing me with knowing looks.

When we were back at the table, I felt her leg rubbing up against mine. I thought nothing of it at first and moved my leg away; it felt nice, but to go along with it could mean disaster. Françoise persisted and there wasn't much I could do. All the time she maintained a cool composure but under the table things were different. I had never been subjected to a seduction like that and thought it very French. What surprised me most was that Françoise carried on as if nothing had happened. As I left, she kissed me on both cheeks in a polite French way but maybe a bit more emphatically than she kissed the others.

* * *

Jean was in dread of introducing Tiziana to his family and asked Christine and me to go with them to the des Touches country house in Velours, a village about fifteen kilometres from Clermont. All of the family would be there: his parents, his sisters and brothers and their children. Tiziana was very anxious about the visit and Christine and I wanted to help her in any way we could. It was a long drive to Clermont from

Paris and we stayed overnight with an old uncle of Jean's who lived about half way between. The congestion out of Paris had been terrible and we crawled along for what seemed like hours. 'Oh, these traffic of jams!' Jean complained.

The house in Velours was ancient and special; when he was a boy, Jean spent much of his summers there. It was built of stone and stood on three levels above a small garden and orchard. It had no electricity and had seen little alteration since it came into the family maybe centuries before. There was no parking at the house so the car was left at the bottom of the drive and we had to walk up to it. As we got closer, we could hear the chatter of people in the open air. The voices grew louder as they came into view. A few of them waved but we were disadvantaged by having to look up to them while they were looking down on us. The introductions were formal; only Jean's sisters showed him any natural affection. I was introduced to his parents. They were in their seventies and had the looks of a couple that had been handsome once and still retained some of their beauty. They welcomed me because I was their guest, but I was an unwelcome guest; it was a welcome tinged with frost.

We had drinks and people circulated. Lunch was served; a good lunch that we ate in the open air. Everything was particular and special: the wine, the food and the manners. After coffee, we sat talking at the table. Christine and I stayed close to Tiziana and for the most part the three of us were ignored. It must have been very difficult for Tiziana but all she could do was tough it out. Monsieur des Touches ignored her completely and made a bitchy comment to Jean, referring to her as '*sa concubine.*' It was clear that Christine and I were not welcome either, especially me as I was the friend from London who had been complicit in Jean's decision to leave the priesthood.

Towards the end of the afternoon, I found myself alone with Monsieur des Touches in the garden. It was an awkward moment but I decided to speak to him. He did not speak in English, although I imagine that he could, so I did my best in French. If he had been English, we could have discussed the weather and moved on, but I knew that wouldn't do, so I chose to mention the garden instead. "Monsieur, vous avez fait un beau jardin," I said. 'Sir, you have made a lovely garden.' He paused to consider his reply then in a firm voice he said: "Non! C'est nest pas *moi* qui a fait le jardin, c'est *Dieu* qui a fait le jardin." 'No! It was not me who made the garden; it was God who made the garden.' And with that put-down he walked away.

Eventually Jean and Tiziana made their peace with the family. Jean inherited a lovely old house in the Massif Central from two of his aunts and they opened a language school. I took Alice and Joe to visit them there and we had a very nice time together. Tiziana cooked a memorable meal of rabbit and we could taste the fresh herbs from the garden in every mouthful. Alice played the piano and we sang. After ten years they closed the language school, sold the house and moved to Clermont where they still live in a flat that they share with one of Jean's sisters. Doreen and I have kept in touch with them and we have had short breaks in France together over the years. Knowing Jean brought so many rich experiences to my life and opened my mind in ways that I never could have imagined. Knowing Doreen and me has enriched Jean's life too and meeting us brought him the freedom that he craved. We owe all of that to my dad and his desire to help a young man who was a long way from home.

THE EDWARDS

One evening in 1960, I was sitting in Rod's car opposite The Church of the Holy Name in Bow Common Lane, when someone tapped on the window. I rolled it down and saw a young man with a dimpled smile and rather good glasses looking in at me. "Hello Joe, I'm Arthur," he said. It was Arthur Edwards. That was when Arthur first came into my life, but Doreen and Rod had known him for a while. They had met through church. Arthur and Ann Heafey, the young nurse who was about to become his wife, were part of a group of young people who went to mass and socialised together. Doreen, Rod, Ann and Arthur became a foursome and forged a friendship that lasted for the rest of their lives. At the time, Arthur was learning his trade as a photographer with John French's studio in the West End, and Ann was a nurse at St Andrew's hospital in Bow. They married and Doreen found them a flat not far from us in Lochnagar Street. When their son John was born, my mum and dad often looked after him while Ann and Arthur were at work or went to see a film.

John was a delightful little boy and my mum and dad loved him. When my dad was on nightwork, we knew we had to be careful because he was never at his best when he woke up. In the morning when he came home from work, he would wake me with a cup of tea and toast: friendly and cheerful, the perfect dad. During the day we crept around so as not to disturb him and when he woke at around five the perfect dad had often been replaced by a grumpy demon. To avoid meeting the demon we would send John to wake him up. "Go and wake Joe," we'd say, and toddler John would climb the stairs and go into the bedroom. There would be a pause and then we would hear my dad say, "Hello, boy…." in the most loving of ways. John's magic never failed; when he woke dad, the demon was nowhere to be seen. By the time their second son Paul was born, Nell and Joe were like surrogate grandparents to the little Edwards brothers. Paul and John were a cute pair: John was pretty with curly hair and Paul was ginger and unmistakeably Irish. "He's Paddy Garvin and I'm Charlie Pickles," John would say.

Arthur left John French and returned to the East End where he worked for a local wedding photographer. To make a little extra money he took match pictures at West Ham. Before the game, I'd see him lugging his heavy camera equipment along the touchline to the goal the Hammers were attacking. At half time, when the teams changed ends, he'd walk the length of the pitch to sit behind the other goal; no one wanted pictures of the away team scoring.

Eventually he set up his own business, Tower Hamlets Studios in East India Dock Road. I designed a small advertisement for it and it appeared on the front page of *The East London Advertiser* every week. I did signage for the studio too. These were great days for me. Arthur would take me around with him in the evenings on jobs and I loved it. "Come on Joe, Ronan Point's collapsed over Canning Town," he said once and we went. "I've got to take a wedding album over to Bermondsey, wanna come?" Arthur did the photographs for Billy McAvennie's wedding and when he delivered Billy's album, he asked him where he was going for his honeymoon.

"We're 'avin a fortnight in Australia," said Bill. "Australia?" Only emigrants went to Australia; it was so far away. "How you getting there Bill?" "By coach," Billy replied. "Do you mean Austria, Bill?" "Well, it might be."

Arthur's dark secret is that, for a while, he was persuaded to be a Tottenham supporter. To put him right I bought John a Hammers kit and taught him to chant, "We want Moore! Bobby Moore!" When Arthur and Ann came back from the pictures one evening, John was standing on our ironing board in full Hammers kit giving it out for the great England captain. Bobby Moore was good to Arthur and often tipped him off about a photo opportunity that could earn him some money. "I'm having me haircut this afternoon Arthur, drop in and you can get a picture." Bobby never asked for anything in return and according to Arthur, Geoff Hurst was the same. These were players who had just won the world cup for England but they managed to stay decent, grounded young men. You couldn't be more of a Hammer than Arthur is today but I doubt if he would ever admit to his early feelings for Spurs.

My dad and Arthur were wonderful together. Arthur constantly sought to wind him up and the banter was relentless. "Where's he taking you for yer birthday, Nell?" he'd ask my mum. "He ain't takin' me nowhere, Arthur, as far as I know." Then he would focus on my dad. "Where you takin her?" "Never you mind." "Go on, where you takin' her?" "I don't have to take her nowhere; she only has to ask if she wants anything." "Go on, you tight sod. Take 'er out. I'll book somewhere for you Nell..." and so it would go on. Arthur and my dad thought the world of one another and Arthur liked nothing more than to get a rise out of him. He called him 'Humpy' if he ever showed signs of displeasure. "What's wrong with you 'umpy? Lost a fiver and found a bob?" My dad couldn't always find a riposte to his goading and would simply say, "I'm watching you Edwards," as if that put them level on points. Arthur's best moment came when my dad was cleaning his car in the road and a bin lorry flattened his bucket. The thought of him holding a flat metal bucket by the handle was something Arthur cherished.

Arthur is a remarkable man. He has charm and nerve. When Aunt Rose moved to Gale Street, he turned up at the door one evening and said, "Rose, I want yer toilet, yer phone and a cuppa tea in that order." "The cheek of it!" said Rose and went off straight away to make his tea. Ann was the perfect foil for Arthur. They bickered and argued and loved each other deeply. I spent hours with Ann when they moved to their house in East Ham. Arthur would be at work in the evenings and when he came home the exchanges would always be the same. "Ann, make me a cuppa tea." "Make it yourself, Arthur." "Ann, I'm jaded. I've been at work all day." "Well, I'm jaded too. I've had the kids all day." Inevitably I'd say, "I'll make the tea" and things would move on. Theirs's was a fine marriage and nothing changed when Arthur became the country's leading royal photographer.

Ann was my confidante; I told her things that I couldn't tell anyone else. "I've found a lovely girl," I said not long after I met Pam. "I think I want to marry her but I've only known her a few days." Ann never told me that I was being foolish or that it might be better to wait; she just listened. Within three weeks of our first date, I asked Pam to marry me and she accepted.

We kept it quiet for weeks; only Ann knew. Arthur took our wedding pictures and their little daughter Ann Marie was our bridesmaid. Arthur took the wedding pictures for Joe and Liz too and recreated some of the poses that Pam and I had taken at our wedding. He took the pictures for Alice and David when they married too. When I look around my house, I see so many photographs that Arthur has taken of us over the years. All of my closest family are there from my grandchildren to their great-grandparents. A poignant thought came to me recently when I was looking at one he had taken of me with my mum: in all of these pictures everyone is looking out at Arthur.

When Pam and I suffered the dreadful loss of our first baby in childbirth, it was just two days before Christmas. The whole experience had been horrific and Christmas Day was heavy and sad. Pam had been given her own room and it helped that we could spend time together in privacy. All around us the hospital was alive with Christmas and that somehow made things worse. People came and went. It was hard for them to know what to say. At about half past five, the door opened and Arthur came in. He had come directly from Sandringham where he had been photographing the Royal Family. Within minutes he had Pam laughing and we were having our own little party. To say that someone can light up a room is a cliché, but sometimes clichés are fine. That day Arthur really did light up the room.

Towards the end of their lives, my parents received tremendous support from the Edwards family. Paul, John and Ann Marie would drop in to see them frequently. Ann Marie jokes that, although it was she who visited them most, it was John whose picture was given the place of honour on top of the television. My mum and dad never stopped adoring John. When my mum began to lose her mind at the end of her life, Ann was wonderful with her. She would talk to her and hold her hand. Dementia had taken hold but Ann said that just before she died my mum had a lucid moment and seemed to recognise her. She raised her head, looked at her and said, "How's my John?" It was the last meaningful thing that my mum ever said. The Edwards were family to us and we were like family to them. When Ann was dying, Arthur turned to me for support and when she died, I put together his tribute to her. It was like a long love letter. I read it on his behalf at the funeral and allowed myself these few words of my own:

"The beauty of Ireland does not only exist within the magnificence of its scenery; sometimes it may be found in the character of its people. Ann was a child of Ireland and she carried that beauty within her and she shared it with us all and for that we must be grateful."

Ann was special and I was fortunate to have had her and Arthur in my life.

THINGS CHANGED

Poplar was overwhelmingly white and working-class. There were Chinese people in Limehouse and a Chinese family who ran a restaurant in Ida Street, but Poplar was neither socially nor racially diverse. There were no black families, but black men were always to be seen at the top end of Chrisp Street where it meets East India Dock Road. These were seamen from the merchant ships that came into the East and West India docks: South Asian men, probably Lascars. Being black, they stood out from the crowd in Chrisp Street. They dressed differently too. They had a clean, tidy look and wore blue denim jackets with Astrakhan hats patterned in twirls of silky black lambswool. The older people were used to them. Lascars had been coming to Poplar since the days of the East India Company, but as a child I treated them with caution and never went too near.

I cannot remember much overt racism in my childhood but, in an all-white community, race wasn't an issue; things would change in later years. Black men like the Lascar sailors were looked upon benignly. People saw them as a curiosity; something different. As children, we called black people 'blackies' and adults called them 'darkies'. 'Nigger' was not a term I heard much and, even when I did, it was rarely used as a noun. More often than not, it was used for description rather than abuse; women would describe a blouse or bag as 'nigger brown.' We never called black people 'coons' either. It wasn't until the television programme *Til Death Us Do Part* was shown in the 1960s, that coon took its place alongside all the other racial put-downs. To my mind, the writer Johnny Speight was responsible for introducing that racist term to millions of people who may never have used it previously. The programme's central character, Alf Garnett, was meant to be mocked for his bigotry. But Speight misjudged the impact of Garnett because the actor, Warren Mitchell, was so convincing a cockney that the character became popular and the gratuitous racism backfired badly.

Viewed from today, it is shocking to think that these racist terms were used at all. I detest racism and have stood against it all of my adult life. Not only is it morally wrong, but it is stupid too; how stupid must one be to take against people not for what they do, but for what they are? Nevertheless, there is a debate to be had about the extent to which terms such as 'darkie' were used merely as description or in a more sinister way to give offence. To use a term in ignorance or innocence is not the same as using it deliberately to hurt, undermine, or subjugate, even if the impact is the same. We must be careful about pointing fingers and apportioning blame, particularly to a generation many of whom gave their lives fighting against the racism of the Nazis.

The first Asian immigrants I knew were Balwindar and Abarjah Singh, a brother and sister who came to Susan Lawrence about 1955. They were made welcome and they were popular. One teacher, Mr Enervor had been in the army in India and was able to communicate with them and give them support. The two seemed contented enough, but I cannot imagine what it must have really been like for them to find themselves in so alien an environment. Ten years later, three Sikh families took houses in Zetland Street just around the corner from where I lived. The impact they had on the neighbourhood was immediate and caused shock and concern for the families living around them. The sight of women in saris and turbaned men with facial hair, sitting on the kerbs and window sills outside their houses, was shocking, coming as it did, out of the blue, to what had been an insular working-class community. When I passed them on my way to visit family in Spey Street, the smell of the cooking coming from the houses was so strong that it made me feel sick.

These families had been uprooted and replanted in an unfamiliar world without any support or preparation. They were not helped to integrate and the community they came into was given no help to integrate them either. That memory marks a moment when things began to change. Two generations on, the grandchildren of these people now run businesses, treat us in hospital, advocate at law and play their part in society in many other ways. And the food that made me retch all those years ago I now relish. Change can be painful and there are phases to go through before rejection becomes acceptance. There has been progress, not enough perhaps, but progress for all that.

* * *

Crime wasn't a problem when I was a boy. The East End had a tough reputation but Poplar was a safe place to live. The crimes that people fear most: murder, physical assault, sexual assault and burglary, never seemed to happen, or at least if they did, we never heard of any. Street doors were left open on warm days and parents hung keys on string through letterboxes so that children could let themselves in if they were not there. But, although crime was low and our house was never broken into, it was vulnerable to burglary. The sash-cord windows onto the back yard were old and loose and could be levered open easily. The back door was flimsy; a good kick could have had it down. The backyard was vulnerable too. Although there were gardens on either side of us, our yard backed onto the debris and there was only a thin wooden fence to screen it. That was never a problem except when travellers came to set up camp on the debris. Then we would be faced with weeks of anxiety until the police moved them on. There could be as many as twenty caravans on the site, each with its own towing vehicle, tools for breaking up cars and oil drums that were used for toilets. The men seemed intimidating and we never went onto the debris when travellers were there.

The traveller women were sent from door-to-door for water. Sometimes they had children with them and it was difficult to know what to do when they asked. Saying 'no' meant denying them a basic need but saying 'yes' could mean facing the same request day after day. Twice we saw men on the fence looking down into our garden; my dad wasn't there and we were scared. Despite these shortcomings, there was a degree of sympathy for the travellers because it was a hard life for them having no permanent homes of their own. But they always let themselves down because when they left, the debris would be strewn with rubbish, overflowing toilet drums and scrap metal. "They're not real gypsies," Nanny Powell would say, "Gypsies are good people; they're just Didicoys."

Although there wasn't much crime, there were plenty of police around. Uniformed officers patrolled regularly, sometimes on their own and sometimes in pairs. Their pace was steady and slow and their hands were always behind their backs. Police cars often came by too, Black Wolseleys, with uniformed officers in the front and a detective in the back. Policemen came by on bikes: big old *Raleighs* with swept-back handlebars and *Sturmey Archer* gears; and street corners had police boxes with telephones that linked directly to the station. Policing was very visible and people liked it. No one ever complained about never seeing a policeman because to say so wouldn't have been true.

Safe though Poplar was, it didn't always feel that way. Sometimes at night one of us would hear a noise downstairs and my dad would spring out of bed to investigate. But our fears were not borne out and we were never burgled. After 1955, when crime rose rapidly elsewhere, things stayed much the same in Poplar; but in the 1960s that began to change. It started with a robbery at the post office. I didn't witness it but I saw the men who did it because, before the robbery, they drove past our door. There were four of them in a black Morris Oxford doing a dry run to check their getaway route. I can picture one of them now. He was in his late thirties with red hair and a green checked shirt. It struck me later how like a villain in a British gangster film he looked. The robbery was like a film too: three of them rushed in, threatened the counter staff, demanded money and fled.

A few years later, Aunt Rose was burgled. She came home from work at lunchtime and couldn't get into her house so she knocked on our door. "The door's stuck," she said. "The key won't open it." I went to try it for myself and I could tell right away that it was bolted from the inside. "Stay here, Aunt Rose," I said, "I'll go round the back." "Be careful, Joey," Rose replied. I climbed over our garden fence into Rod's and then over into Aunt Rose's. Her back door was open and I knew that wasn't right because she always kept it bolted when she went out. I was sixteen and not too sure what I might be facing but there was no-one inside. The burglars had heard Rose trying to open the door and fled. I walked through to the street door, unbolted it and let her in. Then we went from room-to-room to see what the intruders had done. Nothing much had been touched. The only sign of disturbance was in Rose's bedroom where a lighted torch had been flung down onto the bed in haste. As far as we could tell, all that had been stolen was a piggy bank full of threepenny bits.

Rose was very upset by what had happened. "It's not what they've took, it's the thought that they've been in my bedroom," she said. She felt violated by the intrusion and wanted to tell Uncle Charlie. Charlie was her stalwart, the first person she'd turn to when things went wrong. "I ain't no good at phoning, Joey," she said. "If I give you the number, can you phone him up for me?" "Let's call the police first," I said. We walked to the phone box outside Radford House and I dialled 999 and gave the details. Then I took the little piece of paper with Charlie's work number on and dialled Charrington's brewery. It took a few minutes for the office staff to find Uncle Charlie but when he came, I handed the receiver to Rose. "Hello Charl. We've 'ad the burglars in," she said. Despite the awfulness of the burglary, what Aunt Rose said to Charlie made me smile. 'Having the burglars in' was such a funny way of putting it. It sounded like they had been there by invitation. She might have been saying, 'we've had the decorators in' or 'the plumber came.'

It wasn't long before the police arrived; two plain-clothes men from the station in East India Dock Road. They asked a few questions, had a good look around and went on their way. They came back about two hours later with some news. "We've got 'em," said the taller one of the two. "They bought hot dogs and ice creams in the market arcade and paid for them with threepenny bits." "Was it Tony Michaels and Kenny Harrison?" I asked. "How did you know that?" one of them asked accusingly. "Just a guess," I replied.

By the mid-sixties things had declined further. The miserable process of house demolition left gaps and large open spaces that gave a sense of dereliction and neglect. By then my dad had put screws through our window frames to prevent them from being opened. When the Browns next door were burgled, fresh scratches along our kitchen window frame showed us that the screws had done their job.

* * *

The destruction of St Leonard's Road was like the protracted course of an incurable illness; it lasted years. It was demoralising and brutal. The need for slum clearance was indisputable, but the scale of redevelopment went too far and the insensitivity of the process was appalling. Good houses were destroyed. Streets like Ullin Street with trees and fine Edwardian houses were bulldozed flat. Our houses were dilapidated and lacked the most basic amenities; they had to go. Those opposite were bigger, better and in reasonable repair but they went too; in the end everything went.

Even if Britain had not been through a war, hundreds of thousands of houses would have had to be demolished because they were unfit for people to live in. German bombing just made a terrible situation worse, so the task facing post-war governments was enormous. The Attlee government tackled it with imagination and energy; they created new towns and supported innovative housing schemes like the Lansbury Estate. The Conservative government that followed them in 1951 made housing its most important priority after national security and set itself the target of building 300,000 council houses a year.

'Housing is the first of the social services. It is also one of the keys to increased productivity. Work, family life, health and education are all undermined by crowded houses. Therefore, a Conservative and Unionist Government will give housing a priority second only to national defence.'

(Conservative manifesto, 1951.)

Winston Churchill gave the job of achieving these aims to Harold Macmillan, a clever, experienced politician who later became Prime Minister. It was a tough job for him but he did it well. Under his direction 198,000 houses were built in 1953 and by the end of the decade the total number of new homes had risen to one and a half million. There are newsreels of Macmillan visiting housing estates to witness tenants being given the keys to new council homes. He appears confident, smug almost and taking obvious delight in his achievement. It was a time when his party understood what it meant be 'One-nation Conservatives'; to advocate for everyone and not just a like-minded clique.

Tackling the housing problem was difficult and complex. Some people were willing to move away to be rehoused but most were desperate to stay. When our part of St Leonard's Road was due for demolition only a few people considered moving to a flat, most wanted a house and they didn't want to move away from Poplar either. What everyone had in common was a desire to have their basic needs met: a bathroom, an indoor toilet, a roof that didn't leak, more space, dry walls and better light. Providing these basics wasn't a problem because the solutions were straightforward; putting toilets into new buildings and fitting them with bathrooms is much the same in a house or a flat. But the authorities never seemed to have the imagination or intelligence to give families the homes they wanted in the places they wanted to live. Instead, they destroyed communities without first considering how much of them might be saved. In doing so, they ripped apart the social fabric of the country, broke up families, destroyed small businesses and took away a common identity. I can say this with confidence because it happened to me.

The story was the same all over the country and is well-documented in David Kynaston's excellent books *Modernity Britain 1957-62* and *A Northern Wind Britain 1962-65*. Fundamentally the accounts he gives of redevelopment are the same for towns and cities from Scotland to Cornwall. No account was taken of what people wanted because they were never asked. Thousands of families were uprooted and rehoused in flats when they wanted to live in houses.

"Whether they stayed in their familiar district or went elsewhere (especially in the former) many rehoused people finished up living in flats often against their wishes. The 1962 survey of Leeds slum-dwellers showed, among those in the 20-49 age range, only 5 per cent wanting to move into a flat rather than a house. The same year, a survey of the St Mary's district of Oldham revealed that although 75 per cent wanted to be rehoused in the area, that preference halved if they were offered a flat not a house."

© David Kynaston, 2013, Bloomsbury Publishing Plc.

It has been said that the slum clearance programmes after the Second World War caused more destruction to our towns and cities than the Luftwaffe ever did. The evidence is still to be seen in cities like Plymouth and Bristol where bland, uninteresting buildings exist where once stood something better. Exeter is a good example. Much of the High Street in the city was destroyed by bombing but half of its attractive old buildings still stood until the City Council demolished them in the 1970s:

"... perhaps the saddest aspect of Exeter's cultural destruction occurred after the war...Exeter City Council approved the demolition of many partially and undamaged buildings between the 1940s and the 1980s. This was based on the 'Exeter Phoenix' plan devised by architect, Thomas Sharp. Previously listed buildings were secured for destruction..."

(University of Exeter History Society.)

Perhaps the Lansbury Estate with its streets, squares and low-rise flats was a hostage to fortune because it set the bar high and raised expectations. We thought that when our turn came to be rehoused, we would move there or somewhere like it. But as the fifties went on, it became clear that places like Lansbury were not being built. There were to be no more houses in Poplar; we were going to be moved into flats. In 1954 five blocks of nine-storey flats went up around Teviot Street. We had never seen such tall buildings before. "It's getting like America," said Mrs Purton. Hillary House was the nearest one to us and the biggest.

Maura Ryan lived in Hillary House. Maura came to Poplar from Tipperary in 1953 and worked as a barmaid in *The St Leonard's*. She was popular with the regulars and caught the eye of Joe Slater, a decent cockney docker who drank in the public bar most nights. They married and Maura moved in with Joe, his mother and sister in their ground floor flat in Hillary House. I went there quite often. It wasn't much bigger than our house but it was modern and had the essentials of a bathroom and indoor toilet. Being on the ground floor it had advantages: no lifts or stairs, and windows that faced out onto the street. But it also had a sense of being 'wedged in' with flats on either side and above, and it was dark. As the demolition programme edged our way, we knew that when we had to move, it would be to a place like Hillary House and it made us feel uneasy.

The obsession with putting people into flats came from architects, some of whom harboured misguided ideals of Socialism. They saw communal living as something pure, something that people should embrace, and they were in a powerful position to bring that about. So, we got huge buildings that crammed people together onto one site and were told unconvincing stories about the benefits of 'Streets in the Sky.' True Socialism of course should be about serving people and meeting their needs not manipulating and controlling them.

However, the ideological zeal for building high took hold in the 1950s and was made achievable by gullible politicians who were under pressure to clear the slums. They were told that buildings had to be high because land was scarce and houses were more expensive to build than flats. Neither was true. There were plenty of debris in Poplar to build on and plenty of good system-built houses that were inexpensive and easy to assemble. It is telling that Hillary House and the blocks around it have since been demolished and rows of houses now stand on the land they once occupied.

In 1965, a large building began to emerge at the southern end of St Leonard's Road. We watched it rise until it dominated the skyline: high, wide and imposing. It was Balfron Tower, a block of flats twenty-six storeys high and built of concrete. To us it was a threat, something we never wanted to live in but might be obliged to accept. By then we were on the housing list, placed with others on a council register for those awaiting a new home. The list was an abstract. We never saw it or knew our position on it. We had no idea how long it would be until we got to the top of it, but we would never get to the top of it anyway, because to get there we needed housing points and we were never going to get enough points because people with more dependants and people with lots of children would always be given more than us. It was like living in a weird world of uncertainty, a combination of *Catch 22* and *1984*.

We waited years to hear from the housing department and were always in the dark about when our turn would come. Meanwhile, rumours abounded. "The 'ousin woman's genna see Mary Ferry but not 'til next month." "A woman up the market told me they'd offered her one of them 'orrible flats at the end of Aberfeldy Street but she ain't going there.' We got to know the system: when the council wanted you out, a housing officer came to offer alternative accommodation. You were given three choices and obliged to take one. The offers were always for flats and the first was always the worst. The second offer would be better and, if that wasn't acceptable, you were obliged to take the third. There was some room for negotiation but not much.

One by one the houses in our street were emptied and demolished. Aunt Rose saw the housing woman in 1967 and was offered a rundown flat on the other side of the railway. She turned it down. Her second offer was a maisonette in a newly-built block just off Devons Road in Bow. It was in one of four large blocks in a dreary part of the borough close to factories and warehouses. The accommodation was better, but the location had the potential for social decline and in time that is what happened. It was a bitter sweet moment when Aunt Rose moved away and she knew it. She was leaving the house she had grown up in, leaving the neighbours she knew and, although she was not moving far, she would no longer be just two doors away from her sister. In return, she was getting a modern home with a small garden and it was a maisonette too and not a flat.

Hearing nothing ourselves, we took things into our own hands and began a long and demoralising attempt to get a house on the Lansbury Estate. We wrote to councillors, housing officers and Ian Mikardo our MP. We stressed our credentials: we had lived in Poplar all our lives, we had family here, Doreen was a teacher in the Borough and my dad loved his garden, but we got nowhere. Whenever we heard that a house had become vacant on Lansbury, we wrote asking to be considered but every time we did, we were told that it had already gone.

When Balfron Tower was completed in 1967, no one wanted to go there. To reassure them, the architect, Erno Goldfinger, said he was going to live there himself. His decision was met with some admiration and attracted plenty of publicity. Eventually, he moved into a flat on the top floor and declared it a great success, citing the views across London as offering a particular bonus to residents. He lived there for two months and then returned to his home in Hampstead. When Goldfinger moved into Balfron Tower, the lifts were working and the building smelt of paint. A year later, the lifts often failed and the public spaces smelt of urine. How would a middle-class idealist like Goldfinger know what the people of Poplar wanted? How could he know if he didn't ask them? And how could he ask them when he thought he knew better than them anyway? Goldfinger was like so many others in the architectural establishment and Poplar was like so many other working-class areas the length and breadth of the country. It's all there in David Kynaston's books.

In the end we gave up. My mum and dad wrote to the Greater London Council asking to be rehoused on one its estates out of London. They were offered a place at the end of the Central Line in Chigwell and moved there in 1969. It was a system-built house of Swedish design and we liked it from the start. It had three bedrooms, two toilets and a fair-sized lounge. My dad got his garden and it was bigger and better than the one he left behind; there was a front garden too. There are many hundreds of houses like that across the country and they have stood the test of time well. My mum and dad were happy living there but there was, of course, a downside. Doreen and I had a long journey to work every day through heavy traffic; on a bad day it could take an hour and a half to get into the East End. I knew no-one around and felt isolated at times. For Aunt Rose, Uncle Charlie and Uncle Henry, the journey to see us on public transport took nearly two hours. Our neighbours were cold and unfriendly and, although my parents lived there for sixteen years, they never made friends with any of them. How different it was from the days of Aunt Gladys and the 'little gang.'

Our part of St Leonard's Road is a pleasant place today so did it matter that the shabby houses that once stood there were pulled down? My parents were happy in Chigwell, so did it matter that they were obliged to leave the place they knew as children? Yes, of course these things mattered. They mattered because so many lives were made worse by the uprooting of communities. If houses had been available in Poplar we would never have left. If we had not left, we would have been there to look after Uncle Charlie in the last wretched years of his life. It is a story that could be told thousands of times across this country. The destruction of communities in post-war Britain is one of the great social injustices of modern times but it has never been addressed. Maybe this is because it was done to working people who didn't have a voice of their own.

Erno Goldfinger's preference was for height and concrete. His preferred style, 'Brutalism' is acclaimed by some architects and Balfron Tower is now a listed building. Comfortably distanced from the lives of the people who occupy their creations, it never seems to occur to some architects that applying the term Brutalism to social housing is dehumanising and arrogant. What would Goldfinger have known of the people who were to live in his Brutalist creation? Was he thinking about Elsie and Ada Sweet when he drew up his designs? Did he consider Johnny Purton and his pigeons or my dad and his garden? Were Doll Herring and her boys on his agenda, or Old Brum and Jeanie, or Albert Woodyard and his family? Was anyone with children thought about at all when he planned to put families into a building that rose twenty-six flights into the sky?

Architecture has been important to my life ever since I saw the Skylon and The Dome of Discovery at the Festival of Britain in 1951. I love it for its impact and difference. I dislike Brutalism as a term but not necessarily as a style and high-rise flats can be exciting on the eye and good to live in too. What I am against is the determination of architects to put their aesthetic before the needs and desires of the people they are there to serve.

THE IRONS

So what was the East End? From Hackney to Romford, people lay claim to it today, but the East End was much tighter than that. The true East End runs from the walls of the City of London in the west, as far as the River Lee in the east; and from the River Thames in the south to the northern tips of Bethnal Green and Bow. Within these bounds once existed people with a common history, a shared dialect and a way of life that helped them to survive dreadful deprivation through mutual support. I feel fortunate to have known something of that East End, but it exists now only in the heads of people like me and we are a dying generation. The tribe has scattered; it is no longer there. In its place have come immigrant communities who face similar problems of poverty and poor housing to those my family faced. They live near, but not alongside, other newcomers who enjoy wealth and social advantage. The contrast in their lifestyles is, at times, grotesque.

Perhaps we all crave our own history. History forms our identity; it keeps us rooted and reassures us that we are part of something bigger; that we are not on our own. West Ham United has been a part of my history ever since I was twelve when I first saw them play at Upton Park. It is the East Enders' football club. When I was young, many of the players were local boys; some went to my school. Bobby Moore's dad worked in Poplar power station and the bakers in Chrisp Street market made Bobby's wedding cake. In the late 1920s a film showing at The Imperial cinema in Canning Town included the song *I'm Forever Blowing Bubbles.* A few days later it was being sung on the terraces at Upton Park and it is still sung at every Hammers' match today. Not far from Canning Town Bridge, the Thames Ironworks and Shipbuilding Company at Blackwall built *HMS Warrior*, the world's first iron-clad warship. The company had a workers' football team and in 1895 it became West Ham United. The noise of the hammering of rivets gave the club its name of 'The Hammers,' but true supporters also call West Ham 'The Irons,' because the club's first players were workers in iron. West Ham is part of my life. It is my football club. It links me to the East End people of the past and I like it for that. That is not unique in itself; it would be the same for supporters of Glasgow Celtic, or Liverpool or Sunderland or Birmingham City, but it is my club.

In April 1964, my dad and other members of my family went to Bow Bridge to see West Ham parade the FA Cup from an open-topped bus. I was away at college at the time, but in May 1975, I stood with Pam and her mum as Billy Bonds brought the same cup through Stratford. In June 2023, my son and grandson Joe were in Stratford when the Hammers brought the European Conference Cup back to East London. The shirts the players wore for the final had orange and white flashes rising upwards across them. They were there to symbolise the heat and flames of the Thames Ironworks; a thoughtful connection with the club's history.

Many thousands of people waited for the players' bus to pass by that evening and dozens of them were interviewed on television. Most came from the East End diaspora in places like Basildon, Brentwood, Upminster and Hornchurch. Whole families turned out; some were from five generations. The way these people spoke, the obvious closeness of their family ties, their cheeky speculative humour and their basic decency were all so familiar to me. I knew them, I understood them, I was part of their tribe. These were the Massers and the Beards, the Barnets and the Wardells, not bound by geography anymore, but joined in a different way by history and a common set of values.

When my grandson Joe stood waiting for the Hammers by Stratford Town Hall that night, he was standing just yards away from where his namesake Joe Connolly enlisted to join the Northumberland Fusiliers in the autumn of 1914. I have written this book for little Joe and for my three other grandchildren in the hope that they may one day come to know and appreciate the people they came from.

My Great Uncle Joe Connolly who my father, me, my son and grandson were named after.

My Great Uncle Jack Connolly in the uniform of the London Fire Brigade. *'Well...let's just say there was a bank robbery around that time too.'*

July 31st 1919. St Leonard's Road children's party to celebrate the signing of the armistice that ended World War 1. The street had suffered no bombing and is intact. Beyond the terraces to the left is the Spratts' dog food factory. Our house is on the left by the Union Flag. (Tower Hamlets Local History Library and Archives.)

A Heinkel bomber above the East End, 1941. *'A chill went through me the first time I saw it, as I realised that my family were sheltering somewhere below.'*

My dad in his Royal Navy uniform.

My mum and dad, Rye House near Hoddesdon, 1946.

Me with my Great Uncle Harry and Doreen in the backyard of 217 St Leonard's Road, 1946.

Uncle Henry (second right) in front of the cookhouse at Hubble's hop farm, circa 1935.

Nanny Powell (third from right) with other 'hoppers' outside the Bull at Hunton, circa 1949. The lady on the right is her friend Nora.

My family and me by our hop bin, Hubble's Farm, Hunton, Kent 1947.

Doreen and me, a studio photograph 1947.

With Doreen outside 213 St. Leonard's Road, 1949.

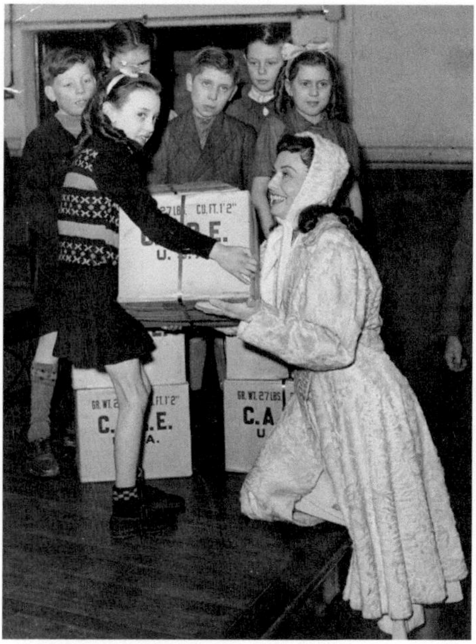

The Hollywood film star Paulette Goddard presents a food parcel to pupils at Alton Street Primary School 1949. My sister Doreen is behind her on the right.

East London Primary schools' country dance party, Poplar Civic Theatre, 1948. Doreen is standing on the left.

A trip to Barking Park with the Five Ways Mission, 1950. Eileen Purton (left in our group) then me, Johnny Purton and Doreen. Miss Ada Sweet is behind us framed by the handle of a pram. I was eating an egg and tomato sandwich!

The elegant staircase leading to the juniors' hall, Susan Lawrence School, 1951. To the left are the long windows of the foyer and through them, a view into the street showing a row of slum houses. A remarkable photograph of Poplar caught at a moment in time; the problem and the solution captured in one frame. (John Maltby / RIBA Collections.)

The Dining Hall, Lansbury Lawrence/Susan Lawrence school today: light, spacious and modern. The school was designed in 1949 and opened in 1951. (Photograph by the author with publishing permission from the school.)

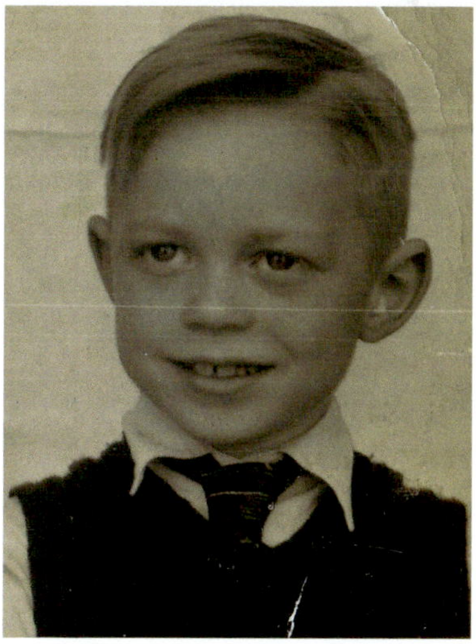

A school photograph aged six. (Hair by Percy Palaver.)

Me (centre) as Neddler the Pedlar. Susan Lawrence School, 1953.

With Johnny Purton. Street party for the Coronation. St Leonard's Road, June the 6th, 1953.

With Margaret Wardell and Doreen, 213 St Leonard's Road, 1954.

Daily Mirror TUES JUNE 22 1954

1½d FORWARD WITH THE PEOPLE

No. 15,736

BULLET IN THE POST BRINGS A DEATH THREAT TO FAMILY

'DAILY MIRROR' REPORTERS

A LETTER threatening to kill a mother and her five children started a gunman hunt ranging across half of England last night.

In the envelope, addressed to widow Mary Ann Bradford, 51, was a bullet wrapped in paper.

The letter said: "This is a present for you, and I have another for each of your family. I will let you have them as soon as possible."

The letter, unsigned and posted in Manchester, was delivered to Mrs. Bradford's former home in Hurford-street, Hoddesdon, Herts.

Mrs. Bradford's daughter, Mrs. Babs Wilson, 24, took it to the county police. The police told Scotland Yard.

And last night—

● More than 27,000 police in London, Manchester and the Home Counties were on the alert for an armed man.

● Detectives sat in a Manchester boarding-house, waiting for a man. And

● Three policemen patrolled around a house in Zetland-street, Poplar, London, where Mrs. Bradford now lives with her father.

All police looking for the wanted man were warned by Scotland Yard: "He has a pistol and ammunition."

Superintendent Leonard ...

'No Trouble in Our Family'

"There has been no trouble in our family.

"I can't think of anyone who would do such a thing. I don't even know anyone in Manchester."

Zsa Zsa's sister comes to town

Bannister's mile record broken

IS THIS LIMIT OF HUMAN ENDURANCE?

"DAILY MIRROR" REPORTER

—and they even talk alike

SHORTING HOME

The Daily Mirror reports my Aunt Nan's dangerous adventure..

With Doreen and my dad. *'That holiday in Whitstable is a treasured memory for me ...two weeks when I had my dad all to myself.'*

119 – 219 St Leonard's Road circa 1958. Our street door is above the saddle of the motorbike. (The London Archives - City of London Corporation).

A knees-up at a 'Gassie' dance, 1955. Left to right: Uncle Henry, Uncle Pats, dad, and mum. Two unknown dancers and then Aileen Robinson. Doreen is on the right at the end of the line. My cousin Janice is in front with her mum, my Aunt Nellie Whitnell.

Susan Lawrence football team with the East London cup, 1956. From the right: John Rodway, Ronnie Kitts, John Hunt (with striped tie), David Wymant, Raymond Holmes, Jackie Painter, Keith Williams (holding the cup), Colin Hogarth and behind him, David Barnett. I cannot identify the boy on the left or the one between the two Davids. Mr Enervor (moustache) and Mr Howell are at the back. (Lansbury Lawrence School archive.)

My Aunt Nan circa 1936. *'...a formidable woman with a strong personality and an impressive physical presence.'*

A Connolly gathering for the Christening of (I think) my cousin Roger, 1947. Back row: Uncle Peter in Navy Uniform and, second from the right, Uncle Danny. Next row: Grandad Connolly on the far left and Aunt Kitt fourth from the right. Next row (centre), my Grandma Connolly with Peter's wife, Rose holding the baby.

Aunt Kitt and Tom Brown circa 1955.

My Grandad William Connolly with three of his sons: Danny (left), Peter and Tom (white shirt.)

Playing for Eltham and Lee Athletic, aged 14. Behind me are my friends Ray Levitt and Tom Tomkins.

With England's ex-captain Billy Wright, Wembley stadium, 29th of April 1961. Ray Levitt is next to Billy and I am next to Ray.

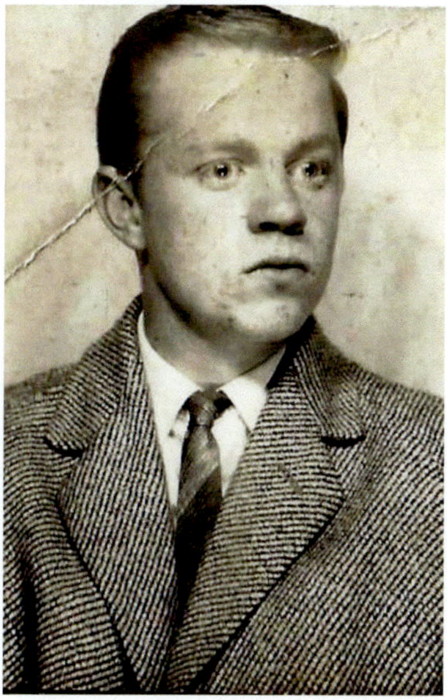

Aged 14. *'Adolescence...the misery of spots on the chin...'*

Aged 15, sporting my 'College Boy' haircut. My dad approved of the style but not of the price: 'Six and six! Lou does mine for one and nine,' he said.

In Ireland with Mrs Clery. August 1961.

The view from my bedroom about 1962. An ink sketch I did showing the land that was once our debris and the houses in Woodin Street. The railway wall runs across the far side and the building on the right is the Far Famed Cake Company where Aunt Kitt was manageress.

The houses opposite ours taken around 1965. Johnny Watton lived upstairs in the fourth house from the left. St Michael's Church with its 'huge witch with yellow eyes' clocktower is at the end of the terrace on the right. (Photograph by Tony Hall, Tony Hall Archive, Bishopsgate Institute.)

Aunt Rose and Uncle Charlie at Gretna Green.

Uncle Henry with my mum and Aunt Gladys at a Bromley Gasworks dance circa 1965.

Arthur Edwards with his sons Paul (left) and John. 213 St Leonard's Road circa 1967.

John Edwards with England captain Bobby Moore at Bobby's house in Manor Road Chigwell. (Photograph by Arthur Edwards.)

An 'ID' picture of me taken in Paris not long after my split with Christine. My dad certainly did not approve of this hairstyle.

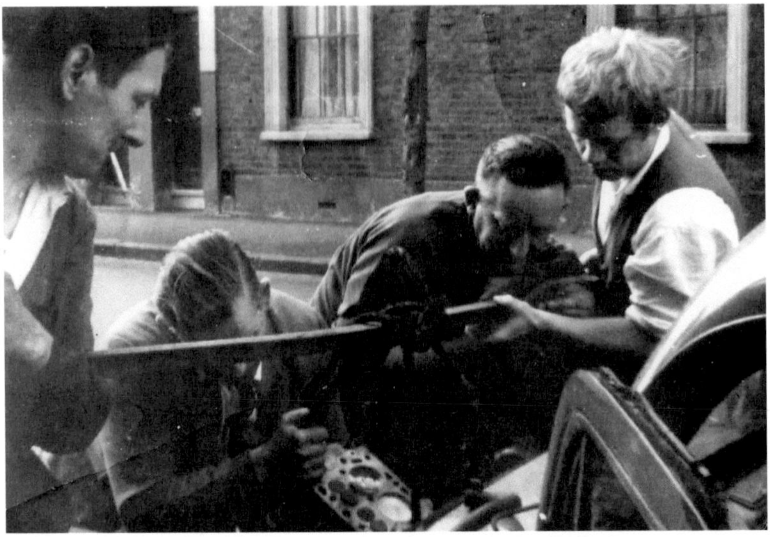

Lifting the engine from my car with Rod (left), Uncle Charlie and Uncle Henry. St Leonard's Road 1966. (Photograph by Arthur Edwards.)

The last days of Woodin Street. '*...demoralising and brutal'* (The London Archives - City of London Corporation).

AFTERWORD

When I was considering the aspects of this book that deal with my time at Susan Lawrence, I became curious to know how the school is doing today. I looked on its website and found a vibrant inner-city school that had been highly rated by inspectors. The website included a link to a film that the children had made about the school's history. It celebrated its special architecture and talked about the Lansbury Estate and the Festival of Britain. I contacted the headteacher and asked if I might visit to take some pictures and refresh my memory of the building. I said that in return I would be pleased to talk to the children and tell them about the day their school opened and what it was like to be a pupil there all those years ago. He agreed and in September 2024, I found myself back in what is now the Lansbury Lawrence school.

The building has been altered over time, but it is still modern and exciting in places, and the reception area and the dining hall are remarkably fresh and appealing to the eye. The pupils I met were ethnically different from those in my day; many were of Somalian origin and others from families originally from Bangladesh. They were bright lovely children, excited to hear about their school and full of questions for me. I feel so fortunate to have had this opportunity; to stand in the classroom where I had been a pupil more than seventy years before and talk to a new generation of Poplar children about what their school had been like in my day. In one class I saw a boy who looked uncannily like me as a boy; in particular, he had my strawberry blonde hair. That he was the only child of similar ethnicity to me emphasised how much the population of Poplar has changed since I lived there. When I left the class, he came running after me, held out his hand and gave me a tomato. It was an act almost painful in its kindness.

I ended my day with a walk through the Lansbury Estate. It was pouring with rain and I had no umbrella so I sheltered in Chrisp Street market for a while and then made my way along Grundy Street as far as the Catholic church. The Lansbury Estate still looked good; the closes and small squares were particularly attractive and the scale of it all seemed to work so well. Good architecture endures.

PLAYLIST

Downloading these songs and performances will get you closer to the people you have read about. They are all available if you search for them online.

'I'll Be Your Sweetheart' – Ann Breen – *The song with the beautiful refrain that Nanny Powell sang to me and I sang to baby Rose.*

'The Eightsome Reel' – Scottish Fiddle Orchestra (YouTube video with dancing.) - *One of the country dance tunes that I enjoyed so much at school.*

'The Spaniard Who Blighted My Life' – The Street Music Singer (also Al Jolson and Bing Crosby.) - *The song my mother sang to make us all laugh.*

'Knees Up Mother Brown' – Unknown chorus group (YouTube) - *The cockney anthem we danced and sang to at every gathering. I still love it.*

'With My Little Stick of Blackpool Rock' – George Formby – *Rude and funny. George Formby's music brought me and Uncle Henry together despite our clash of musical tastes.*

'Waiting For the Robert E Lee' – Al Jolson - *Jolson was Uncle Henry's favourite and this was the song he liked best. Al Jolson is not to my taste but he performs this song with great expression and originality.*

'Sugar Bush' – Eve Boswell – *A 1950s song of its time. At the PTA dances Mr Hunt would shout "Play Sugar Bush again!"*

'The Poor People of Paris' – Winnifred Atwell - *Brilliantly performed, Keith Carter played it to a drunk who stopped us as we were carrying a gramophone across the Chrisp Street bridge.*

'Treat Me Nice' – Elvis Presley – *The record that change my life. I played it one Saturday morning and could not believe how exciting it was.*

'Til I Kissed You' – The Everly Brothers – *The first record I every bought. Perfect harmonies that still sound fresh today.*

'It Doesn't Matter Anymore' – Buddy Holly – *The record I got for swapping 'Til I Kissed You'. Buddy's music has enriched my life.*

ACKNOWLEDGEMENTS

I would like to thank my sister Doreen Clery for filling in some of the gaps in my memory. Arthur Edwards for his help and patience with the photographs. My daughter-in-law, Dr Elizabeth Connolly, for describing the symptoms and possible consequences of Sepsis. The late Eileen Fisher for explaining the 'Panel' system and pre-NHS healthcare. Jean Hands for applying her brilliantly forensic eye to the text. Chris Martyn, my own personal sage, for his on-going help, support and careful scrutiny of the draft. The staff and children of the wonderful Lansbury Lawrence school in Poplar and in particular, Owen O'Regan and Saleh Ahmed. I am also indebted to Johnny Purton for reminding me of the story about the missing baby Herring.

My thanks also go to the Bishopsgate Institute, The City of London Archive, Lansbury Lawrence School, Tower Hamlets Local History Library and Archives and the Royal Institute of British Architects (RIBA) for permissions to reproduce photographs from their collections. I would also like to thank Bloomsbury Publishing Plc for permission to reproduce an extract from David Kynaston's *Modernity Britain 1957-62*.

BIOGRAPHY

Joe Connolly was born just after the Second World War and was educated at Susan Lawrence School in Poplar, the Roan School in Blackheath, Camberwell School of Art, Bath Academy of Art and London University. After teaching at secondary schools in East London, he joined the schools' inspectorate and went on to hold senior posts in education at the Suffolk and Cambridgeshire Education authorities. For five years he was external examiner in post graduate teacher education at London University and was also external examiner in teacher education at Goldsmith's College. Joe presented the BBC2 *Art in Society* programme and was also a programme consultant for the BBC. After retirement, he took an active interest in the National Health Service and chaired the Harlow and District Healthcare Forum. He is currently a member of the Visual Arts Advisory Panel at South Mill Arts.

Also by Joe Connolly: *'Journeys from Innocence'* and *'Poplar and Family Sayings.'*